"Allie Contrera a true "bass singer" which was a rarity in those days; one fifth of the silky smoothest harmony of Brooklyn's best, The Mystics; a lifelong friend and now a wonderful story teller/historian about what it was like to live the "impossible dream" in the world of Doo Wop ...a fascinating read!!"

Vini Poncia

"Al was on the front line of rock and roll history when it all began.... His front row view gives us a perspective into the power these artists had (either knowingly or unknowingly) who forged the way for all who followed...."

Kenny Vance

""Rock On" back with Allie Contrera to a fabulous time in Rock 'n' Roll and remember the good times of a fabulous era."

"Mr. Music" Norm N. Nite

"Al Contrera gave me my first break into the music business by introducing me to Vini Poncia who was a very successful Record producer. I had the pleasure of being the backup band (as The Brooklyn Dreams) to the Mystics on a few gigs. In this book, you will find great stories of Rock and Roll History. I'm proud to know you Al, and thanks for taking the time to share this historic story..."

Joe Bean Esposito

From my friends who grew up singing on the street corners of Brooklyn in the fifties, I frequently heard, "you had to be there." Now I feel like I was. This book transports you to a time and place in history that defied description... until now.

- Joe Mirrione, Creator of "Pop,
Rock & Doo Wopp Live!"

This is the real history of the Brooklyn group The Mystics as seen through the eyes of the original bass, Allie Contrera. It's a must read for all Rock N Roll fans.

Don K. Reed formerly of WCBS
FM,NY and the original Doo
Wopp Shop.

AL CONTRERA

HUSHABYE

The Mystics, the Music, and the Mob

BALBOA
PRESS
A DIVISION OF HAY HOUSE

Copyright © 2018 Al Contrera.

All rights reserved. No part of this book may be used or reproduced by any means, graphic, electronic, or mechanical, including photocopying, recording, taping or by any information storage retrieval system without the written permission of the author except in the case of brief quotations embodied in critical articles and reviews.

Balboa Press books may be ordered through booksellers or by contacting:

Balboa Press
A Division of Hay House
1663 Liberty Drive
Bloomington, IN 47403
www.balboapress.com
1 (877) 407-4847

Because of the dynamic nature of the Internet, any web addresses or links contained in this book may have changed since publication and may no longer be valid. The views expressed in this work are solely those of the author and do not necessarily reflect the views of the publisher, and the publisher hereby disclaims any responsibility for them.

The author of this book does not dispense medical advice or prescribe the use of any technique as a form of treatment for physical, emotional, or medical problems without the advice of a physician, either directly or indirectly. The intent of the author is only to offer information of a general nature to help you in your quest for emotional and spiritual well-being. In the event you use any of the information in this book for yourself, which is your constitutional right, the author and the publisher assume no responsibility for your actions.

Any people depicted in stock imagery provided by Getty Images are models, and such images are being used for illustrative purposes only. Certain stock imagery © Getty Images.

This book is a work of non-fiction. Unless otherwise noted, the author and the publisher make no explicit guarantees as to the accuracy of the information contained in this book and in some cases, names of people and places have been altered to protect their privacy.

Print information available on the last page.

ISBN: 978-1-9822-0027-5 (sc)
ISBN: 978-1-9822-0029-9 (hc)
ISBN: 978-1-9822-0028-2 (e)

Library of Congress Control Number: 2018903685

Balboa Press rev. date: 04/10/2018

DEDICATED TO:

The Mystics: Phil Cracolici, Albee Cracolici,
Bob Ferrante and George Galfo
The Classics: Emil Stucchio and Teresa McClean
The Passions: Jimmy Gallagher, Albee Galione,
Tony Armato and Lou Rotundo

My cousin Anthony Conigliaro

Our manager Jim Gribble

My Parents Lee and Joe Contrera
My wife Florence Lucky Contrera; my brother Rich Contrera;
My children: Christine Contrera Longette, Dina Contrera Messina;
My grandchildren, Vanessa Longette, Angela Longette,
Gianna Messina, Nico Messina, and Angelo Messina. My great
grandchildren: Mila Rosario, Gabriel Rosario, and my extended
family, Frank Messina, Michael Valentino, and Jose Rosario.

ACKNOWLEDGEMENTS

Editor: Catherine Hiller: Thank you for your
guidance, skill and understanding.
Photography: John Gagliardi and Lily Ann Sciametta

Technical Assistance: John Gagliardi and Christine
Contrera Longette and Tony Testa.

Inspiration: Phil Cracolici, Albee and Roberta Cracolici, Bob and Georgian Ferrante, George Galfo, Emil Stucchio, Vini Poncia, Pete Anders, Kenny Vance, Hope Devenuto, Linda Ardigo, Maryann Sciametta, Joe Esposito, Eddie Hokenson, Joe Mirrione, Ben Cammarata, Marc Eliot and Jerry Rosenberg, John Roper, Lou Adesso, Steve Flam, Dr. Anthony Gribin, Joe Contorno, Frankie Lanziano, and Richie Ticarelli.

FOREWORD

By Dr. Anthony Gribin, PHD
Author of The Complete Book of Doo Wop

Anyone who knows what doo-wop music is, has heard "Hushabye" by the Mystics. It's as much of an anthem as it is a song. And although their other sides are not as well known, they are just as good. Songs like "All Through the Night," "Darling I Know Now" and "Don't Take the Stars" made minor impressions on the charts, and "The Bells Are Ringing" and "Why Do You Pretend" weren't heard much on the airwaves, but all of these are as good as "Hushabye." This group of five Italian guys from Brooklyn had close to perfect harmony and, given slightly different circumstances, could've been as well known as the Four Seasons.

Al Contrera, the bass of the group, tells us the story of five young men. He takes us through their formation, their recording and touring career, as well as their successes and heartbreaks. As a bonus, we learn about the fine line between the music and the mob, and how peer pressure and the temptations of fame got in the way of at least one of the guys. As we all know, doo-wop music has had nine lives and the songs of the Mystics, as well as their neighborhood buds, the Classics and the Passions, are still in demand. This book is a must for anyone who loves the sweet sound of doo-wop harmonies of the 1950s. Crank up the sound of the Mystics on your iPhone or on YouTube and start reading.

You won't be disappointed...

CHAPTER 1

OH WHAT A NIGHT

On Saturday, June 13, 2009, the weather in Rutherford, New Jersey, was chilly. The forecast called for a slight chance of rain, with the temperatures in the high fifties. At the Izod Center, the marquee announced, "Richard Nader's Original Summer Doo Wop Reunion XX, starring Little Anthony and The Imperials, Kenny Vance and the Planotones, Gene Chandler, The Cleftones, Larry Chance and The Earls, Speedo and The Cadillacs, Clay Cole, and Emil Stucchio and the Classics."

I was a Classic, looking forward to playing tonight's show and seeing Clay Cole again.

That "slight chance of rain" became a rainstorm, cancelling the afternoon outside festivities in the parking lot of this huge auditorium in The Meadowlands complex. We were supposed to sit at an outside table and "meet and greet" the hundreds of Doo Wop fans waiting on line for a picture and an autograph of their favorite acts from the fifties and sixties. Also disappointed were the a cappella groups waiting to perform on the "Outside Tail Gate Party Stage," hosted by former CBS-FM disk jockey Don K Reed, adjacent to the autograph table.

Inside the auditorium, the usual hustle and bustle went on as the house band prepared for sound check. The booming sound of technicians checking the microphones filled the cavernous auditorium: "One-two, one-two." Once in awhile you would hear "three." The empty room echoed the sound like a tiled subway station. The musicians were gathering at the stage area with the usual handshakes and hugs. The show's musical director, Mark Baron, who usually worked with The Duprees, tried to get them in place but gave up and joined the handshakes and hug banter.

Mark is an accomplished musician and conductor with numerous credits in both Broadway and rock music. Finally, he got everyone to focus, and the rehearsals began by sorting out the music charts. As the acts arrived backstage, they found their dressing rooms via computer printed signage attached to the doors with scotch tape. Backstage looked a little sterile and unwelcoming. Just off-white walls, linoleum tile squares on the floor and a never-ending array of exposed piping and electrical wiring where the ceiling tiles should have been.

I got there at 1:30 pm, a few minutes before the rest of The Classics, and hung my suit bag in the appropriate dressing room. There was a large table, several folding chairs and hooks on the wall for hanging up clothes. At the time, I was 69 years old, an original member of The Mystics and a member of The Classics. I sang bass with The Mystics and have been singing bass and baritone with The Classics for the last 23 years. I have had more than my share of tough times but still manage to be upbeat and even funny at times. I experienced the tragic loss of my wife, something that has never left my mind, due to a cancerous brain tumor in 1995. I have always felt that singing with a group, especially since they are my closest friends, saved my sanity.

Emil Stucchio and Teresa McClean, the other members of The Classics, walked into the dressing room ten minutes later and found their clothes-hanging spots on the wall. Emil is the original lead singer and founding member of The Classics. "Till Then," recorded in 1963, went into the top 20 on the national charts. Quite a feat considering the initial British assault on the American music scene started then. Emil had always been the lead singer of The Classics except for one year in 1989 when he sang with The Mystics, and he shared singing lead with Phil. "Emil still has his pipes, in fact he continues to improve" is what many promoters said.

With the same amount of dark brown hair, he had when he was a young man (the magic of chemicals!), Emil also looked younger than his 65 years. Like me, he fought the same weight-on, weight-off battle. A confident and alert man who has a memory like an elephant with a computer, Emil recalls everything. He has a unique ability to read people and is the driving force of The Classics. He retired from the NYC Police Force in 1972 after 25 years. That was the job, according to Emil, that was supposed to "just pay the bills until the music kicked in again." He and Teresa drove in from Long Island, and like every gig, it was "a drive from hell." There came a point where it didn't even pay to talk about how bad your commute to a gig was because there was always someone with a more horrific traffic story.

Teresa joined The Classics a few years ago, replacing Mike Paquette, and immediately proved to be an asset. She'd sung with a girl group called The Chicklets that often opened for the Classics, and when Mike Paquette and then Scott LaChance left the Classics after 15 years, Emil and I had the same thought: "Let's ask Teresa to sing with us. She's got the right personality and she can really sing." This change would set the Classics in the direction that they'd wanted to go ever since they started the Classics again in 1986.

Teresa is a very attractive woman in her early forties with a feisty Irish spirit who is not struggling as much as the other two thirds of The Classics with her weight. She comes from a musical family and has had some experience in theatre groups and Broadway shows, which made her the perfect fit. She joined right in with the onstage impromptu jokes and antics between Emil and me. The dressing room was now alive with conversation. As usual, I set off to find some food. The catering was always good at these events. They would serve a light fare type lunch with salads and sandwiches and a variety of soft drinks, teas and coffee.

On the way to the so-called "green room," which was not green but just another room with food for the performers, I ran into Kenny Vance, and we shook hands and patted each other's shoulders during the quick hug thing. Kenny always started with an earnest soft spoken, "How are you doing"? He spoke in a barely audible monotone, and since most of the people back stage, at this stage of the game, are almost deaf, it was hard to hear him. Sometimes I think that's why people hug when they meet, so they could hear better. With Kenny, you really felt the sincerity in the question. He really cared about how you were doing. Kenny, at a lean 6'2, had to bend a bit to hug most people. He, too, is fighting the on again off again battle with weight, but he's winning. He always wears black and always wears a hat, both off and on stage. Kenny and I have known each other for fifty years. We met in Jim Gribble's office in 1959, when Jim was The Mystics' manager and Kenny was singing with The Harbor Lights. The group was named by Kenny Vance for the lights that were visible across the harbor at night in the Far Rockaway section of Brooklyn. This was the first of many innovative titles and songs in an amazing career. Kenny is a founding member of Jay and The Americans, which started in Jim Gribble's office, but I will get into that a little later. Kenny always appeared to be thinking about something – although, perhaps, he wasn't.

Clay Cole walked over and now the three of us did the hug and "I can hear you now" ritual. Clay, who had lost the on-again off-again battle with weight, promised to continue the battle. Kenny had not seen Clay in decades. Actually, no one in the music business, except for Ray Ranieri, and me, had seen Clay. This was his first live appearance in 39 years. Clay dropped out from the music scene around 1968 at the height of an incredible ten years of hosting television shows in New York City. He stayed in New York until 2001 writing television shows and even managed to win two Emmys for an award show special, and then he suddenly decided to move to North Carolina. Clay and I had always stayed in touch over the fifty years we've known each other and at the very least exchanged Christmas cards. When the return address on Clay's card read "North Carolina" instead of West 57th Street, New York, I knew something was wrong. Sometime in 1967, Clay felt that because television was changing into something he did not want to be part of, he was not going to be part of it. He quit a successful TV show in New York on channel 11. Under the management of Ray Ranieri, who eventually became a close friend of Clay, he got involved with some night clubs and live shows for a few years and eventually disappeared into the shoreline of North Carolina, where he began to work on his autobiography, *Sh-Boom*, which, by the way, is an awesome book. He writes about his fifty plus years in the music business with personal stories about the artists he met and the friends he made.

I first met Clay in Providence, Rhode Island, in 1959 where he was Al Rucker, his real name, doing the Al Rucker Show on WJAR-TV. The Mystics had the number one song in Providence at the time with "Hushabye" and were contracted to appear at the tenth anniversary outdoor block party of WJAR-TV, with Al Rucker as the host in downtown Providence. It was a steamy hot July 7th. We had just finished a 24-city tour in the Midwest with other artists, including Johnny and the Hurricanes. We got home on July 6th and drove to Providence the next day. The other acts on the Al Rucker show were Connie Francis, the Four Lads, Lou Monte, Jerry Vale, Jack Scott, Carl Dobkins Jr., George Hamilton IV, and the Videls, who became very close friends with us in the years that followed. The Videls, who did not have a national hit yet, were hometown favorites and opened the show with a sensational set.

We were scheduled to go onstage just before the headlining and closing Connie Francis, and by this time the crowd had grown to over 50,000 people. The house band began playing the music to our opening song, and I remember seeing a sea of people from building to building across the main street, and it went back about six or seven blocks. We all looked at each other with astonishment as we walked out onstage and saw this huge crowd. The people were packed in shoulder to shoulder. It was impossible for anyone to move.

Halfway through our third song, "Oh What a Night," I noticed two guys in the audience starting to have a fist fight. I motioned to the other guys, who were all watching from the stage. The two brawlers were swept by the crowd into opposite directions. They had no control as to where they were going while their arms were still swinging in the air. It was scary. The audience created a constant blaring sound that drowned out the band and much of the conversation onstage. A group of policemen were huddled next to the stage stairs, which started to shake. They were shouting at each other, so they could hear themselves, As we finished the last verse of "Hushabye," the police and fire department officials decided to shut the show down. At that point, the crowd had nowhere to expand except towards the stage, which was a wooden structure about six feet higher than the street. Al Rucker made the announcement, and the crowd went wild pushing towards the stage . . . and moving it! Feeling the stage start to move, we got out in a hurry. Then the instrumentalists jumped up, gathered their belongings and fled, right behind us. Al Rucker was now the only one on the mike, trying to calm the crowd down, but it was too late, it was out of control. No one was listening, so he calmly walked off, shaking his head. If anyone had passed out in that crowd, they would never have hit the ground. There simply was no room to fall. The show moved into the television studios, where Connie did a few songs on live TV in the producers' attempt to save the day. Connie never got a chance to get onstage. Al Rucker interviewed the acts and explained to the TV audience why the show had to be shut down. It took hours for the crowds to disperse.

The next time The Mystics and Al Rucker would meet was September 4, 1959, back stage at the Alan Freed Tenth Anniversary show at the Brooklyn Fox theatre – only now, Al Rucker called himself Clay Cole. We all became very close friends over the next few years.

Now, fifty years later, Clay Cole and Kenny Vance and I filled up our coffee containers and grabbed some snacks from the make-believe green room and settled in some chairs with Emil and Teresa. It was still a little early for sound checks, so we settled down to conversation, with the "Fifty years gone by" as the subject. Kenny whispered, "I can't believe we know each other fifty years" and stopped. Usually a statement like that would be followed by a profound expression of life from Kenny. After a meditative silence, he continued "How are all the guys in The Mystics and how is Phil Cracolici doing"?

I answered, "He's fine; just spoke to him the other day."

Clay turned to Kenny "You know when you said that about fifty years ago, I thought about that incident with Phil. It's hard to believe that actually happened."

Emil responded with "You know, if that didn't happen, who knows where The Mystics would be today."

Kenny added, "That's exactly what I was thinking about."

By now, Teresa was really puzzled. All this talk about an incident fifty years ago, before she was even born. She finally asked a perfectly natural question, "OK, what happened?"

They all turned to me, Kenny adding, "Yeah what really happened? I remember hearing that Phil was arrested for killing someone but then no one really talked about it that much back then."

I took a sip of coffee and said "Well he was arrested, but he was only a witness to a killing. It's a really long story."

"We have some time," said Clay, moving his chair a little closer to the circle of chairs. I began telling them the story. But before I could get to the gas station homicide and its consequences for Phil, I had to go back even further.

YOU'LL NEVER KNOW

Tony "Punchy" Armato walked into Pop's luncheonette on 17th Avenue and 80th Street in Brooklyn, New York to meet his girlfriend, Maryann Addesso, one of the most attractive girls in the neighborhood. Maryann and her younger brother Lou lived directly across the street from me at 1735 79th Street when we were younger. By coincidence, the Addesso family moved across from my family in 1956. I now lived on 84th Street and they moved to 85th Street. There was a common driveway in the back of the houses, so I saw both Lou and Maryann often. After all these years, I'm still in touch with Lou.

Punchy got his nickname after he went into the Golden Gloves and won a few fights. Punchy looked like Andy Williams with blue eyes and was far from being punch drunk. He was very handsome and always upbeat and happy. He loved to help people and loved to go out with pretty girls. His engaging personality left you with liking him after a short conversation. New Utrecht High School was right down the block on New Utrecht Avenue, between 79th street and 80th street.

I was sitting at the counter in Pop's store with my best friend, Angelo "Scapper" Rubano. Punchy came in, sat on the stool next to me and asked Pop for two cokes. While Pop was there, I asked, "Can I have another egg cream?"

Punchy looked over at me and said, "Hey you have a really deep bass voice, are you with a group?"

I said with a laugh, "No, I don't sing."

Scapper continued the conversation, introducing me to Punchy as Allie, my nickname, and reminding me that Maryann was Punchy's girlfriend. We talked a little about the coincidence of me living near her not once but twice. Punchy got up and went over to the jukebox, put some coins in and pressed D-5 and B-8. Scapper whispered to me, "Punchy's one of the Bath Beach Boys and he's also in a singing group." I really didn't know much about the singing groups, but The Bath Beach gang was legendary in the neighborhood. That made Punchy a neighborhood celebrity.

I knew the current music, like every other teenager, but never thought of actually singing it. I only sang to myself and usually the bass parts because I did have an unusually deep bass voice for a sixteen-year-old.

Punchy came back to the counter as The Platters' 45 record dropped on the turntable and Herb Reed's bass voice sang, "You'll Never Know." Punchy asked me, "Can you hit that note?" I didn't know what he meant, and Scapper told me, "Sure you can sing that, go ahead, try it, you got the voice." Scapper didn't know if I could hit that note: he just saw an opportunity for me, and as a friend, tried to push me into it. I thought, what the hell, and when the next "You'll never know" came up, I sang it with Herb Reed and the Platters.

"Holy shit!" Punchy was grinning. "You *are* a bass." I was a little bewildered. "I am?" Scapper was smiling ear to ear with a look of I told you so. The other song that Punchy played started with a bass part, too. "Don't Go, Please Stay" by the Drifters. "Try this one," he said. I took a deep breath and out came a perfect copy of the "Don't go" part. While Punchy, Maryann and Scapper were laughing about how good that was, I thought that if this guy thinks this is good maybe I can sing. I also noticed that some of the girls sitting in the next booth were impressed and looking over at us. It seemed that once you were perceived as being a singer, or in a gang, you were special. Suddenly I was intently interested in becoming a bass singer. Looking back, this was a turning point in my life.

We were having a conversation about singing and which songs we liked when suddenly the front door opened, and in walked Tarzi Barilla with Ralphie Rest, Frankie Rice and Jerry the Jew. Tarzi had a crazy look in his eyes like he was looking for trouble. He was built like a grizzly bear and always had a weird sardonic smile. Ralphie's arms were like tree trunks with tattoos. Each one of the Bath Beach boys, including Punchy, had a skull and crossbones tattoo on their forearms: the tell-tale symbol of The Bath Beach boys. The skull had a top hat that was slightly tilted to one side with "Bath Beach" written underneath. Jerry was very serious. His grey sweater vest stood out against his white tee shirt. Punchy waved to them, and they waved back, like a secret greeting, and Punchy continued to talk with Scapper and me. Tarzi went up to the counter as Pop was turning around with an egg cream in his hand and said, "Hey, Pop, you wanna see time stand still?" The other guys started harassing the girls, except Maryann who moved a little closer to Punchy.

Pop was used to the pranks these guys would play. He was a nice old man, with grey hair on the sides of his bald head. He looked like a real Elmer Fudd with a white ice-cream-stained apron on which he wiped his hands. Tarzi reached behind his shirt and pulled out a gun. Most of the kids in the store had never seen a real gun, including me. We all thought it was a joke, and some started to laugh. Scapper and I looked at Punchy, who was not laughing, and that scared us. Punchy stared intently at Tarzi's face. Tarzi pointed the gun at Pop's chest. Pop hands were frozen to the stainless-steel ice cream counter top covers and my egg cream was on the floor. Pop started to shake. His skin turned as white as his apron. Beads of sweat started rolling down his forehead. Tarzi leaned over the counter and was looking right into pop's eyes. The next record dropped onto the turntable, "Down Down Down Down Down down di doobie" breaking the silence. Frankie Rice burst out laughing, then Tarzi, Ralphie and the rest of the kids joined in. Punchy wasn't laughing, and neither was Jerry. Tarzi slowly raised the gun as Pop's eyes followed it up and over Pop's head. He pointed it at the red and white Coca-Cola clock on the wall behind Pop. He pulled the trigger and the clock shattered into a thousand pieces of plastic and glass. The noise was deafening. The girls were screaming and trying to get out of the store without going near Tarzi. And then Pop collapsed. Everyone was silent except Jerry, who was now slapping the counter with his hand and laughing hysterically.

Punchy starting yelling at Tarzi, "Are you fucking crazy?"

Tarzi looked satisfied, like he'd just finished a great meal. Scapper, real name Angelo Rubano, who always talked about being a doctor someday and did become a surgeon, ran behind the counter, got a cold rag and started wiping Pop's face and neck while holding him. Punchy and I tried to assist Scapper, but he had it under control. Punchy suggested we all leave the store, and everyone complied except Tarzi and the crew, who started helping themselves to ice cream and soda, making a mess behind the counter. Pop sat up and started yelling, and they all left, laughing. The only one left with Pop was Scapper.

Punchy met me outside and asked me if I would be interested in singing with a group. He explained that they were starting out and that he would help me. I really didn't know what to say, but it was oddly interesting, and with my new-found talent as a bass singer, I agreed. We exchanged phone numbers, and Punchy said he would meet me at 7:00 by my house and we would walk over to meet Jimmy Hudson and his group. Jimmy got his nickname because he drove a 1953 Hudson, and he was the lead singer because he had a decent voice. Naturally, his group was called The Hudsons.

Punchy, Maryann and I went back in and checked with Scapper. Pop was feeling much better. He kept saying that he was going to sell his goddamn store and move to Florida. Punchy explained to me that he was helping this new group, The Hudsons, because of his friendship with a guy named Conig. I asked if he meant Anthony Conigliaro because Anthony was my cousin, and he said, "Yes, that's the same Conig. His father owns the Hollywood Terrace."

When we all met later on, Conig was surprised to see me. "You sing, too?" Conig asked with a big smile.

I replied, "Well, Punchy thinks I would be a good bass. I never did this."

Bobby Ferucci was the second tenor, Jimmy was the lead singer, Conig was baritone and Punchy did first tenor until they could find someone else. Punchy asked me to sing the "You'll never know" part that I'd sung earlier at Pop's, and everyone was stunned. "Wow," Conig said with his usual smile, "You're a fucking bass, my cousin's a fucking bass!" We all laughed, and I felt so good because Conig was there, but I still didn't have a clue as to what to do.

The song we were trying to learn was "Sentimental Reasons" by The Riveliers. The method of learning to a sing a song with a group was to first play the record and sing along until it sounded like the record. Not so simple. We listened intently, over and over, trying to pick out each of the harmony parts. Actually no one exactly knew what to do, it was a hit and miss process. Punchy had some experience from singing with his group, but it was still dicey. Jimmy would sing along with the lead of the recording and the rest of us would try to emulate the background vocals. It was clear to me that the background, with the harmony, was difficult. It sounded okay as long as we were singing with the record, but when we tried without the record it did not sound so good. We didn't understand music, and Punchy was trying the best he could to explain harmony to guys who knew nothing about it. Luckily, Punchy had a lot of patience. Teenage vocal groups everywhere were utilizing the same method. Without any training, there was no other way to learn harmony.

Once we had the format of the song down pat, we started working on the harmony parts. Punchy asked Conig to hit a baritone note and just hold it as steady as he could. Bobby Ferrucci would try to harmonize with that note. When it sounded right, Punchy filled in the tenor note, and it sounded like nice harmony, but only if no one dropped off his note. It was hard to do. Punchy showed me where to fill in with the bass notes, and it sounded a little better. We didn't know it then, but there were only three harmony parts that made up the simple backgrounds we were imitating. The bass part was always an octave below one of the three harmony parts and made the harmony sound fuller.

Jimmy started his lead part, "I love you," and we countered in harmony, "I love you." This was the first time I had heard live harmony, and I was totally blown away with the fact that we accomplished this on our own, in only three hours. It was difficult for some us to stay on the note and keep the harmony going. It was also the way guys were weeded out. Some just knew that they were not meant for harmony and quit on their own, while others, like me, were totally infatuated and decided to hang in and do the best they could. The real harmony would come later, with a lot of practice and a lot of patience. You just kind of developed an ear for what sounded right and what didn't. Some people had it, and most people didn't. It was a little like rhythm. Some people can naturally feel it, while others have a really hard time. I was lucky: I had natural rhythm. Harmony took a little while, but at least I didn't have tin ear.

CHAPTER 3

GEE

Tony "Punchy" Armato was part of a group that was started by Bobby Ferrante called The Enchanters. They started to sing on the corner of Bay 19th Street and 86th Street in the Bath Beach section of Brooklyn, NY. Yes, I mean on the corner, because that's where most of the singing groups started, outside while everyone was hanging out. Phil Cracolici was the lead singer, Philly Campano, the bass, Tony "Punchy" Armato sang second tenor, with Bobby Ferrante on first tenor and Albee Cracolici doing baritone. They all hung out in Kelly's pool room on Bay 19th Street, which was directly across the street from the exit stair side of the Loew's Oriental movie theatre on 86th Street.

While writing this, I had a conversation with my friend Ben Cammarata, who also sang with us in Brooklyn. While reminiscing about the neighborhood and Kelly's, Ben told me that the Loew's Oriental is now a Marshall's store. Ben is the presently the Chairman of the TJX Companies; he founded TJ Max in 1976 and then acquired Home Goods and Marshall's. Ben recalls that when a real estate person in his company asked if he would be interested in the Loews Oriental property in Brooklyn, he immediately went to see it – and bought it. Perhaps it was out of nostalgia. Ben made sure that during the renovation they kept the old marble staircase intact. We all loved that theatre. It brought back so many fond memories.

Kelly's Billiards was in the basement of the building across the street. There were about 20 green felt-topped pool tables, each with a light fixture hanging over the middle of the table. Two 100-watt light bulbs lit up each table, to eliminate shadows, and raising the oppressive heat. The place had an eerie look; cigarette smoke hung in a low cloud, with an aroma that was a mix of cigarettes, old wood, beer and sweat. The smoke cloud moved with the wind from the fan when it changed direction every few seconds. There wasn't any air conditioning, just a couple of stand-up fans that didn't help much.

Air conditioning was new in public spaces. Most places that installed central air conditioning would advertise that they had it by hanging a sign that showed a glacier with the words "Air Conditioning" proudly displayed. Everyone smoked. It was cool to smoke. The pro pool players shot pool with a lit cigarette dangling from their lips while the smoke made its way up their faces, making their eyes twitch. When they tired of shooting pool and there were enough guys to form a group, they would usually go directly across the street and sing. There was a small alcove in the side of the tan brick building, which was part of the Loew's Oriental that provided the landing for a huge black metal fire escape. This is where they sang because this was where there was an echo.

A cappella always sounded better with an echo. That's how the group started, with an echo. In 1956, Bobby Ferrante was singing to himself in the laundry room of his building and realized it sounded much better with the echo from the walls, like singing in the shower. He thought it sounded like a recording. Bobby loved to sing. He shared this new-found echo chamber with his friends, Tony Carosella and Phil Cracolici, and they started trying to harmonize, and to them it actually sounded like the harmony on the records by the groups they listened to. From that point, there was no stopping them. Bobby borrowed a tape recorder from his uncle, and they recorded their harmony in the laundry room. They sang "Gee" by The Crows. Bobby brought the tape recorder to Kelly's pool room and played it for some of the guys. Everyone in the pool room wanted to be in the group. Albee Cracolici and Punchy were interested and friendlier with Bobby so they decided to join Bobby and Tony and Phil in the singing group. It was mostly hit and miss in the beginning, as they were trying to duplicate songs that were on the rhythm and blues radio stations by groups like The Penguins, The Wrens, The Nutmegs and The Harptones. They would soon find out that without formal music training this was an incredible task, but they didn't have much of anything else to do. Nobody was really interested in school. In 1956, it was an accomplishment to graduate from high school, and college was for the rich kids.

The street corner became the urban college for those teenagers wanting to sing in a group. They studied their asses off, continuously going over the harmony parts over and over until it sounded right. They sang every chance they could. Bobby had a pretty good ear for music and assumed the role of arranging the harmony parts. Phil was singing the lead part because he had the most melodic voice and he knew most of the lyrics to the songs. Bobby did the first tenor, Punchy did second tenor and Albee had the right voice for the baritone part. They recruited Phil Campano for the bass because he had the deepest voice. Although Phil was not thrilled with the idea of singing, he was actually pretty good. Tony Carosella realized, with the help of Bobby, that although he wanted to sing, he had a tin ear, and so he left the group.

Nobody made fun of them in the pool room because they were the tough guys. Imagine a group of would-be juvenile delinquents forming a singing group with the farfetched intention of becoming recording stars. Imagine trying to learn how to do harmony without any formal training or schooling.

They needed a group name, and Bobby came up with The Enchanters. After a few weeks of nightly harmonizing practice, they started to sound good. It was the constant practice that did it. They didn't realize it, but they were in school. Self-taught, but nevertheless very school-like.

One night, Phil Cracolici broke the news that he had decided to join the Navy. They would have to get a new lead singer. Phil had dropped out of high school like a lot of the other guys and saw no real future in the neighborhood, especially when most of his friends were preparing themselves for a life of crime. He wasn't interested in the crime scene, and he didn't see any future in hanging out every night. He didn't do well in school and thought about going into the Army or the Navy, so he could learn a trade, which was very forward-thinking for a young man. He passed by a Naval recruiting office one day, walked in and they talked him into becoming a sailor.

The other Enchanters were annoyed but not discouraged. The group thought they were going places. They had no idea how difficult it was to get a hit record. Bobby's friend Johnny Bellsano (Johnny Bell) a nickname that, like many, came from his last name, was going out with a girl from 50th street and 12th Avenue, and she said that her neighbor, Joe Strobel, was a good lead singer. Bobby told the guys and arranged a meeting with Joe and found him to be not only a pretty good lead singer but a song writer and guitar player as well. They met Joe at his apartment in the afternoon, and he sang a few songs that he knew. It was rare that someone from the neighborhood played an instrument. Not too many families could afford the lessons. Joe wasn't a great player, but he owned a guitar and that was worth something. Joe was frustrated with the group he was with, and after hearing the Enchanters' harmony he agreed to join their group.

Joe was of German decent and although he was outnumbered by Italians, four to one, he did have a unique voice and some musical talent. It seemed like a good match. Joe was about six-foot-tall, with a lean body frame. He had blondish hair and a strong chiseled face that set him apart from the dark-haired Italians. After getting to know everyone, Joe figured out that Bobby was the group leader/spokesman. Bobby had the gift of gab, and Joe knew he was no match for him as a leader. Still, he thought that he should run the group since he was now the lead singer. That started an internal rivalry that would eventually lead to the group's breakup.

The Enchanters sounded good after only a few weeks of practice. In fact, they sounded better than most of the other groups that had been singing for a while on just about every street corner and subway station, for the tiled walls in the subway train stations also provided good echo. Joe hated the name The Enchanters and told the guys it sounded like a girl group name. He said that there was a group of girls he knew from Avenue U that called themselves The Enchanters. They didn't sing, they just were a sort of social club. They wore pink satin jackets with "Enchanters" in script across the back. Once the guys saw that, the name was history. But they got to know the girls through Joe and started developing some relationships.

Bobby felt that they should have more of a musical sounding name like The Cleftones. They voted on a few names and settled on Joe's pick. They were now The Overons from Bath Beach. They were the singing descendants of the infamous Bath Beach gang. Bobby kind of liked the name but did not really like Joe Strobel.

The Bath Beach section of Brooklyn, New York, was part of the original town of New Utrecht and was close to the shoreline and Coney Island. After the stock market crash of 1929, when affordable housing was built in Bath Beach, many Italian and Jewish immigrants moved to this area from the Lower East Side of Manhattan. The completion of the Belt Parkway in 1939 made it easy to travel by car to the area. The Italians brought many talents to the neighborhood. Cooking, gardening, music, building skills – and the Mafia. It was the kind of neighborhood where you could walk around at night and not worry about being mugged because the would-be muggers were afraid they might hit on someone "connected."

Music of the early 1950's continued the big band sound of the 1940's. Artists like Perry Como, The Four Lads, Louie Prima and Keely Smith all had their musical roots in the forties. The music changed as younger people listened and put their own spin on what they liked. The teenage music of the early fifties added the black sound of rhythm and blues. This led to groups like The Drifters, The Platters, and Fats Domino doing their version of that mix of forties and fifties music. Done by young people for young people, this music caught on like wildfire. DJ Alan Freed picked up on it, played it and named it "rock 'n roll."

And so, music was forever changed, and so were the lives of thousands of teenagers who wanted a piece of fame and fortune. It looked easy, so they formed a group and sang. The Overons were no different. They had gone to the shows at the Brooklyn Paramount to see 13-year-old Frankie Lymon and the Teenagers singing about teenage love. They saw The Cadillacs from Harlem with their slick harmony, choreography and electric blue suits singing "Gloria" and "Speedo." The Platters, with Tony Williams on lead, sang standards from the forties, and with a touch of falsetto and bass transformed those into rock 'n roll songs. They listened to Freed on his radio show playing this new music by the teenage generation, and every teenager thought: I could do this too. So, the Overons started, just like every other teenage group singing on the street corners of Brooklyn at night trying to emulate their idols. Even though they were tough kids, they found this special feeling when they made harmony. It was like the camaraderie of a gang without the dire consequences. It was the beginning of lifelong friendships.

This wasn't the only group these boys belonged to. Prior to and including the Enchanters and the Overons, many were part of the Bath Beach Boys, a tough teenage street gang. Throughout the New York area, teenagers, usually from the same neighborhood, formed gangs out of boredom and desperation, since there wasn't much to do after school. The Rampers from Bay Ridge, The Hawks from Bensonhurst, The Chaplins from the Bronx, and the many motorcycle gangs like The Hells Angels, The Pagans and The Outlaws, some of which still endure, were just part of a vast number of teenage groups. Many of the teenagers' parents both worked, and there was a lot of unsupervised time. Some moms, like mine, worked in dress shops and factories in sweat shop conditions. Work was available if you wanted it, but you had to work hard, so many teenagers were left alone after school.

Most of these gangs were formed as social clubs, but the Bath Beach boys were more than a social club. They planned and pulled off robberies. The leaders, Frank "Tarzi" Barilla, Ralphie "Rest" Galione, Frankie Rice and Jerry "The Jew" Rosenberg, were well known in the neighborhood. Not every member participated in the robberies, but all of them were involved in the gang fights. If a member of another street gang entered the neighborhood or talked to somebody's girlfriend, there were consequences. It could be in the form of a fight between two individuals, but it usually meant a gang fight.

In the summer of 1957, teenagers hung out at luncheonettes like Freytag's, Chookie's and Mom's in Bensonhurst and Bath Beach and ordered cokes and egg creams while they fed nickels to the juke box to hear their favorite songs. These were our daily hangouts before, during and after school. My favorite place was Mom's Sandwich Shop, which was directly across the street from New Utrecht High School on 79th Street and 15th Avenue. Mom's made the best potato and egg hero sandwiches in the world! Scrambled eggs mixed with crispy home fries, in olive oil, on a half-loaf of Italian bread. Awesome!

Bill Haley and the Comets and The Platters were on the pop stations but the R & B stations, on the high end of the AM radio dial, FM was not invented yet, played The Harptones, The Nutmegs and The Turbans. I was one of those kids who listened to those groups. I thought they were fantastic.

The Overons practiced every chance they could. Listening to groups that had records out at the time, they put a lot of effort into capturing that harmony sound. Bobby Ferrante having the most musical talent guided the guys with the harmonies. "That's too high" he would say to Tony. Then they would try it again. "Okay, Albee, a little lower." They kept doing the same parts over and over until it sounded right. It was like learning to play a musical instrument, the more you rehearsed the better you got. This was quite an accomplishment for teenagers who'd never sung harmony before. They just knew when it sounded right and when it was on. Joe sang "Oh what a night" and the background followed with "To love you, dear."

"Perfect" Bobby said.

Tarzi, Ralphie Rest, Frankie and Jerry the Jew had other aspirations. They were always planning their next scheme to make money illegally. They would hang out at Freytag's Ice Cream parlor on 79th Street and New Utrecht Avenue, sit in a booth and plan their next heist. I lived up the block from Freytag's on 79th Street and would see them in there occasionally. I would usually hang with Louie and Butchie Valerio, Angelo "Scapper" Rubano and Nicky Zagami, play the current 45s and talk with the girls. Although I was already singing with the Hudsons my friends and I dreamed of starting a vocal group of our own and would call ourselves the Bellbottoms, because wearing Navy issue bellbottom jeans was popular. Growing up in Bensonhurst was amazing. We played stickball, punch ball, stoopball, boxball, kick the can, Johnny on the pony, and many other neighborhood games. Living a few blocks away from New Utrecht High School allowed us to use the school handball courts, and so many a day was spent hitting the pink Spalding ball against the concrete walls on the court. Well we weren't, actually allowed, there was a hole in the chain link fence. As a kid, that pink Spalding was part of my life. I can still remember the smell.

When you walked through the front door of Freytag's, the first thing you would see straight ahead, across the off-white tile floor, was a large Wurlitzer juke box. It had all the trimmings: the colored bubbles in glass tubes, the curved glass dome, the numbered buttons, and most important, the 45 records. The counter, to the left, had about 10 black-leather-covered stools trimmed in chrome. Behind the counter were the gleaming stainless-steel ice cream holders. And there was Lillian, a most memorable waitress who was everybody's favorite mom. Lillian's son Phil was taking drum lessons and I thought I would like to try that too. Phil introduced me to his drum teacher and for two dollars a week I was taking drum lessons. I had to pay this out of the money I earned by working in my father's shoe repair shop on Saturdays. Of course, it was completely impractical to think I would ever own a drum set. I practiced my lessons on a homemade rubber pad with the drums sticks that Phil lent me. I eventually got myself a new set of drumsticks.

We lived in a two-bedroom apartment on 79th Street and I shared a bedroom with my brother Richie. We each had a single bed and I had to move my bed to get into the one closet. That's when it dawned on me that in order to be a drummer you had to live in something larger than a two-bedroom apartment.

Just past the juke box were the wooden booths, each capable of seating four to eight people. Freytag's made their own ice cream in the cellar of the store. It was so good! I still remember the tutti-frutti flavor, a combination of vanilla and strawberry ice cream with tiny pieces of fresh fruit. It's amazing how a song, a taste, and a smell can stay in your memory and when unlocked reveal where you were and what you were doing, how you felt and the people you were with.

Ralph Galione had two nicknames, Ralphie Rest and Ralphie the Hat. Ralphie the Hat because he always wore one everywhere. It was a grey fedora, the kind just about every grown man wore when outside. But Ralph wore his hat inside, too. At 21, he was prematurely balding and never took the hat off. Ralphie Rest because he ended every conversation with "take a rest," which eventually became just "rest." It was one of those sayings that caught on in the neighborhood. We would tell someone to "rest" when we thought they were bullshitting. Ralph dropped out of high school to work construction and was now a trim 160 pounds of muscle. After meeting Tarzi, he decided to join the gang. Ralphie had a great lead voice and would sing with the Hudsons once in a while.

CHAPTER 4

BIG BROWN EYES

The Overons auditioned for a singing group contest at the Loews Oriental movie theatre in November 1956 after Albee saw the sign go up on the marquee asking for singing groups to participate. The theatre manager, Robert Bergerman, wanted to give local teenage singing groups a chance to perform after he saw a group of kids singing by a storefront on his way home. He knew Albee's reputation and was too scared to refuse him, but after he heard The Overons sing, he felt better about it. They sang their original up-tempo song, "Big Brown Eyes." The audition took place on the stage of the theatre in the morning before the movie started. This was a big theatre which was originally built for stage shows and now showed movies.

Philly Campano, the bass singer, was freaking out. A 185-pound muscular teenager who was not afraid of anybody had the most awful stage fright. Sweating profusely, he leaned over to Albee and said, "I can't do this." Albee's answer was, "Come on, Philly, just get through this one song and then we'll talk about it." They walked from behind the curtain and had their first view of the theatre from the stage. The spotlights were so bright they could only see the first three rows of seats, and although nobody but the theatre manager, his assistant, and a few ushers were out there, it was still a new and exciting event for all. Looking down at the floor, Philly Campano nervously started with his bass part after Bobby gave him a note from his pitch pipe, and the rest of the group chimed in with their harmony parts. Joe Strobel started his lead, with his fingers snapping the fast tempo. He sang, "Big brown eyes, I love you so-oh" and they all became a little more relaxed, except for Phil Campano, who was still in a state of shock and continued to stare at the floor. Joe was on one mike and the other four crowded around the other mike. This was the first time they'd sung with microphones on a stage in front of people. The sound system was not the best, but it was loud and reverberated throughout the theatre. They did not have monitors but hearing themselves on the house speakers was thrilling. When they finished, Robert, the theatre manager and Bruce, the assistant manager, clapped and shouted out, "Good job guys, nicely done."

Three other groups did their songs while the Overons watched from the audience and quietly commented to each other. Philly Campano was still nervous and made up his mind that if this is what he had to do to be in the group he wanted no part of it. His T-shirt was soaked from sweating so much. He told Bobby that he was not sure he wanted to do this. When Robert Bergerman offered them a spot in the contest, Campano's knees got weak.

After the audition, they all went to the diner across the street to celebrate, but not Philly Campano, who went home instead. The remaining four Overons sat in a booth discussing the other groups they'd just heard. The Baybops from Bay 20th Street sounded okay but were not as good as The Overons. Neither were The Flames or the C-notes. None of the young groups had a bass singer. Bobby told the guys that if they were going to do this show in two weeks they would need a new bass singer, because Campano was too scared to perform. They all agreed. Punchy had told Bobby about this kid Allie, who had just started to sing with a new group that he was coaching but said he would have to check with Allie's cousin, Conig, first. Joe asked if Allie was as good as Philly and Punchy assured him he was. Bobby suggested they let me try out and Punchy set it up.

Frankie Rice and Jerry Rosenberg were at the next booth, having coffee with Billy Botts. They overheard the boys discussing the upcoming contest. Jerry asked, "What's the prize if you guys win?" At this point, he had no interest in the singing, even though he was also in a group, but if there was money involved that was another matter. Bobby told him the first prize was fifty dollars and that Robert Bergerman and Bruce Schwartz were running the contest. "This kid, Bruce, he must have money," Jerry mused.

"I think his family is loaded. They live over in that rich section of Flatbush," answered Bobby. Billy, Frankie Rice and Jerry decided to go to the movies. Bobby and Albee thought they were going to try to get in on the group competition, and they had a good laugh since they'd heard their group sing. Jerry was the lead singer of The Blue Notes, and although they looked good and had all the right moves, they had very little harmony sense. The Blue Notes did a few shows at the 19th Hole bar on 86th Street, because that's where they hung out, and all their friends would go to hear them and support them.

Billy spotted Bruce in the lobby. Bruce was in his late twenties and a mild-mannered mamma's boy. They grabbed him by the arms and ushered him down the side door to the boiler room in the basement where they tied him to a drain pipe. Bruce started to cry. "What's going on, come on this ain't funny."

"Aw shut up you fucking pansy" answered Jerry.

They got Bruce's home number and called his mother. "Is this Bruce's mother?"

"Yes, it is whose calling?"

Jerry continued, trying to disguise his voice. "Don't worry about who this is and worry about your son Bruce. If we don't get two hundred in cash today, you won't see Bruce tomorrow." The conversation went on, including her hearing Bruce crying in the background, and she agreed to pay the money. Billy went to her house and picked up the envelope from the garbage can as agreed. He then jumped into the waiting car and he and they sped off, removing the handkerchiefs that covered their faces. They let Bruce go with a warning that if he told anyone they would get his whole family. Bruce never went back to the Loews Oriental. His mother eventually called the police, but Bruce was afraid to say anything or identify anyone and, so it became history.

Detectives, Kevin Riley and Angelo Carelli knew who did it from general questions but without proof or an eye witness, there was nothing they could do. They could not get Bruce to talk about it and quit his job. The Detectives would have to wait a little longer.

A few days after the incident, the two detectives caught up with Jerry and Frankie sitting with Bob Ferrante in Al's Luncheonette on Cropsey Avenue and Bay 17th Street. "So now you're into kidnapping?" asked Riley. Neither Jerry nor Frankie looked up from their burgers, as if they didn't know who Riley was talking to. Bobby really didn't have any idea what this was all about, so he did what they did and stared at his burger. Carelli and Riley in their typical dark suits, white shirts and ties were standing directly in front of Jerry. "There is nobody else here but you guys, so don't act so surprised" said Carelli. Jerry looked right into Carelli's eyes and said, "I don't have the foggiest idea of what you're talking about" in a kind of mocking English accent. Riley, feeling like he should say something that would register, said, "You know, you guys are smart. Why don't you do something responsible with your lives? Go to school, get a job, and learn a trade. I'll bet if you put half the effort that you put into your bullshit stuff into school, you could be something special." Frankie never looked up, he just kept on sipping his coke and eating his hamburger and fries. Jerry moved his eyes to Carelli's and said, "Gee, detective, how nice of you to care, and that's exactly what we were discussing when your friend here started accusing us of bad things. I was thinking of becoming a judge."

Frankie started to laugh under his breath but made it sound like he was choking on the soda. "Yeah, I'm gonna be a doctor." Riley hit Jerry with a backhanded slap across the face and then got real close with both hands holding on the table and his tie dangling very close to the ketchup sitting on top of an order of French fries. In a real serious tone, he said, "You guys are destined for jail and I am gonna be there when you get booked."

Jerry shrugged off the pain as his face turned red from the slap and answered as the detectives were leaving, "Hey, Carelli, you forgot the check, it's your turn to buy, you scumbag. Nice to see you again, drop in any time, assholes." Bobby was a few years younger than Frankie and Jerry when he met them in Al's luncheonette around 1951, when he was 15 years old, and he started hanging out with Jerry mostly because he liked Jerry and they made each other laugh. Jerry liked Frankie Rice because he was a tough guy. Carelli said to Riley as they got into their car, "I'm gonna get all those fuckers." Then he wiped some ketchup from the tip of his new tie.

Jerry had a 1950 red Plymouth Belvedere that his parents gave him for his 18th birthday, and he would pick up Bobby and Frankie Rice at Al's diner and they would go to Coney Island. Jerry's father was a wealthy businessman and could never understand why his son had to go around getting into trouble. Once in Coney Island, Jerry loved to pick up girls on Bay 14, and then they would all go to Nathan's and then to the fun house where in the dark they would make out with the girls, sometimes for hours. Jerry always paid for everything; he always had a roll of cash. Sometimes on the way to Coney Island, Jerry would make stops and leave Frankie and Bobby in the double-parked car. He would say "I got some business to take care of." He would reach into the glove compartment, take his gun and go into a grocery store. He would come back in ten minutes, throw the gun back into the glove compartment and drive. That always made Bobby a little nervous, but he never questioned Jerry.

The singing contest was set for December 7, 1956 and the Overons still needed a bass singer. Punchy was supposed to set up a meeting with me and my Cousin Conig. Nobody in the Overons knew me except Punchy, but they all knew Conig. Conig was considered one of the guys in the neighborhood that you never messed with. He had a great sense of humor and the heartiest laugh in the crowd and would fight at the drop of a hat, and usually win. Punchy, Bobby and Albee decided that Bobby would talk to Conig. He called Conig, and it was decided that I would try out for the Overons, but I didn't know it yet.

Conig called me at home that afternoon and said he was going to pick me up at 6:30 and that we were going for a ride and get some food at Mitchells. I wanted to know why we were going there, but he said he would tell me later. When I got in the car, Conig told me about the conversation with Bobby, and the Overons situation. I was stunned because Conig and I were already in a singing group, the Hudsons. I said, "Hey, I don't want to leave you guys flat."

Conig answered in his most serious tone, "Look we ain't got nothing going on, our harmony's not really making it. At least you have a real shot with the Overons." We were on our way to Mitchells. On the way, Conig filled me in on what had happened with Phil Campano at the Loews audition. I was starting to get nervous. Singing with the Hudsons was kind of easy, as everyone was at the beginning stages. No one was expecting anything special. The Overons were a different story: the best vocal group in the neighborhood and considered the most professional. I was only singing about five weeks. I was both nervous and strangely calm, like I knew this was meant to be. I thought, well I don't have anything to lose. I might as well give it a try.

CHAPTER 5

COME GO WITH ME

We pulled into Mitchells about 6:45 PM. Mitchells was the most popular drive-in restaurant in Brooklyn. It was located on the corner of 86th Street and Seventh Avenue, and cars were constantly going in and out. There were 1954 Mercs, 57 Chevys showing off their bull noses, skirts, candy-apple-red paint- jobs and loud engines outfitted with custom mufflers, which the drivers would blast as they paraded through the group of parked cars. There were lots of teenagers hanging in and out of cars.

It was a little chilly outside, sweater weather. Conig backed his 1955 Ford into a parking spot, shutting off the engine and leaving the radio on. A carhop that we knew named Marie came over smiling and hung a metal tray on the driver's side door. She bent down to see who was sitting in the car, exposing the tops of her breasts. As "Oh What a Night" by The Dells played on the radio, she asked, while chewing gum, "Hi, Conig, whaddaya want?" She knew she was going to get a wisecrack answer, and she did. "Your tits on a bun," Conig said with a big smile as he stared at her chest, which was eye level. He laughed so heartily that she couldn't get mad and laughed out loud herself. Conig had a way of making everyone laugh.

He and I talked a little and noticed a black Oldsmobile pulling into a spot across the lot. "That's them!" he said. We finished our cokes and walked over to Albee Cracolici's car. Conig knew everyone and introduced me to Joe Strobel, Bob Ferrante and Albee Cracolici, who were all sitting in Albee's car. I already knew Punchy. We all shook hands and exchanged "how ya doings." I tried to say it in the deepest voice I could muster, which did get facial reactions. I felt a little more comfortable when Punchy invited me to sit in the back with him. We made a little small talk and then Albee asked me what songs I knew. Punchy answered, "Let's try 'Come Go with me,' he knows it."

Bobby had a shiny round pitch pipe that later became affectionately known as the kazoo. He blew a note and Joe started singing, snapping his fingers to the beat, "Down Down Down Down Down down di doobie," and then it was my turn. I came in with the bass notes I had studied at home listening to the Dell Vikings, "Down down down down down." This felt good. The rest of the guys started singing their harmony parts, and Bobby said, "Holy shit, this is great." I was astounded at how good their harmony was and how my voice just fit right in. It was smooth and creamy harmony, and we all knew it. That night, singing in a 1953 Oldsmobile with some guys I'd never met before, changed my life forever.

Albee and Joe turned around so that now we were all facing each other. Each of us was smiling as we went into, "Oh What a Night." An amazing thing was happening. I was swept up in the music we were making with our voices. I glanced over at Conig who was right outside, leaning against the car by the open back window, beaming. Kids started gathering around the car to listen.

Frankie Rice and Jerry the Jew were passing the drive-in and saw all the kids around Albee's car. They stopped right in front of the car and jumped out, thinking something was wrong. As they got closer, they heard the harmony. They popped their heads in the open windows in a weak attempt at joining in but gave up when they realized that what they were hearing was good harmony. "Hey, you guys are good," Jerry said to Albee. Albee just smiled as he continued to sing. Jerry looked at me and nodded his head, yes. He didn't know who I was but knew I was the new guy. Jerry and Frankie got back in their car, found a spot and ordered some food, while waiting to speak to Albee, Punchy and Bobby about an idea they had for a hold-up. Then we sang some more. After a few songs, they told me to leave the car, so I waited outside with Conig as they voted. It was decided – I would be the new bass. Conig was telling me how great we sounded – Conig and Punchy could not have been happier. I was thrilled. Not only was I part of a singing group, which elevated my status to the top of the social ladder, but I was with the premier neighborhood group. And, as an added bonus, Bobby, Punchy and Albee were part of the Bath Beach boys, which meant I automatically had immunity.

It crossed my mind that I was getting tight with some tough older guys, but in this neighborhood, it was not unusual. I had no intention of getting involved with any of their hold-ups or other crimes. And I was reassured because my cousin Conig knew everyone in the group.

Later, Jerry asked Albee and the other guys to join them in a holdup they were planning for the following night. They said they could not go because they had set up a rehearsal. Albee explained that the Loews theatre contest was next Friday night and they needed to practice with their new bass singer (me). They didn't realize it at the time but turning down Jerry and Frankie Rice because they wanted to practice was the first step towards saving their lives. This new thing, this bond between young men striving to learn something together, was taking over. It was like a religious experience. Group practice and music became a major part of our lives. To get better, we knew we had to rehearse a lot. The better we got, the more we realized that we could be even better. There was so much to learn, and we were committed. There were other groups in the neighborhood that were also rehearsing. What we didn't realize at the time, was that there were thousands of teenage groups all over the city as well as the rest of the country rehearsing and trying for that golden ring, the magic recording contract. It was like an American Idol contest, but the judges were the record companies and managers.

Around March of 1957, Bobby Ferrante's cousin Champie introduced Bobby to Jeff Pearl from the Neons. Jeff invited us to one of their rehearsals on 39th Street in the Borough Park section of Brooklyn where they lived. The Neons had just released their new recording called "Angel Face," which became a New York hit. We were very impressed with their harmony, and I think it influenced our subsequent style. Jeff offered to come to our rehearsal and helped us out with harmony parts that we didn't know existed. A week later, we learned "Angel Face" and did it as a warm up for rehearsal.

The only other famous group from the neighborhood was the Three Heartbeats, who later changed their name to the Three Friends. In 1955, they recorded "Blanche," which was also a big New York hit. They were all from New Utrecht High School, and one of the members, Joe Villa, went on to write and record "Short Shorts" with the Royal Teens in 1958. The song was co-written by Bob Gaudio, who went on to sing with Frankie Valli and The Four Seasons.

Bobby Ferrante was dating a girl named Annie from Avenue U, and he asked us to go with him to meet her friends. They stayed at Fat Sid's candy store, affectionately called "The Rathole," on Avenue U. Fat Sid was at least 350 pounds and usually sat in a big chair by the front door. From this position, he would collect money from his customers. He had a few teenagers working behind the counter and serving the four tables. He rarely got up. He would only get up to go to the bathroom, and that would take an hour. The girls were part of a club and called themselves the Allures. They wore pink satin jackets with "The Allures" in black script. We met Carol Ardigo, one of the Allures, who was dating a guy named Tommy Shack, who, she told us, played the guitar. (I met Tommy again many years later, in the seventies, when he played as a part of a backup band for The Mystics.) Carol introduced him to Bobby and Bobby asked Tommy if he wanted to play guitar for us. Bobby and Albee were getting annoyed with Joe Strobel's guitar playing while he was singing. He would miss lyrics because he was concentrating on the guitar. Tommy invited all of us to Carol's parents' house on West 6th and Avenue U to rehearse in the basement. Carol's parents were very generous. Tommy got Johnny Black to bring his drum set over and now The Overons had a band. A guitar and a snare drum. Not a very good one, but a band. I was positive that Johnny Black did not live in a two-bedroom apartment.

Carol's basement was typical for two-family houses in Brooklyn. It had a boiler, a hot water heater, a clothes line, and a couple of folding chairs. None of us cared about how it looked, it was better than singing outside and it was nice of the Ardigo family to let us rehearse there. That's when I met Carol sister, Linda, who was fourteen. I didn't pay much attention to her because she was just a kid. Only a few years younger than me but nevertheless a kid in my eyes. (We met again a few years later when she wasn't a kid anymore.)

Jerry Rosenberg found out where we were rehearsing and stopped in one night to listen to the new guitar player. Jerry always felt close to Bobby and would do anything to help. Jerry came down the basement and said, "You guys don't even have a decent chair to sit on." He lit up a Lucky Strike and listened for a few songs, and when his attention span maxed out he said, "Listen, meet me tomorrow at 10:00. My uncle owns a moving company and he has some old furniture we can have, but we have to pick it up." Tommy asked Mrs. Ardigo if it was okay and she agreed. The next morning Jerry pulled up with a Bath Beach Movers truck and handed us Bath Beach Movers shirts. "Put these on" Jerry said, with his signature sardonic smile. "We're gonna get some furniture!"

The four new moving men climbed into the truck with Jerry, and twenty minutes later we were in front of one of those fancy apartment buildings on Ocean Parkway. Jerry jumped out of the truck, saying, "I'll be right back." He went into the lobby and spoke to the doorman while waving some paperwork in his face. He told him management was changing out the furniture and that we were here to pick up the old furniture because the new stuff was arriving on another truck in about an hour. He gave the doorman the paperwork and ten dollars and motioned for us guys to come in. Jerry started barking orders. "All right, you two get the couch; you two get the chairs and the lamps." The doorman held the door open for us. Within twenty minutes, the lobby was empty. We even rolled up the fancy Persian carpet in front of the couch. Two hours later, Jerry was sitting on one of the Ocean Parkway chairs in Carol's basement smoking a cigarette; flicking ashes into the new chrome ashtray stand and listening to The Overons rehearse. Carol's mom was shocked. She couldn't believe that all this nice furniture had been donated by Jerry's uncle just because he liked The Overons so much. She would always offer – and we never refused – meatball sandwiches and cokes.

Later that day Detectives Carelli and Riley saw a report about the brazen robbery on Ocean Parkway in a residential building. They went to talk to the doorman, who couldn't remember what they looked like except the one in charge, who was very handsome and charming. They showed the doorman photos of Jerry, and the doorman, realizing that Jerry was in trouble with the law, said he couldn't really be sure. He was sure they were wearing "Bath Beach" shirts. The report also stated that a Bath Beach moving truck had been stolen from Bath Avenue the night before.

"That cocky son of a bitch," Carelli said. Then he smiled. "What a pair of balls on that skinny little prick." They decided to talk to Jerry and spotted him the next day having hot dogs with a few guys at Nathan's in Coney Island. Jerry's real uncle was the hot dog server at the counter and verified that Jerry was with him helping on the day in question. Two of the other Nathan's employees cheerfully verified the alibi. Jerry said, "Hey, guys, let me buy you some hot dogs." The detectives walked away, hate growing inside them. "Hey, you two scumbags forgot your fucking hot dogs," Jerry yelled. They turned and gave Jerry a long stare as Jerry slid a hot dog in his mouth with an in and out motion. Everyone at the counter broke out laughing.

Including my friends at the 2009 Nader Reunion show. Some gestures are always funny. We still had a few hours to kill before show time, and since everyone was so interested I went on with the story.

We took a short break while Teresa and Clay got a cup of coffee, and then I continued.

The Overons (1958)
Left to Right, Bob Ferrante, Tony (Punchy) Armato,
Joe Strobel, Albee Cracolici and Al Contrera

BOB FERRANTE
TONY ARMATO

JOE STROBEL

The Overons
VOCAL GROUP

CLOVERDALE 9-3867

ALBEE CRACOLICI
ALLY CONTRERA

The Overons Business Card

CHAPTER 6

IN THE STILL OF THE NIGHT

Most of my summer was spent on the beach at Coney Island, and a good part of that was under the boardwalk on Bay 15 at the Bop House. The Bop House was a small store snuggled under the boardwalk that sold soda, beer, hot dogs, French fries and other beach foods. It was located between Raven Hall, a pool club, and Steeplechase, a self-contained amusement park famous for the parachute ride, which is a landmark and still stands. The Bop House had a jukebox that blared rock and roll music while the kids danced on the sand. Almost everybody wore a bathing suit except for Jerry, who never wore one. He was always in a pair of dark grey dress pants with a white T shirt and a light grey vest. Most of the guys wore jeans and T-shirts with a bathing suit underneath just in case. The girls wore brightly colored tight pants and blouses over their bathing suits. The sand was cool and clammy under the boardwalk and was decorated with cigarettes butts and gum wrappers. The concrete columns that supported the boardwalk were covered with lipstick and chalk graffiti which was highlighted by the stripes of sun that filtered thru the thin openings in the wooden planks of the boardwalk, where hundreds of people walked by. "Kilroy was here" was a popular saying to put on a column and there were lots of hearts with announcements, like Vinny loves Mary and Joe loves Brenda. Maybe Joe didn't love Brenda, but it was there for all to see. The sun stripes looked like lines painted in the sand. The jukebox always blared at maximum volume, "In the Still of the Night" was playing while a group of the kids danced the Fish. This was a dance where the guy and the girl got as close as possible and danced as slow as possible and pressed their private parts into each other as hard as possible in a grinding motion. Most of the guys would walk away with a boner after the dance was over, and the girls would giggle. Some couples would drift away after a few slow dances and find a quiet spot where they could be alone and make out for hours, some vertical and some horizontal, some on blankets and some on the bare sand. We would usually find some girl friends that had blankets laid out in the sunny side of the boardwalk and sing a cappella. This would draw a crowd of blanketed beach teenagers, mostly girls, who would listen and make requests. This was a treasured additional benefit of singing with a vocal group: the girls. It was amazing how we went from being normal teenagers to special teenagers because we sang. Girls that I wouldn't even consider asking out were now asking me out. The Overons were getting a reputation as one of the best vocal groups around and we loved it. Other singing groups would stop by and listen to see if they could pick up some tips or hear some mistakes. The Bop House was known as being the Bath Beach Boys' hangout, as well as the Rebels motorcycle gang, who were friendly with the Bath Beach Boys.

One hot afternoon, a rumor started that the Chaplins, a notorious black motorcycle gang from the projects who had an ongoing rift with the Rebels, were on their way to the Bop House to kick their asses. The word spread quickly, and all gang members from the Rebels and the Bath Beach Boys started heading for the Bop House. Augie, one of the owners of the Bop House, started handing out the stored chains and bats from behind the counter. Wooden cases of empty coke bottles were lined up for easy access. The girls headed for the sunlight. Of course, Albee, Bobby and Punchy were going to be part of this probable gang fight. Joe Strobel and I were not so sure we wanted to be involved in this, but at this point we really did not have much choice. How could we not stand with our group? The scene was set, and the players were coming.

There were about forty guys preparing to do battle when they heard the noise from the Chaplins' motorcycles as they approached Bay 15th Street. The street ended at the boardwalk. There were two concrete ramps, one on either side of the street that went under the boardwalk and met the beach sand. This became the entryway for the Chaplins. Their bikes were parked on the opposite side of the street of the Rebels' bikes. Tarzi, Frankie Rice, Albee, Bobby, Vinny Mook, Blubberhead, Punchy, and Jerry the Jew were barking orders to the rest of the guys, who were positioned at the bottom of both ramps. As the Chaplins got closer, they started hitting the concrete ramp and then the steel hand rails with their bats in an eerie rhythm of a percussion marching band. It sounded like a dull bell. They put on their traditional red bandanas around their necks. Even with the temperature in the high eighties, most of the Chaplins had black motorcycle boots, jeans with motorcycle belts and T-shirts. They took off the belts and wrapped them around their fists, so the large metal buckle would show on the outside. Some of the Rebels were in T-shirts and some of them left their motorcycle jackets on for the added protection. On the back of each of their jackets were the words "Chaplins" in blood red Gothic type lettering. The sound of 30 bats and chains echoed throughout the boardwalk while "Church Bells May Ring" was playing at full volume, giving the scene a surreal feel.

People walking to the beach area realized what was about to happen and began running the other way. Some of the store owners on the boardwalk pulled down their shutters and called the police. As soon as the first Chaplin hit the sand, the Rebels and the Bath Beach boys started backing off, drawing them deeper into the darker area. Coming from the bright sunlight, their eyes did not adjust quickly – and then a barrage of thick glass coke bottles hit them from both sides, taking down at least a dozen Chaplins. Blood spurted from some of their heads as bottles met bone. The sound of bottle against bone was like a loud crack. The jukebox changed its record and Little Richard stated singing "Gonna tell Aunt Mary 'bout Uncle John." The yelling and cursing intensified as the gangs merged with bats and chains finding their marks. It looked like a gladiator movie. Tarzi was screaming at the top of his lungs, hitting every Chaplin in his way with a baseball bat. Jerry leaped into a bunch of Chaplins with a broken bottle in each hand, like a wild animal slashing skin and flesh. Johnny Black, a 6'5 Rebel member and half owner of the Bop House had a bat in each hand and was pounding the tops of the red bandana'ed heads. Two minutes and 10 seconds went by, and another record dropped onto the turntable as the sound of sirens blared in the background, The Channels started singing, "The Closer You Are."

In seven minutes of brutal fighting, about twenty Chaplins and a dozen Bath Beach boys were seriously hurt. Some were unconscious; some weren't able to move. The rest hopped and staggered to their motorcycles, helping the wounded get up the ramps. I was in a state of shock. That was the first actual gang fight I had ever seen. At 16 years old and 118 pounds, all I could offer was throwing coke bottles at the Chaplins. I was scared shitless. I don't know where Joe went, but when he came back he was as white as a ghost. Albee stood by me, to make sure I was okay, and hit a guy so hard that he rolled backward into the sand, unconscious with his nose split open. The sirens were getting louder, and everyone started running away from the scene.

Most of the motorcycle riders made it off the block before the police came. Those who didn't were pounded again, only this time by the police with night sticks. Then they were cuffed and thrown into the waiting paddy wagons. Most of the Bath Beach Boys made their way out into the sunlit beach area, scrambling to find blankets to share with the girls, who were more than willing to share. The guys quickly stripped to bathing suits and lay down on blankets. Officers Joe Cleary and William Ryan spotted Tarzi and Jerry sharing a sandwich and a coke with a few girls on a blanket and walked over. Joe Cleary had arrested both Jerry and Tarzi Barilla for a robbery which didn't stick in court. It was about ninety-one degrees out in the sun; the sky was a beautiful blue with very few clouds. The sound of waves breaking and radios playing, the soft summer breezes and the smell of Carmel popcorn and hot dogs after what just happened was bizarre. Theresa was rubbing the blood stains off Jerry's arms with suntan lotion as the officers approached their blanket. Of course, Jerry still had his pants on but did not have his shirt or vest on they were tucked under the blanket.

"You guys are gonna wind up in jail or dead if you keep this shit up," said Officer Ryan, using his night stick as a pointer. Jerry politely replied in his phony British accent while forcibly squinting because of the bright sunlight in his eyes, "Why Officer Ryan, what could possibly be wrong, we are just getting some sun with these beautiful girls." The blankets were close to each other, and everyone began laughing. Officer Cleary didn't care about the laughing – he was too pissed at what had just happened. He walked across a few blankets, ignoring the jeers of the kids complaining about the sand he was spreading, over to where Tarzi was getting his back rubbed with lotion. His shirt, which was in Maryann's beach bag, was covered with blood. She quickly covered the bag with a towel. "And you," Cleary said, "I should take you down to the station house for questioning, but I know it wouldn't do any good. You guys all stick up for each other, which is the only goddamn good trait I've seen in any of you."

That night we all showed up as usual at the Hollywood Terrace, on 78th street and New Utrecht Avenue, for the Saturday night dance. The Hollywood Terrace, formally the Hollywood Theatre, where I spent many a Saturday afternoon watching movies as a younger boy, was now a catering hall that held dances with live bands. Tito Puente's Latin band was one of the favorites. We all dressed for the occasion. The men wore suits and ties and the women dresses and skirts. The young men's style suits included peg pants, sometimes with saddle stitching, and a high-rise for the pants. This meant that the pants would end about two inches above the belt line. The belt was very thin and just fit through each of the belt loops. The peg happened when a tailor narrowed the pants at the bottom cuff which would give the rest of the pants a drape look. The suit jacket had one fabric covered button and the lapels were wide and ended at the button. Extra shoulder padding insured the desired "V" shape. One of the most popular colors in the late fifties was power blue and that's what I had, a powder blue "Hollywood" style suit specifically tailored to my specifications that looked like everyone else. Oddly enough, the Hollywood style suit had nothing to do with the Hollywood Terrace. Tables were set up along both sides of the room and we rarely sat down, except to talk with a girl. The bar was always crowded, and this is where I tried my first seven and seven, Seagrams Seven whiskey and seven-up in a cocktail glass suggested by my cousin Tony Conigliaro. Tony's father Jimmy, was one of the Hollywood's owners and so I felt comfortable and rarely paid for a drink. Dancing was popular, but not everyone was a dancer. This is where I met Marcia, who taught me how to dance. My drink taste changed later on to Scotch on the rocks, mostly because that's what my Father drank.

Inevitably a fight would breakout and the bouncers, who were usually off-duty cops, would swoop in out of nowhere and breakup the fight ejecting both fighters into the street. If you were thrown out, you were not allowed back in that night. Most of my friends would leave about 2:00Am and we would wind up at one of the "after-hour" clubs in the neighborhood where we would continue drinking and dancing until 4:00Am and then go to a diner for breakfast. Needless to say, we drank a lot.

CHAPTER 7

SLEEPWALK

The Overons had a show planned with their new band at The Embassy Terrace, a catering hall on West 10th Street on a Friday night in November 1957. This was owned by Jimmy Conigliaro, Conig's father and my cousin. We had rehearsed for weeks, and Joe insisted on playing guitar, which eventually led to an argument between Bobby and Joe. Bobby, Albee and I left rehearsal, and Punchy stayed with Joe to try and talk some sense into him. Joe convinced Punchy that everybody was quitting and leaving Bobby without a group, so Punchy called Bobby and in a confusing conversation said he was leaving, too. When Albee found out what Joe did he called his brother, Phil, who had just come out of the Navy, and asked him to be the new lead singer. Punchy found out a few days later that Joe had lied to him, and he called Bobby and Albee and set a meeting to get back in the group. Albee was pissed that Punchy would side with Joe and told Punchy that he already called his nephew, George Galfo, to try out to fill in Punchy's second tenor part. Punchy really felt bad and eventually they resolved their differences, but George made the group and Punchy was still out. Punchy got pissed at Joe Strobel and told him that he was on his own. Later that week, Punchy called Albee Galione, who also sang with all of us when we started, and they decided to start a group with Vinny Ascierno as baritone, Benny Cammarata doing tenor, and Vinny Margi on lead. The group made some more personnel changes and the final version consisted of Tony "Punchy" Armato (first Tenor), Vinny Acierno (baritone), Albee Galione (second tenor) and Jimmy Gallagher on lead. They called themselves the Sinceres but eventually they became The Passions.

With all the new singers in place, the Overons now consisted of Phil Cracolici doing lead and tenor, Bob Ferrante (first tenor), George Galfo (second tenor), Albee Cracolici (baritone) and me as bass. We couldn't do the Embassy show because now we had to rehearse with our new singers. It was like starting from the beginning, only this time everybody knew how to sing harmony. It was just a matter of putting it together. We dropped the instrumentalists – we would just do vocals – and looked for a new place to rehearse. Between going to school and working, we had to rehearse at night. One of Albee's friends suggested we go to St. Finbar's Church on Bay 20th Street, off of Benson Avenue, which was my church and had Sunday school classrooms. Our intention was to ask at the Parish Directory for permission.

We went one night to check it out and everything was closed. It was cold outside, and since there was no one around, we jimmied the lock and got into one of the classrooms. We put on the light, set up the tape recorder and started singing. The echo was fantastic. Singing in a room without soft surfaces creates an aurally pleasing sound, like singing in a tiled bathroom. The reverberation or echo creates overtones which naturally enrich the human voice. Five voices singing in harmony was just crazy good. Listening to perfect harmony with all those Overtones gave me a high. We always recorded each song and listened to critique the harmony as we went along. It sounded so good and we weren't disturbing anyone, so we collectively decided that this was a perfect place to practice. We designated every Monday, Wednesday and Friday as practice nights. We would get there about 7:00 and practice for three hours. On Fridays after practice, we would usually go out for a late dinner at the diner or the drive-in except when we had dates. Sometimes we would double date. Bobby was dating Georgian, Albee was with Barbara, Georgie was going steady with Gerri, Phil was dating Eileen and I was with Marcia. Life was good.

We got a surprise visit the third week as Father Donegan, who noticed that the lights were on in one of the classrooms, walked in and asked us what we were doing. Bobby, who had the gift of gab, apologized and explained how much we loved music and how we were trying to get a recording contract and how it was difficult to find a place to rehearse and how it sounded so good here. Father Donegan, although angry that we'd broken in, saw an opportunity to help us in a spiritual way. He also realized how serious we were. There were only the five of us there: we made it a point not to invite girlfriends or other friends, so the place remained a secret.

Father Donegan invited us to all sit down and spoke to us in a level tone about how bad it was to break in and that we could have been arrested. We knew that and apologized, this time in unison: "Sorry Father." This made him laugh. He said that he loved the idea that we were trying to do something constructive and asked us to sing a song for him. Maybe he just wanted to be sure that we really were a vocal group. After listening to our version of "That's the Way It Goes," he gave us a standing ovation, a blessing and left us with a key to the classroom. We promised to take care of the room, which we did, and promised to show up for Sunday mass, which we did not.

The next couple of months we had serious harmony rehearsals. We were getting better and more polished. Father Donegan would stop in and listen to us rehearse and sometimes brought some of the other priests, who all promised to pray for us. They loved the harmony and the fact that we were off the streets. In hindsight, all those prayers might have helped. We spent so much time rehearsing and planning that we didn't have time to do anything wrong.

We realized we were sounding better every week. After much discussion, we decided that the only way to make a record was to go directly to the record companies and audition, like a lot of groups did in 1958. Bobby looked up the names of some record companies in the phone book, and off we went to the city. We got to the Brill building at 1619 Broadway, looked at the lobby directory and found Gee records, which had The Teenagers and a few other famous groups. We got into the elevator, which had an elevator operator, as automatic elevators were not in any buildings yet. At the 12th Floor, we walked into the office of Gee Records.

"We're here to audition," Bobby said, with the rest of us right behind him. The secretary, who was obviously so used to this, asked Bobby if he had an appointment, and of course Bobby said no. The next week was spent making appointments and doing auditions. We went back the following week and sang for George Goldner, the head of Gee records.

Gee Records was a New York-based American record label formed in 1953 as a subsidiary to George Goldner's Tico Records and Rama Records labels to honor the million selling hit song "Gee" (1953) by the Crows. Gee records was reactivated as a division of Roulette Records (Dinah Washington, The Playmates) by president Morris Levy in early April

1961, The Cleftones' hit "Heart and Soul" (1961) became Gee Records' first release.

George introduced himself as we approached his huge desk, and we all reached across to shake hands. There were two other men in the office who did not identify themselves nor offer to shake hands, but they were dressed in suits and ties, and if I hadn't seen the Gee Records sign on the glass door when we walked in, I would have thought we were going to a Mafia meeting. These two guys looked just like the wise guys that stayed by the Nineteenth Hole bar in our neighborhood.

George seemed pleased at the harmony and was particularly interested in where we were from. He liked our look. We got an offer from George Goldner in the form of a secretary handing us a standard recording contract from a stack of them and wishing us good luck in a monotone voice. Goldner said that we had nice harmony in such a matter of fact way that we all got turned off. We weren't very happy with the contract, as it had so many restrictions and paid only 2% of record sales. We had heard from The Neons that we should not settle for less than 3%.

There were three groups waiting in the hallway when we left. It looked like Goldner was giving contracts to every group that auditioned. Bobby felt that we wouldn't get the personal attention that he thought we should have. One of the record company secretaries who took a liking to Bobby told him that we should be bringing in original songs on a "demo recording." She said that record companies pay more attention to a group that has a demo. That was the first time any of us heard about a "demo."

We were hanging out with some of the guys in the neighborhood that night, discussing the audition and how frustrated we were with this "demo" thing, when Jerry Rosenberg suggested that we see this guy Frankie "Mouth." He got his nickname because he could talk anyone into anything. Frankie was a wise guy, and Jerry thought he had some connections in the music industry. Everybody knew that the mob-controlled parts of the music industry. Frankie Mouth hung out at the 19th hole with many of the *connected* guys. Jerry Rosenberg insisted that Frankie help his friends, the Overons, make a record. Frankie said to Jerry, "You know you can bullshit with the best of them, you should become a lawyer."

The meeting was set up for the following afternoon and we sang for Frankie Mouth at the 19th hole. Frankie was a tall, good-looking, dark-haired, fast-talking Shylock with, as suspected, ties to some record companies. He had a slick dark grey mohair suit that probably cost more than it would take to pay for the recording. I had seen him always hanging out on the corner, but never knew who he was. We sang "That's the Way it Goes," originally done by the Harptones, and Frankie, who knew the song, was impressed. So was Jerry, who had not heard the new Overons with Phil and Georgie.

Frankie Mouth said, "Okay, you guys can sing, I'm gonna set youse up with Jimmy Doyle and he will bring you into a studio to make a demo." When we heard him say "demo," we thought he really knew about the music business. Frankie went over to the pay phone, and in 20 minutes Jimmy Doyle showed up. Jimmy Doyle, as we found out later, was a two-bit record producer and musician who never really amounted to anything. We sang a few songs for him in the back room and he was pleasantly surprised. He told us that we really had a nice sound and that it would probably cost us five hundred dollars for studio rental and musicians and of course the finished "demo."

Five hundred dollars was like asking for five thousand dollars. Minimum wage in 1958 was a dollar an hour. Jimmy Doyle was in his late forties, with long grey receding slicked back hair that curled up in the back. He had a permanent stoop. He told us that a garbage truck had backed into him, and he was suing the NYC Sanitation department. When his case was settled, he would move to Miami. He looked a little like Hoagy Carmichael. He said when he was younger; he had worked on big band and jazz recordings as a trumpet player and had met Hoagy Carmichael, which made us smile. He really didn't have a feel for this new rock and roll music, but he needed to do this so he could give his share of anything he made to Frankie Mouth to pay his gambling debts. Frankie, after conferring with Jimmy, decided that if he was going to open some doors in the music business for us that he should be our manager. Jimmy told us that he would prepare a contract and that when we got the money together to call him.

We didn't have that kind of money, but we knew wanted to do this, so Bobby decided that we would take a loan from a bank and we could pay it back over time. We tried the Dime saving bank, but they said we needed a co-signer, so Bobby's father co-signed for the loan, and Bobby gave the money to Jimmy Doyle. What we didn't know, and found out later, was that the recording session would only cost $250.00.

Jimmy told us to meet him at the Broadway Recording Studio at 10:00 am on the following Saturday and learn the four songs that we wanted to do really well. In the meantime, he suggested we change our name to something classier, like "The Courtesans," a name that he'd thought up. When we met the next day for rehearsal, Bobby told us that he'd looked up "courtesan" in the dictionary and it meant "prostitute." We agreed to all come to the next rehearsal with suggestions for another name.

That afternoon, Albee and Bobby paid Jimmy Doyle a visit. When Jimmy opened his apartment door, Albee pushed Jimmy into the wall and said, "What the fuck are you doing? I ought to punch your fucking lights out!"

Doyle was startled and thought that we'd found out he was pocketing some of the money. Then Albee asked, "Do you know what a courtesan is?"

Doyle was relieved that his secret was still safe and apologized for the mistake. He told them that he saw the word "courtesan" while reading a book about King Arthur and liked how it sounded. Happy with the explanation, Albee and Bobby left.

CHAPTER 8

A PRAYER TO AN ANGEL

The next day at rehearsal, the five suggestions for a new name were written on pieces of paper, which were folded and put into a baseball cap. Bobby picked one of them. It was my suggestion, which I'd found by browsing through the dictionary. So, we were now officially The Mystics.

We rehearsed every night that week, and finally Saturday came. We recorded the four songs we wrote during our rehearsals at St. Finbars at Pat Jacques Broadway studio: "Big Brown Eyes", "The Bells Are Ringing", "Prayer to an Angel", and "Why do You Pretend." They were done a cappella at first. Then Jimmy Doyle ran down the songs with the bass, piano, drum and guitar players with the playback a cappella tape. Our harmonies were smooth as silk. This was the first time we heard ourselves at a professional studio. It was so different from the home tape recorder. The playback had some echo included which made it sound so much better. We were overwhelmed and completely hooked on pursuing this. The second hour was recording with the band, which was made up of jazz musician friends of Jimmy and did not have a real feel for rock and roll. It was a little rough at first, but then the band got the hang of it, and we finished after a few takes per song. Jimmy Doyle was very impressed with our harmony and praised us for knowing the songs so well. He said that Pat, the recording engineer, would give us demos if we waited for him to run them off. Jimmy took off with the musicians and reminded us that Frankie Mouth wanted to hear the demos when we got back to Brooklyn. Demos were made by hand, with a cutting machine out of some type of brittle acetate material much like the 78 RPM records of the thirties and forties. Pat typed the song title labels and put one on each recording. Seeing how anxious we were to listen to them at home, he made us all copies.

Pat Jacques was a nice guy and realized that our group had talent. He also liked us, and while the demos were being copied, he gave us a little education in the music business. In his experience, he told us, "There aren't too many good harmony groups. Besides you are all really good-looking kids and that means a lot in the music business." He explained that we really had something and that we would be wasting our time with the likes of a Jimmy Doyle. After the discussion with Pat, who knew Jimmy Doyle's reputation, it was evident that neither Jimmy Doyle nor Frankie Mouth was going to do the group any good in the music business. Pat suggested that we see a manager that he knew, Jim Gribble, up on the 10th floor. He said that Gribble was currently managing the Fiestas, who were on the charts with their hit song, "So Fine." This was very impressive.

We overheard Pat's phone conversation. "Hi, Jim, listen, I have a group of guys down here in my studio that you would love. They call themselves The Mystics and they just finished a demo. I think you should give it a listen." Jim took the elevator down, and 15 minutes later he was listening to our first studio recording of "A Prayer to an Angel".

We liked Jim right away. He was about 6'4 and had fair skin and dirty blond hair. He looked to be about forty, but it was hard to tell because of his ruddy complexion. He wore a dark grey suit and a blue tie with a white shirt and appeared to be the real deal. He had a nice smile and a good-natured southern drawl. The first words out of his mouth were "Hello, boys," his voice dripping with southern hospitality. He was from Memphis and said he'd been involved with The Grand Old Opry in his younger days, although as time went by, it never became clear to what extent. He rarely brought it up.

Jim took an instant liking to the Mystics. He asked us to come up to his office, so we could have a conversation without disturbing Pat, who was getting ready for another session. We all thanked Pat and wound up on the 10th floor in room 1008. On the way up, Jim asked where we were from, our school status and our ages. He was pleasantly surprised to hear that Phil and Albee were brothers and that George was their nephew. Bobby told Jim how we got to do the demo but never went into the details about Frankie Mouth, especially the part about Frankie being our manager with a signed contract. He didn't want to ruin this new relationship.

We talked for a while, and after hearing a few more songs "live," Jim praised us for our singing talent, but he seemed especially impressed with our looks. As we sang, he took a deep drag on his cigarette and studied us, taking long looks at each face. It was a little disturbing, but this was all new territory for us and we just kept singing. We were looking at each other while we were singing, and I could read everybody's mind. Is this guy a nut?

Jim took another drag, and the end of his cigarette glowed red like a hot poker. When he exhaled, only a bit of smoke came out of his nose and mouth, and it drifted up along the side of his face. We talked about those long cigarette drags for years. It seemed as if the cigarette burned down to half its size with one drag. Jim's fingers had the yellow nicotine stain that heavy smokers had. On his desk was a huge glass ashtray filled with cigarette butts. Everybody smoked, but nobody smoked like Jim Gribble.

Jim was a realist. Talent was only part of the deal. He knew that the "pretty boys," as he called them, like Frankie Avalon, Bobby Rydell and Fabian, would sell more records because it was teenage girls who bought most of the records. Jim felt that he had five pretty boys, and they could sing, too. It was just what he was looking for. He told us he was fed up with the antics of the Fiestas. They were not showing up for gigs, which made it was difficult for him to promote them. We listened very carefully. I wanted to reach up, make a fist, pull my arm down and yell "Yes!" but I didn't. I waited until I was alone.

It was now early afternoon, and as we sat around in his office, excited and impressed, Jim suddenly picked up the black phone on his desk, listened for a dial tone, and as he dialed the rotary numbers he motioned for us to hush. We went completely silent. In a real sweet southern accent, he said, "Hi, honey, I'd like to talk to Gene Shwartz, its Jim Gribble . . . Hello, Gene. I have five pretty boys here in my office" – as he looked at each us one by one – "and they can sing their asses off. Are you available?"

We all looked at each other. Our eyes were asking, who the hell is Gene Shwartz? The phone hit the cradle. "Okay, boys, first we'll get some lunch and then we're going to audition for Laurie Records."

We were dumfounded. Laurie Records –Dion and The Belmonts – holy shit! We were on a cloud of anticipation and excitement as we floated down Broadway with our new manager. We stopped for burgers, cokes and fries. Jim watched intently as we ordered and ate our lunch. We didn't realize it, but he was watching our manners and our attitude. After his experience with the Fiestas, he wanted to make sure that we were stable and presentable. He picked up the tab and we liked him even more.

Jim introduced The Mystics to Gene Schwartz and Elliot Greenberg, who listened as we sang. They both had nice things to say. Gribble told us months later that Gene liked Phil's lead because it was like Dion's and that The Mystics seemed very respectful and easy to work with. Both Jim and The Mystics didn't know it at the time of that audition, but Gene Schwartz had big plans for The Mystics, and he didn't want to make any mistakes.

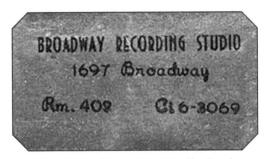

Broadway Recording Studio Card

The first studio picture of The Mystics (1959)
Left to Right, George, Al, Phil, Bob, Albee

The Mystics with Jim Gribble
Left to Right, Bob, Albee, Jim, George, Phil, Al

CHAPTER 9

HUSHABYE

"When did you have that hit 'Hushabye?'" asked Theresa. "Was I even born yet?"

"Very funny," I said. We often teased each other about our age difference.

Emil said, "Yeah you were just a baby".

"So, here's how it happened."

This may sound strange, but "Hushabye" was born when the songwriting team of Doc Pomus and Mort Shuman sang, "Why must I be a teenager in love" Morty played the piano and Doc sang the lyrics in the New York office of Laurie Records. It was a March day in 1959. Standing and listening were Elliot Greenberg, Laurie's musical director, and Gene Schwartz, its president. Also present were The Mystics and Jim Gribble, our manager. Gene was very excited, and he yelled out to his brother Bob in the next room, "Bob, come in here and listen to this. This is a smash!" Gene and Bob had modified crew cuts and usually wore a suit and ties. Gene sometimes wore a bow tie, which made him look studious. They looked alike, slightly built, around 35 years old, with Gene being the older brother. It was always obvious that Gene was in charge. He had a unique business sense, especially when it came to picking hit records.

Bob came into the small office wondering what was so important. The small office had a slightly used upright black grand piano against one wall and a professional type reel-to-reel tape recorder on a small grey metal table by the other wall. Doc and Morty started at the top, "Uuu uuu wah uuu . . . Each time we have a quarrel it almost breaks my heart." Morty continued to sing. Bob Schwartz turned to The Mystics and said, "What a great song!" Bob did not really know if it was good or not, so he waited for someone to agree with him. "Oh, yeah!" said Georgie. Albee said, "Wow, this is a hit!" Gene, with the biggest smile I have ever seen on his face, asked Morty to start teaching us the song and left the room with Jim, Bob and Elliot. We liked the song but never realized how good it really was. We were just anxious to record something. We were ready. We had already recorded "Adam and Eve" and "Wimaweh," but Gene didn't think they were strong enough to break out through the hundreds of would-be hits by other hungry groups. We found out later that Gene would always try to record three songs at each session. He was still looking for his smash.

We sang "Teenager in Love" on the subway going home, standing around a pole, hands holding on to steady us from the rocking subway ride. That was an incredible feeling. The train wasn't crowded but none of us wanted to sit down. I felt so close to all the guys. We were like brothers. Perhaps the other passengers in that subway car thought we were crazy teenagers, but they applauded when we finished. Life was good. The first part of an incredible dream was about to happen. We all felt it. There was not any one time since we'd started this group that felt as good. All the countless hours of practicing were about to pay off. We had great, not good, but *great* harmony from all the hours spent practicing the perfect harmony with the perfect five guys. All the trial and error sessions lasting well into the night to hammer out harmony were about to pay off. Of course, it did not hurt that Phil and Albee Cracolici were brothers. Their voices were meant to be in harmony. Georgie being related had similar vocal qualities. In addition, of course Bobby, a friend of Albee and Phil from elementary school, could harmonize with anyone. The addition of my bass voice rounded out the smooth, creamy harmony of The Mystics.

I couldn't wait to tell my parents, my kid brother Richie, my cousin Conig and my friends.

That night, Jim Gribble called Bobby and said that Gene wanted the group at his office the next day at 1:00 pm. On the way in, we imagined that Gene had found an even better song for us. When we walked in with Jim, Gene asked everyone to grab a chair as they went into the music room. Sitting at the piano was Morty Shuman looking a little sad. I knew Morty from the neighborhood. He was a few years older than I was and lived on 79th Street and 18th Avenue. George also lived on 79th Street but more towards 15th Avenue. He passed my house on his way to the 79th street train station. He just would give a little wave like a "hi kid," as he passed, not knowing that we would ever be in the same room, with him as a songwriter and me as part of a group about to sing a song he wrote. That thought blows my mind. Doc was in his wheelchair alongside Morty as Gene spoke. "I really hate to do this to you guys but Bob, Elliot and I had a meeting about 'Teenager in Love.' We feel that this song is an incredible smash hit, and Laurie needs a big hit badly."

At this point, nobody except Bob and Elliot knew where Gene was going with this, but concern was starting to spread through everyone's mind as he continued. "You see, guys, The Mystics really don't have a track record at this point for advance sales, and that's what we need." Gribble lit up another Chesterfield and shifted in his chair. He took one of his long ten-second drags, crossed his legs and tilted his head so he could hear better. He did not look happy. In an up-tempo happy voice, as if he were giving us a gift, Gene said, "So we would like Doc and Morty to write you guys another song."

Gene Shwartz was a real nice man and I guess he truly felt bad, but business was business. He knew that by allowing The Mystics to record "Teenager in Love," Laurie would have a hit – but not as big a hit as Dion and the Belmonts might deliver. Since Dion had just come off two decent charted records, this could be a monster. "So," Gene said, "We're going to let Dion record 'Teenager in Love.'"

The room went completely silent. My jaw dropped. Jim lit another cigarette from the match that Bobby and Albee had just used to light their cigarettes. It looked like a wake, with people just staring into space. It was a very awkward silence, which Gene finally broke. "I'm sorry, guys, but I really have to do this." Gene looked over at Gribble, who was in the middle of another drag, but spoke to Doc and Morty. "I'd like you guys to come up with something along the style of 'Little Star' for the Mystics." Obviously, he had put some thought into this new decision.

(Of course, Gene was right. "Teenager in Love" by Dion and the Belmonts would go to number one on all the charts.)

We all said that we understood, although we really did not. It was not our company; so how would we know the business end of this? Years later, when I went into my own business, I totally understood Gene's decision. Jim consoled us on the walk back to his office with a lot of "Don't worry and things always work out for the best." We weren't buying it. We'd been screwed. Disappointment was an understatement. We were devastated.

On the way back to the neighborhood we barely spoke and did not sing at all. Usually we would sing at least a dozen songs while going home.

What was missing the most were the laughs. Bobby did not tell one joke. We always had a good time while we were together, telling jokes, kidding around and singing. Bobby was so good at telling jokes we would ask him to repeat the jokes and we would all laugh even harder. But there was a somber atmosphere on the way home that day. Albee dropped us off at our houses, and we decided to meet the next day to rehearse. The next morning, Bobby got a call from Jim Gribble asking the group to meet again at Laurie's office that afternoon. Bobby called everyone, and we met at 12:00 and were in the city by 1:00. Everybody who was there the day before was there again, all sitting around the piano with Doc and Morty and Jim Gribble sucking down Chesterfields. On the way in, Georgie said, "Maybe they changed their minds." Albee agreed, "Yeah, maybe we got that song after all." Our spirits started to lift. By the time we got to Laurie's office, we were sure we had "Teenager in Love" again and were on the road to stardom.

Doc Pomus (Jerome Felder) and Morty Shuman, both in their thirties, became songwriting partners about six months before writing "Teenager in Love." Doc was stricken with polio as a child and used crutches and a wheelchair. He was heavy-set with a thick black beard. He looked like he could have been a pirate in another life. Doc was the lyrics part of the team. He started as a blues singer in the early fifties with moderate success in the Village. Doc was a likable guy – not what you'd expect from a successful songwriter. Morty was a tall, lean, good-natured musician who studied piano at the New York Conservatory of Music for years. Their song-writing career would go on to include, "Save the Last Dance for Me" (the Drifters), "Turn Me Loose" (Fabian), "This Magic Moment (the Drifters), "Suspicion" (Elvis Presley) and dozens of other major hits. Quite a songwriting team!

Doc and Morty felt terrible about Gene's decision. They had written "Teenager in Love" with The Mystics in mind and really felt it was a perfect fit for Phil's unique teenage-sounding voice. There were not too many Dion-sounding voices out there, and Gene thought that was Laurie Record's signature sound. Jim told us that Gene did not like the attitude of the Belmonts and found them hard to work with. So, he saw a similar sound with a group of eager kids and thought this would work. Doc and Morty really liked us and tried to write something fresh for us. As it turned out, riding in the car on their way home the day before, they came up with an idea, and they finished it when they got home. They called Gene in the morning and now were ready to play it for the Mystics. They thought this new song was a better fit because it featured Phil's falsetto, which they liked very much.

Once everyone was settled down, Gene announced that Doc and Morty had written a new song for us. Jim took out a fresh pack of Chesterfields, tapped it until he was satisfied all the tobacco was tight. Then as everyone waited for him to get settled, he opened the pack, took one cigarette out and lit it with the one he had just finished. At this point we were feeling a little sad. I did not think they would be able to top or even equal "Teenager in Love." There was another one of those awkward silent moments, which was broken when Gene asked Doc and Morty to start the new song. Morty started playing the piano, with a kind of cha-cha shuffle, and sang "ooooooo" in a baritone tone and then repeated it with a falsetto tone, saying "This is Phil" and then sang "Hushabye, Hushabye." Now he said, "This is everybody – 'Oh my darling don't you cry.'"

We were stunned. Morty motioned to the group to come over to the piano. Doc was singing the background parts as Morty sang the lead part, kind of indicating where the harmony would be and where the unison parts would be. We started singing with Mort. Doc's face lit up with a huge smile. The only part that they did not have figured out was the background part behind the main lyrics. Albee suggested "Shang, shang-a-lang," which was similar to a Channels background part that he remembered, and that became the part. Elliot was poised to show us the harmony parts, but we were way ahead of him. We automatically fell into our signature harmony. As we got more and more into it, we realized that this was an incredible song. We learned "Hushabye" in about thirty minutes and perfected it with all the harmonies in about an hour. Everyone was ecstatic. Jim loved the song and had the biggest grin on his face that we ever saw. The ashtray next to Jim had a pile of spent butts. Gene was stuttering over praises about this fantastic song and the amazing songwriters. "I think we're ready to go into the studio right now," declared Gene. Elliot did not get the joke and added, "But, Gene, I have to write arrangements first." Jim Gribble sucked on his cigarette, rolled his eyes, and started laughing aloud. We all joined in on the laugh.

We had acquired quite a bit of studio experience thanks to Jim's insistence that Gene use us for background vocals on some of Laurie's recording sessions for other artists. We got our first professional pay check, a whopping $275.00 for the entire group, for a back-up session. We did quite a few sessions with various new Laurie artists. We were so happy with that! Jim did not want to take his ten percent manager's cut because he wanted us to earn some money.

Our first studio background session was sometime in April 1959. Judy Allen sang "Don't Sit Under the Apple Tree" ("Sentimental Me" was on the B side). Elliot arranged the background parts and rehearsed with us until it was perfect. Elliot had a lot of patience. He understood that we were not professional singers, but I felt he was impressed with not only our sound but also our heart. We were so driven to make this happen. "Don't Sit Under the Apple Tree" was recorded at Bell Sound Studios, which was much more professional than Pat Jacques Broadway recording studio where we did our first demos.

We dropped in on Pat occasionally to say hi. He was so happy for us. We never forgot that if it were not for Pat introducing us to Jim Gribble we would not be recording for Laurie records.

There were professional musicians at the Bell Sound sessions, and they all read charts that Elliot wrote while he conducted the band. We were thrilled to be introduced to the musicians by Elliot. There was Panama Francis on drums. Panama drummed on many Elvis Presley demos, and he is featured on hits by the Four Seasons ("Big Girls Don't Cry" and "Walk Like a Man"), the Platters ("Only You", "The Great Pretender", "Smoke Gets in Your Eyes" and "My Prayer"), Bobby Darin ("Splish Splash"), Neil Sedaka ("Calendar Girl"), and Dion ("The Wanderer"). Bucky Pizzarelli on guitar, was a staff musician for NBC, playing with Skitch Henderson. In 1964, he became a member of The Tonight Show Band on the Johnny Carson show. During his time performing for The Tonight Show, Pizzarelli accompanied guest bands and musicians playing through a variety of musical genres, even playing with Tiny Tim (after tuning the performer's ukulele) on the day Tiny Tim married Miss Vicki on Carson's show. While professedly not a big fan of rock and roll, during this period, Bucky performed on seven hits with Dion and the Belmonts. I believe he was a good friend of Elliot's. Al Caiolla, on guitar had prominent pop hits in 1961 with "The Magnificent Seven" and "Bonanza." And Milt Hinton, on bass, was a famous jazz artist who did a lot of work as a studio musician. He was part of a large group of studio musicians who played on dozens of hit records by songwriters who worked at the Brill Building. Hinton was responsible for the opening bass line on The Drifters' "Under the Boardwalk" as well as playing on dozens of hits recorded by Neil

Sedaka and many others. These musicians were responsible for key "licks" that were not written in the music sheets. These musical phrases were things that they felt fit and, in many cases, became part of the "hook" that made that song a hit.

Both Elliot and Gene, who was in the booth with the engineer, showed us where to stand and how to work the microphones. We were eager to learn these new techniques of studio protocol. Prior to this, we only had experience at Pat Jacques studio. Bell Sound was impressive. Our first recording session there was an inspiring experience. Listening to the playback tapes was overwhelming. The huge speakers had so much clarity. Gene knew we were "green" and was continuously praising our harmony. This wasn't even our recording. We were just the background. I didn't even hear Judy's lead vocal at first, although she was much louder than we were. I was completely focused on the incredible harmony coming out of those massive speakers hanging over the huge recording board.

The sound engineer looked over at us and winked. "Nice sound, guys." I'll never forget that. It made us feel good. It bolstered our confidence. Judy, also new at this, was usually kind of shy, but she couldn't help herself. "Oh my God, that sounds so good!" We felt this was where we belonged, doing what we did well and being appreciated. I thought to myself, how cool is this? We did that. I could have listened to the playback all night. After "Don't sit under the Apple tree" was released, DJ Peter Tripp played it on WMCA. This was the first time we heard ourselves on the radio. We didn't get credit on the recording or on the air by any disc jockeys, but we knew it was us. It sounded so good. We were all in Albee's car at 7:00 PM when Jim had told us it was going be played on WMCA. At 7:00 PM, Peter Tripp announced a new recording by Judy Allen and we witnessed the greatest two and one-half minutes of our lives so far. No one spoke a word while this new song played over the tiny speaker in the dashboard of an Oldsmobile. The bond between the five of us just went up another notch.

Gene and Elliot were happy with us doing background and often left it up to us to come up with the background sounds. They felt that since we were teenagers we would naturally sing what other teenagers wanted to hear. So, we just did what we always did. We made up sounds, put in ooos and ahhs, and they thought we were geniuses. In the months prior to "Hushabye," Gene had us doing background vocals on a variety of artists, such as Rusty Lane (Carl Hanna Jr), a rockabilly songwriter under Jim Gribble's management who recorded "Karen," a nice recording that went nowhere. Rusty wrote "Adam and Eve" for The Mystics while hanging out in Jim's office. We also arranged and sang background for Scott Garrett's recording of "Love Story" and Don Press's recording of "Ask the Robin." Although some of these were good recordings, none of them went anywhere, even with air play. We were beginning to see how difficult it was to get a hit.

The lobby was bursting with teenage talent. Songwriters, male and female vocalists, acoustic guitarists and singing groups would occupy the lobby's chairs and couches and spill out into the hallway to Jim's office.

"Adam and Eve" was the first studio recording that we did as The Mystics. We also recorded "Wimoweh," which was originally done by The Weavers with Pete Seeger in the early fifties. Elliot Greenberg was a fan of The Weavers and felt that the falsetto part was a perfect fit for the Mystics' tight harmony, especially with Phil's unique falsetto. The Weavers version (and ours) had no lyrics and was fashioned after the original African folk version meaning "The lion sleeps tonight." After recording the song, Gene felt it was just not strong enough to release. In 1961, songwriter Bobby Feldman added lyrics to "Wimoweh" for the Tokens and it became a number one hit, a few times.

"You mean, you almost sang 'Teenager in Love' and 'The Lion sleeps tonight?'" asked Clay. "Ouch, that must hurt!"

"It does," I said. "Even now, fifty years later, I still think "Teenager in Love" should have been ours!"

The Mystics studio promo photo (1959)

Mort Shuman and Doc Pomus

CHAPTER 10

ADAM AND EVE

After the disappointment of losing "Teenager in Love" wore off, we prepared to record "Hushabye." Thanks to the insistence of Jim Gribble, we now knew our way around the recording studio. The recording method was always the same. Learn the song with Elliot, make sure the parts were right, and then rehearse it until we knew it cold. I often wonder how my brain remembers all these songs. "Adam & Eve" was our very first professional recording, a typical slow rock and roll tune. Albee, Phil, Georgie and Bobby started with an a cappella harmony part and then I said in my bass voice, "Down through the years in this old world there was always a boy who loved a girl." Then the Laurie records signature saxophones followed with the rest of the band. This was like the Dion and the Belmonts' recording of "Pity Me" with similar saxophone harmonies. Phil did a great lead and our harmonies were also great, but I think we all knew "Adam & Eve" was not a hit. It was the same for "Wimoweh." It was a great song with fantastic harmony but not a hit.

It seemed to be just another typical March day in 1959 when we went into Bell Sound Studios on West 46th Street off 8th Avenue to record "Hushabye". We had no idea that this recording would change our lives forever. Until then, our personal lives were pretty much the same as before we'd gotten the recording contract. Bobby and I were working as draftsmen in an engineering firm on Whitehall Street in New York City and went to work together every day on the train. George had just started working for American Express in the city. Phil and Albee were working in construction. We usually rehearsed three times a week, with Bobby setting up the practice sessions. Most of the time, we went to Albee and Phil's place on 86th street next to the Loews Oriental theatre. We saved the weekends for family and girlfriends.

Gene, Elliot and Jim were already at the session. It was an impressive place. The lobby had pictures of so many famous people that recorded there. We were led into the main studio and were thrilled to see some of the same musicians that were at some of the other recording sessions that we'd done for Laurie. We met the same group at our first session with Judy Allen. Bucky Pizzarelli was on lead guitar. Al Ciaolla on rhythm guitar and Milt Hinton on stand-up bass. Panama Francis was there on drums. Up until now, we had done about five different recording sessions for Gene, and these incredible musicians were on most of them. We said our hellos to everyone and got to work. Gene explained how he wanted to get a kind of "Little Star" feel. Gene asked us to sing Hushabye a cappella for the band and then he played a bit of The Elegants' "Little star." He told Panama that he wanted to get the exact tempo and Panama said, "I got it, man." Gene took out a metronome with which he cloned the exact "Little Star" tempo and played it for Panama. Panama just rolled his eyes in our direction, and we all broke out laughing, partly from being so nervous. It broke the ice. We weren't pros, but we knew that you don't tell Panama Francis how to play drums. The look on Panama's face was priceless, and so was the look on Gene's face, since he didn't get it.

Although Elliot's charts had the basic chords, he relied on the musicians to come up with the right feel. He would know when it was right. He really did have sixth sense for music. Bucky took the lead, started with a real nice twangy guitar feel, and as if by magic, the others got into the groove. It was heavenly. I don't think they even looked at the charts. Under the direction of Elliot, we started over and ran it down, off the microphones, while standing with the band. He made some minor changes and said to Gene, who was sitting behind the glass in the recording room, "Do you want to try one"?

Then we heard Gene's voice over the speakers. "Are you boys ready to do one"? We said "Sure-Yeah-Ok-yes and uhhu" all at once and we all laughed. Then we heard Jim's deep sweet drawl, "OK boys, let's calm down and do one." Jim already knew, from the previous sessions, that if left alone we would just break out into laughter at every silly thing that happened. After some sound testing for each of us to get a good balance between the voices and our individual distance from the microphones, Gene announced, "'Hushabye' take one." We sailed through the song; we could all see each other. It was not at all like the recordings that are done now, where the artist is wearing earphones for separation. Every microphone was open. All the voices and music leaked into each microphone so if any one musician or singer made a mistake we would have to start all over. I believe this is what gave vinyl that special warm sound. After the first take was done, we heard Gene on the speaker say, "All right boys, that was great, come on in and take a listen." I thought that maybe one take was enough – but that was impossible. We knew from our past recording experience, with Gene and Elliot, that there had to be at least three, and there were times that we did ten takes. There were also false starts. If one person, musician or singer made a mistake, we all started over. I remember the time when we backed up Scott Garrett, one of Laurie's artists. His lyrics were supposed to be, "Where there's a moonbeam there's a rainbow." He kept singing, "Where there's a rain beam there's a moon glow." After Gene stopped and corrected him for the fifth time we all lost it. Phil went to one knee and Georgie's eyes were tearing. Albee and I could not look at Bobby, as his expression made us laugh even more. It took about 20 minutes to get ourselves back to normal. Even Gene and Elliot laughed, and that was rare. We restarted but we could not look at each other or we would crack up again. I laughed so hard I had tears in my eyes and a pain in my side. I miss laughs like that. Both Gene and Elliot were patient with us. But, when we were finally serious, it sounded great, and that was what they wanted, perfection.

We gathered in the sound booth and the engineer started the tape. These were reel-to-reel tapes set on a huge soundboard with what appeared to be hundreds of levers, dials and meters. Gene was standing next to Elliot while Jim was sitting towards the end of the console, sucking on a cigarette, his nicotine-stained fingers holding the cigarette while a cloud of smoke hung over his head like a halo. This was the third time we'd recorded at Bell Sound, and we were still impressed with the place, we were blown away when our voices came out of the giant overhead speakers. It was beautiful. Phil sounded amazing. The harmony was perfect. The music was perfect. There was a pause for mutual congratulations and then Gene said, "Allie, you have to get a little closer to the mike, Albee and George back off a little, Phil and Bobby relax and just do the same thing. OK- let's try it again." Since the whole group was on one track there was no way to change it after the fact. Not like today's recording sessions, where each person and each instrument often have their own track. Today's method of recording allows everything to be blended electronically. The sound engineer has complete control. When we recorded, it was up to everyone

Hushabye

to maintain the same distance and intensity for each take. Elliot made a few minor adjustments with the musicians and we did three more takes in a row. Gene came out this time, asking how we felt about the takes so far. He said, "I think we're good but let's just do one more for the hell of it." We knew from past experience that in editing they could cut and paste the best parts of various takes, but Gene was a purist. He really wanted a complete perfect take. Knowing we had done a great job on the last few takes, we were a little more relaxed on the last one. We were now confident that we knew the harmonies, the timing and our levels. I knew that this last take was the one Gene finally selected for the actual recording, because towards the end of this, and only this take, I added a little extra bass part in the fade out at the end of the song.

And so, with three recordings, "in the can," we were ready. A few weeks went by, and we found out that Gene, and Elliot had selected "Hushabye" as the A side, (no surprise) and "Adam and Eve" as the B side for our new single. "Wimoweh" was set aside for another day or maybe as an album song. Two weeks later, we were called into the office to pick up our copies of our new record. Gene was thrilled to play it for us in his office, but his enthusiasm was not even close to ours. We were ecstatic! We looked at the record label, Laurie record number 3028. Time: 2:30. There it was-plain as day, the title, a simple "HUSHABYE" and directly under, THE MYSTICS on the Laurie record label. A beautiful thing and one of those sights that stays in your mind forever. We listened to an actual 45 record that had "Advance Copy" printed over the actual label on the small record player in Gene's studio and were thrilled. This was the advance record that was sent to the DJs for their use. It was not for sale. It was the sweetest record we'd ever heard. We played the B side and loved it, too, but there was no comparison. "Hushabye" was a clean bright teenage sound. I always had a sense of which new recordings were going to be hits, and I knew about this one.

Gene and Jim explained how we would start doing some record hops to promote the record with the local DJ's. I am not sure if we even understood what they were trying to tell us. We each got a box of 45's for our personal use to give out to family and friends, which we did as soon as we got back to Brooklyn. We had our usual lively conversation on the way home, only this time we were high on life. We had a real actual recording. What could be better than this? I remember calling my cousin Conig and my friends Scapper, Guy Penna and Ben Cammarata and telling them to come over

61

to listen to "Hushabye." In the meantime, my Mom and my brother Richie, who was 14 at the time, listened and loved it. Of course, they had heard the songs repeatedly from all the times we'd rehearsed in the house, but this was the real thing. My father listened to it when he got home from work and for the first time acknowledged that The Mystics had accomplished something. I think he and my Mom thought of music as a passing fancy, not a real job. If I had grown up in a household of musicians, their reaction would have been different, but my parents never thought of music as a real career move. They never went to college, they just worked hard all their lives. Having gone through the "depression", I guess they wanted me to do something with a little more substance, like the engineering I was taking in college. Ben Cammarata and I started going to community college right after graduating from high school. We both landed part-time summer jobs. Ben went to work for Mays department store, and I worked at Guardian insurance. Later, Bobby got me a job where he worked at an engineering firm on Whitehall Street in New York city. Every morning we met at the 18th Avenue subway stop at 7:30, talking about everything but mostly wondering if our new record was going to be a hit. There was a record shop on the street level of the building we worked in and we would stop in there almost every day and browse the new records. One day, I asked the owner if he had the new record "Hushabye" by The Mystics. He said he had not heard of it but would check it out. I didn't tell him Bobby and I were in the group.

 A few weeks went by and it was now sometime in April of 1959 when Jim called us into the office to give us a schedule of record hops to do. He told us that "Hushabye" was starting to sell in various markets around the country, especially Connecticut, and that DJ's were starting to play it. He said that Alan Freed, the premier Rock N Roll DJ, in the country liked "Hushabye" and wanted us on his Saturday night TV show. We were completely floored. I had often watched that show and dreamed about being on it, as well as on the Dick Clark show and on Alan's live shows at the Brooklyn Fox theatre. We also found out that Peter Tripp, from WNEW radio, and a few other popular DJ's were going to play the record starting the following week.

 WMCA's DJ, Harry Harrison and some of the others started playing it. "Hushabye" got great reviews on Cashbox and Billboard magazines, which were the bibles of the music world. We hoped to get on the Top 100. That would be a miracle. The weeks that followed were unbelievable. For several weeks, Freed closed his Saturday night TV show with "Hushabye," which shocked Jim Gribble and Gene Schwartz, as Gene said he didn't have any relationship with Freed. Some record companies had relationships with DJs to play records. These relationships included cash payments or "pay to play," commonly known as payola. But our record was getting airplay without any of that.

Alan Freed started playing rhythm and blues music in 1951 on his "Moondog House" radio show in Cleveland, Ohio, billing himself the "king of the moondoggers." He was credited with promoting the first "live" Rock and Roll concert, which was a huge success. The Rock and Roll Hall of Fame was built in Cleveland in recognition of Freed's involvement in this music. He eventually coined the phrase "Rock and Roll" for this new form of music that teenagers loved. Freed moved to New York City, where he began spinning records on "1010 WINS New York." By 1959, he was internationally famous and had starred in several motion pictures. As time went by, Rock and Roll changed, and so did its title. By the time the 90's rolled around, the Rock and Roll of my adolescence was called "oldies" and "doo-wop."

Back in April 1959, The Mystics were ecstatic. Our friends and family would call to say they'd heard "Hushabye" on the radio. I went back to the record store in the building where we worked and asked how "Hushabye" was doing. The owner replied, "I had to reorder that record several times, it's great. Do you want me to reserve one for you?"

I answered, "No thanks" and walked out with a big smile. I never told the owner that I was a Mystic. I don't know why.

We were all getting the same feedback from everyone we knew. Right after that crazy week Jim called us to come into the office for a special meeting.

He started by saying, "OK, boys, it looks like we got a hit on our hands." We just stared at him. He realized that we really didn't comprehend what that meant so he clarified. "Listen, you're all going to quit your jobs because I just booked you on a 3-week tour in the Midwest, which starts in June." We were shocked and thrilled at the same time. Having grown up in a time where everyone had a job, it was hard to accept that we could quit our jobs. It took Jim a while to convince us that music was now our new job. With a satisfying grin he said, "You boys are now recordings artists, this is what you wished for and now it's yours." I was not sure I was ready to hear this, nor did I know how to respond. All I could do was look at the faces of the four guys I was spending most of my time with and feeling overwhelming happiness.

I didn't think my parents would understand the concept of music as a job. All I ever heard from them was, "You have to go to college and get a good job." They didn't get the fact that music could be a career. How could they? No one we knew had a career in music. I hardly got it myself. It seemed like too much fun to be a job. The other guys were getting similar feedback from their parents. Georgie's parents, who became friendly with my parents, were having discussions on the subject.

Of course, no matter what anyone said, we were going through with this anyway. As young as we were, it was obvious that this type of thing did not come along every day. Every time we showed up in Gribble's office there were new kids wanting to try out. And I realized we were getting extremely popular. We talked amongst ourselves and were convinced that this was what we'd worked so hard for and that we should go for it. Besides, we were going to be famous. What could be wrong in that? Jim laid out a short-term plan, which consisted of the Midwest tour in June, a series of tri state record hops, a Saturday night show on the Freed show on May 16, 1959, and a shot at the Dick Clark Saturday night show, also in June. We were overwhelmed!   Our trips to Laurie became more serious. We had to scrap our first 8 x 10 promo photo and make an appointment for more professional shots. Our first photo session had been with my friend Angelo (Scapper) Rubano's brother, Bobby Rubano, who was starting out as a photographer. We had gone to Alley's Men's shop on Bay Parkway and bought matching black pants, black shirts, and white velvet jackets for the photo session. Bobby set us up in the basement of his family's house on 78th street and 16th Avenue and with one large lamp shot our first "professional" 8 x 10.

Jim and Gene set us up with a promotional woman who took us to Phil's Men's shop on 3rd Avenue in Manhattan to buy three new matching outfits: a dark tan suit, a gold jacket and dark pants, and a black and white plaid jacket with black pants. All outfits were to be worn with white shirts and ties. She also picked out white cardigan button down sweaters for us that became one of our favorite outfits. We felt so special. Imagine! We were buying outfits to do TV shows, we had our own shopping professional, and Laurie Records was footing the bill. We found out later, when we got our commission statement for record sales, that Laurie only fronted us that money. They took it off the top of our statements. Amazing!

Hushabye

Our shopping expert walked us over to the London Character Shoe store on 46th Street and Broadway and helped us pick out brown, black and white shoes for our outfits. With the white sweaters, white shirts and black tie, black pants and white shoes, we looked like five Italian Pat Boones. Having found out who we were after selling us 15 pairs of shoes, the shoe-store owner, Lew Kestenbaum, asked us for a signed picture for his 14-year-old son who loved "Hushabye." We all signed it and addressed it to Art Kestenbaum.

Twenty-five years later Art Kestenbaum showed up at one of our shows with the same signed 8 x 10. We're still friends with Art.

Jim set us up for our third photo session, with a photographer on 46th street and Broadway. Everyone who was somebody in show business went to him. We had done a previous session with another New York photographer," who was good but not as professional. The photographer suggested we use theatrical pancake make up for the photo session. This, of course, became another laughing session. We wore our brown suits and ties for the face shots and the white sweaters for the full-length photos.

Pete Mastropaolo, Tom Schizzano, Mary Beth Ryan, Tony Ventura and Joe D'Angelis, all part of our backup band called Coda, walked into the dressing room to announce that they were going to get a snack before starting sound check and rehearsal with the acts.

We chatted for a few minutes and off they went to the "Green room."

The rest of us were caught up in the past. I continued.

The Mystics (1959)
Left to Right, Bob, George, Phil, Al, Albee

The Mystics (1959)
Top L-R, George Phil, Albee; Bottom L-R, Bob, Al

CHAPTER 11

JUST TO BE WITH YOU

"**H**ushabye" was climbing the local charts. What was hard for us to fathom was that it was on its way to becoming a national and international hit. It was hard to process the fact that our first release was a hit record. Hundreds of recordings all over the country were being released with the intention of becoming a hit. Why else would anyone record? And here we were poised to get a hit!

On March 9, 1959, we did a record hop in Livingston, New Jersey, and were thrilled to see the response from the kids. Record hops were nothing more than a DJ playing records and teenagers dancing in an auditorium. The DJ's were usually somewhat famous on their local radio stations. At some point, the DJ would introduce the act and the act would lip-sync their record. We didn't realize it at the time, but we were being rated by the record company and the distributer, who had a representative at the hop to judge our presentation and the audience reaction. We did few more hops in New Jersey and one in Brooklyn, at the Albermarle Towers, a catering hall, on May 9. Oddly enough, this was around the corner from the apartment building from which a few years before we helped Jerry the Jew remove all the lobby furniture. The kids went crazy there, lots of screaming from the girls.

It was our first real taste of fame. We were the same guys that we always were only now we were a recording group with a song being played on the air. It was hard to understand the adulation, but it was nice. On May 16, 1959, we did the Freed TV show in NYC. At this time, "Hushabye" was not on the national charts, though it was noted in Cashbox as an up and coming record and in Billboard as "bubbling under the top 100." Being new in the music business we had no idea how hard it was to get a hit record. Just to be mentioned in Cashbox or Billboard magazine was a major feat.

This was our first TV show. We showed up at the studio with Jim Gribble, who looked and acted like the manager he was. He was an impressive sight in a blue suit with a white shirt and a reddish tie. He guided us through the process and we followed like ducklings. He told us to wear our new brown suits and ties, and with the advice of our new promo-lady, insisted we wear makeup. That was funny. Watching each other get make up applied by the make-up professional was too much to bear. Think about five streetwise guys from Brooklyn getting made up! Between the makeup and our nerves, we broke out into our usual fits of laughter. Bobby would make such funny remarks that we couldn't help but laugh. Jim calmed us down and gave us a "look professional" talk, which we adhered to immediately.

This was our first visit to an actual TV studio. Freed came into our dressing room, introduced himself, complimented us on how we looked. He said he loved "Hushabye," shook our hands and disappeared. We could hear the music playing in the studio where the kids were dancing on a "live" set. I had seen this show many times but never dreamed I would be on it. Our dressing room door opened, and the music was much louder. A young woman producer introduced herself and asked us to follow her. This was it. We had practiced our choreography repeatedly and of course; we knew how to lip sync our own recording. We followed the young women and weaved thru the wires scattered on the floor attached to the cameras, with earphone-wearing men looking through lenses as if they were about to launch a torpedo. We moved around to the semi-lit area while looking at the main studio, which was lit up like an operating room.

It was just before a commercial break, and we could hear "Dream Lover" by Bobby Darin and saw, through various monitors, kids dancing a sort of odd cha-cha step. Looked like an American cha-cha to me. I was used to dancing the cha-cha and mambo to the Latin bands like Tito Puente. A few of the kids saw us and starting cheering, I'm not sure if they actually knew who we were, but five young men, in a TV studio, in the same suits meant something was going to happen. We were handed off to an older man with earphones and mikes hanging off his neck, who guided us to a blank wall where he had us line up and face the cameras. He gave us our instructions, "When the red light on that camera goes on – you're on." Bobby verified our positions and re-stated the instructions we just got. We were a little nervous but handling it well. There were three TV cameras and we got a little confused as to where to look. We could barely hear Freed, who began announcing us from his podium on the dance floor after coming back from the break. In those few seconds, I thought of my family, friends and relatives at home watching their televisions, waiting to see The Mystics' TV debut.

Suddenly, a lot of bright lights went on, the red light on the middle camera went on, and we heard the familiar sound of us singing in unison the opening of "Hushabye." It took about a half second to focus but we got into the song and looked at the red light. We stood in a semi-circle with Bobby on one end next to George, me on the other end next to Albee, and Phil in the middle. The recording was loud, but we'd learned from previous record hops that singing aloud helped us stay together and look like we were actually singing instead of lip-syncing. I always wondered if anyone watching was surprised at the absence of microphones and instruments.

When we started singing, a few girls started screaming, for no apparent reason. But by and large, the audience, made up of teenagers, was polite and gave us an enthusiastic round of applause when we finished. We could see the outline of our 6'4 manager watching every second of our performance from behind the cameras. As no smoking was allowed in the studio, I knew that Jim must have been dying for a cigarette, Although "Hushabye" was not on the National Cash Box charts yet, it was selling very well and getting played on local radio stations throughout the country according to Gene, his brother Bob and Jim. On May 30, 1959 "Hushabye" debuted on Cashbox at number 74 with a bullet. The Cashbox charts listed the top 100 selling records in the country. If record sales of a particular record made a sharp upward move, based on information compiled by Cashbox from the leading retail outlets, the number it jumped to would have a red dot, called a bullet, around it. Entering the top 100 at number 74 was a big deal. The number one song was "The Battle of New Orleans" by Johnny Horton. "A Teenager in Love" by Dion and the Belmonts was number 8.

On May 23, 1959, we did a record hop at Temple Beth Emeth in our own neighborhood, where we met many of our friends who came to say hi and see for themselves what we were up to. It was weird, to say the least, to be dressed in jeans hanging with your friends one week and the next thing you know you're in a suit and tie lip-syncing a hit recording front of cheering teenagers. We were not hanging out with our friends as often as before because we were always doing something in New York or doing a record hop somewhere. Rehearsing became very important. It started to become part of our lives, kind of like a job but a job we enjoyed very much. Jim Gribble wanted us to dress well and look good on and off stage and especially on TV. He strongly suggested that we wear dress slacks and sport shirts instead of jeans and tee shirts when we showed up at the office or to a gig. Our socializing became more focused on ourselves and our girlfriends. We all had girlfriends in our lives and we often double-dated. Our world was rapidly changing. We did a show at WHOM radio for Alan Fredricks, a popular NYC DJ on May 22nd. The next day, we did a similar type show in New Jersey; the following day The Hy Litt Show in Quakertown, Pennsylvania. On these shows we usually were interviewed by the DJ for his radio show and then lip-synced "Hushabye" for the audience. It felt like we were campaigning for a political office. The more people saw you, the more records you sold. On May 31th we did a show in Patchogue, New York, at Dodge City, a western style amusement park with DJ Murray Kaufman. The Bellnotes, a group from Long Island, were also in the show. I remember that some of our families were at this show and were impressed with the audience reaction to our performance. It was kind of weird signing autographs, but we got the hang of it. We signed shirts, hats, jackets, arms, legs, necks and lots of programs. Jim was with us every step of the way.

Up to this point we really hadn't earned much money. Just before "Hushabye's" release we had done a few recordings backing up some new Laurie recording artists. We got $275.00 for a Don Press recording "Ask the Robin" b/w "More than Ever," and $275.00 for a Scott Garrett recording "Love Story b/w Graduation Souvenirs." That was $275.00 for the whole group. So that came to a total of about $100 each after Jim's cut. Considering that the minimum wage in 1959 was $1.00 an hour and we worked approximately four hours on each recording, we actually earned about $6.00 an hour. In today's money that would come to approximately $60.00 an hour before tax. It was a good thing we were all living at home with our parents.

We also backed up Connie Francis on her recording of "Tommy." This song was written by Stan Vincent, one of the young guys who started to hang around Jim Gribble's office. Jim befriended Connie Francis's vocal coach Al Meyer, whose office was next door to Jim's, and persuaded him to show Connie "Tommy" and also got him to agree that The Mystics would be an asset on the recording. We worked with Al to develop the background parts for "Tommy" and another song. When Connie showed up on the day of the session, we were a little nervous, but she was very gracious and friendly. Still, the session did not go well. The musicians were making errors, Connie didn't like the way the vocal background was arranged and wanted to add the three girls that normally sang background for her to our vocals. The other song went well but "Tommy" didn't work out that day. She came over to us and apologized for all the confusion and asked if we could come up with something on our own, which we did. It was simpler than Al's arrangement, and we finished our part, singing alongside the girl background singers, in a few takes. Stan stayed with Jim Gribble and took over his operation after Jim Gribble passed away in the mid sixties. Stan wrote "Teardrops follow Me" by the Del Satins who were managed by Jim (1962) and produced the Earls' hit record "Remember Then" (1962). Stan also had a few of his songs recorded by Connie, notably the hit singles "Drownin' my Sorrows" (1963) and "Looking for Love" (1964). Stan's biggest successes came when he wrote and produced "I'm Gonna Make You Mine" for Lou Christie in 1969 and "Ou-ou Child" by the Five Stairsteps in 1970.

Freed got so much good feedback from our appearance on his TV show he asked us to do another one on June 9th. I think this was unprecedented. He was still closing his television shows with "Hushabye." During this show, he spent a little more time with us and asked us, while in our dressing room, to join him at his show at the Brooklyn Fox Theatre in Brooklyn starting September 4th. We were gushing with appreciation. Then Dick Clark invited us to do his Saturday night TV show on June 20th. Incredible! The only rub was that we had already agreed to a General Artists Midwest tour from June 12th to July 5th (24 different shows in 24 different cities). Incidentally, our entire fee for 24 shows was $3000.00. Our airfare and hotels and transportation were paid by the tour, but food was on us. We didn't eat much for three weeks. I was still 120 pounds.

We spent the next couple of days preparing. Jim gave us as much information as he could. We would be flying out of Idlewild airport on June 10th and meeting a GAC representative at Chicago's O'Hare Airport later that day. This would be the first time any of us would fly on an airplane. We rehearsed our new show for the tour which was going to be live, not lip synched. Johnny and the Hurricanes, currently at number 28 on the Cashbox charts with "Crossfire" would be playing for all the acts on the tour, who, by the way, all had current records in the top 100, except for Barbara Evens, the only girl on the tour, who peaked at 100, with her recording of "Souvenirs." Frankie Ford was number 68 with "Sea Cruise," and Freddy Cannon's "Tallahassee Lassie" was number 9 and climbing. Carl Dobkins Jr.'s recording of "My Heart is an Open Book" was at number 24, Gary Stites was at number 29 with "Lonely for You" and we, the only group on the show, were at number 41 with a bullet. "Teenager in Love" had climbed to number 6. It still bothered me that we didn't record "A Teenager in Love".

A week before we left, we went shopping on 86th Street for some new clothes to wear for our trip, as well as a suit carrier. It's hard to believe that we went away for 24 days with one suit carrier for each of us: not a suitcase but a folding suit carrier. I remember going into a men's store on 86th Street with Bobby, Albee, Georgie and Phil and buying some of the latest paisley print shirts and new pants. The store owner had heard "Hushabye" and was thrilled that we were shopping in his store. We signed an 8 x 10 photo and he hung it up on the wall right behind the register. We were local heroes in the neighborhood!

Jim Gribble's office was getting busy. It did not take long for word to get around that he was looking for acts. He held auditions almost every day. We were his prize pupils: living proof that it was possible to get a record deal and a hit record. Jim would sometimes have us sit in on the auditions and give an opinion. It was like sitting on the panel for American Idol. Some of the kids were not that good, but some were very good or at least worthy of recording. As we learned, it was not only how you sang, but also how you looked. Jim liked to pick out real good-looking kids: the Fabian/Frankie Avalon syndrome.

Shortly after we first met with Jim, we invited our good friend Tony (Punchy) Armato to meet Jim and talk about getting an audition for his group, The Sinceres. This was a another local singing group that Punchy got involved with prior to my joining the Overons. The Sinceres, at this time, consisted of Tony (Punchy) Armato, Albee Galione, Vinny Ascierno, and Robert Fabano on lead. Despite Tony's efforts, the group never really got going. Bobby and I would sometimes stop by their rehearsal, out on the street on the corner of 84th Street and 16th Avenue. We tried to help, but it was obvious that they were lacking a good lead singer. They had great harmony, but they had to find a lead singer. Tony didn't want to audition with Jim until he was sure he had the right singers in his group. He had heard that there was a group in south Brooklyn called The Runarounds that had a great lead singer named Jimmy Gallagher. Tony, Albee and Vinny knew where they were rehearsing, which was usually on Carol Street in South Brooklyn, and they decided to check him out.

In those days, many groups would travel to other neighborhoods to listen to different groups sing. It was both checking the competition and finding new talent. The visiting group would always introduce themselves and just listen or sometimes join in. Many of the groups knew that The Sinceres were good friends with The Mystics who were now slightly famous just because they had a manager and were signed to Laurie records. After listening to Jimmy sing, Tony was convinced that he was the right lead singer for his group. The Sinceres weren't sure how to approach Jimmy, especially in front of the other singers, so they followed him home after the rehearsal and knocked on his door. After convincing his mother that they wanted to sing with her son, not mug him, the foursome went to a nearby park. It was a great match, and they ended up harmonizing for hours. Tony told Jimmy that he had an audition lined up with The Mystics' manager and that they wanted Jimmy to join The Sinceres. Jimmy told them that he was not happy with The Runarounds and that this would work out just fine. They were now a quartet, with Jimmy on lead, Tony on first tenor, Albee on second tenor, and Vinnie on baritone. They looked for a bass, but there were not too many kids with a bass voice. Tony had already met Jim and was considered our close friend. Jim liked Tony and was waiting to hear his group. Right after the audition with the new Sinceres, Gribble signed them up and renamed them The Passions. He gave them a demo that was sung by a duo of studio singers who called themselves The Cousins. The song was "Just to Be with You," written by Mary Kalfin. The Cousins were Paul Simon and Carole King.

Released in August 1959 on Irving Winkler's Audicon label, The Passions' impeccable harmonies and Gallagher's beautiful lead put "Just to Be with You" on radios across America. It was a top 20 hit in many eastern cities and it charted nationally, rising to number 69 on Cashbox and Billboard. A great accomplishment – and even more impressive considering that The Passions and The Mystics were neighborhood friends. Jim Gribble's reputation went up a couple of notches.

The Passions' follow-up on Audicon was twice as good. Both sides, the harmony-filled "I Only Want You" and the beautiful Billy Dawn Smith ballad "This Is My Love" got great reviews and radio play but did not do well on the national charts. Nevertheless, The Passions were considered a hit group. By the time the group recorded "Gloria," Vinny had left and been replaced by Gallagher's neighborhood friend Lou Rotondo. The Passions and The Mystics usually hung out with each other. In 1960 Lou Rotondo and Albee Galione, along with me, Albee and George Galfo, sang behind Clay Cole's recording, "Here, There, Everywhere" (Roulette), a single that became popular in the New York area. Audicon Records' next Passions release, was entitled "Made for Lovers." The group recorded a few more sides for Audicon' which were leased to Jubilee and Octavia records for distribution. By 1962 their recording career was over.

The Passions (1959)
Top - Jimmy Gallagher, L - Tony Armato, R - Albee Galione, Bot - Vinny Acierno

CHAPTER 12

TILL THEN

In the summer of 1959, the hot news in the vocal group world of Brooklyn was that the Mystics, from the Bath Beach section of Brooklyn, had just hit the charts with "Hushabye" and their friends the Passions were also recording for The Mystics' manager, Jim Gribble. It was amazing how fast this news travelled in the neighborhood. "Hushabye" was being played on all the radio stations and this was inspiring to every group in Brooklyn. There was an "If they could do it-so could we" feeling. The Classics were friendly with a hot local south Brooklyn group called The Del-Rays, who were considered to be a really good singing group. Emil Stucchio, who was friendly with Louie Rotundo, the lead singer of The Del-rays, would often go listen to them at the local church dances.

There was no formal rating system for how good a group was, it was a word of mouth thing that was surprisingly city-wide and accurate. If you had great harmony with a great lead singer you were at the top of the list. The Mystics had both, and even before "Hushabye," as the Overons, we were considered one of the best harmony groups around. When I would hang out at Jim Gribble's office, I would see groups from every borough auditioning for Jim. Jim would often ask me and the guys to sit in on the audition to render an opinion of the group that was trying out for a recording contract. It was weird, as some of the groups were not very good, and I felt funny giving an opinion, even though it was only to Jim after the auditioning group left. Jim would give out recording contracts like candy to groups, especially if they were good looking boys or "pretty boys" as he called them.

Louie Rotundo, who left the DelRays in 1959, replaced Vinny Ascierno in The Passions in late 1959. Once Lou joined The Passions, who were riding high with "Just to Be with You" and felt confident enough, he brought Emil and his group, The Classics to audition for Jim Gribble. Emil always talks about how the audition went for them. He remembers that five groups were auditioning that day, and while they were waiting in the outer office they could hear each of the other groups audition through Jim's office door. Everyone was better than The Classics in Emil's mind, and it was intimidating. Not only were they older and more mature, but they were singing more involved harmonies. He couldn't fathom how they would be able to compete with these groups. They almost left and scrapped the audition but thought why waste the trip? We have nothing to lose. Once inside the office and finally meeting Jim Gribble, Emil recalls that Roger Sherman from Dart records was also sitting in the office. Jim asked if they could sing and Emil assured them that they could. Jim took his signature drag from his cigarette and asked if they had any original songs and Emil told them they just finished writing a song called "Cinderella." Gribble asked Emil if those were his own eyelashes. Emil assured him they were, never realizing what he meant. Gribble then turned to Joe Sherman, winked and said, "Joe it looks like we have a group of pretty boys here." Apparently, handsome young men sold more records to the young girls buying public than older artists. The other groups who auditioned for Jim were better vocally, but Jim liked the looks of The Classics. After they sang "Cinderella" and "So in Love," Gribble informed them that they would be recording both sides next week. The Classics were ecstatic. They had secured the ultimate prize, a recording contract. They didn't ask what the contract would say or how much they would be making. They just could not stop talking about their good fortune. They all couldn't wait to tell their families and friends. So in 1959 under the auspices of manager Jim Gribble, they recorded their first single on Dart Records for Roger Sherman. A few months later "Cinderella" made the "Bubbling under the top 100" chart in Cashbox.

 The Classics' new release made it to the the top 20 on the local charts. It was number 5 on the New York WMCA radio station chart spearheaded by Peter Tripp, a DJ known as "The curly-headed kid in the third row." Their next release, "Life is But a Dream," fashioned after The Harptones' hit, did fairly well. This prompted the usual series of record hops and road trips to promote the record. During one of these shows, Andy Leonetti, who produced and managed The Chimes of "Once in a While" fame, took a liking to The Classics and approached the boys with a proposal. Andy asked them if they had a contract because he would like to record them.

At the time, Jim Gribble was not giving out long contracts unless groups had hits, so with their Dart record contract almost up they decided to go with this new charming producer in the latter part of 1962. Andy assigned producer Larry Lucie to The Classics with a plan to record an old standard like what the Chimes did with "Once in a While." Larry and Andy proposed "Till Then" to The Classics. Emil knew that this song was recorded in 1944 by the Mills Brothers because, like most teenagers at the time, he had heard the song from his parents. They rehearsed, and in January 25th of 1963 went into the studio to record.

Larry was a seasoned jazz guitarist and trying to capture the teenage sound of the time, asked Jamie to do a bass part that he thought up. He went up to Jamie and said, 'Your part is do-um, dodo-um" then turned to Emil and gave him the lead part timing to come in with "Till Then." The harmony arranged by Larry fit in with the live band and the recording session went on. After hearing the first playback Emil felt that they finally had something that would become a hit. "Till Then" (B side "Enie Minie Mo on the blue label of Musicnote Records, produced and arranged by Larry Lucie and Andy Leonetti, hit the national charts a few months later and shot up to the 20's. Another teenage dream fulfilled.

The Classics (1963)
Top L-R, Jamie Troy, John Gambale; Bot L-R, Emil Stucchio, Tony Victor

CHAPTER 13

PEGGY SUE

We went to the airport with an entourage of family members on the morning of June 12, 1959 to begin our first professional tour. A few hours later, we landed in Chicago and got in a taxi to the GAC (General Artists Corporation) offices located in a downtown office building. We stepped off the elevator and were met by GAC representatives and introduced to the other acts that were going to be with us including our tour manager Hal Charm. The walls were covered with 8 x 10 photos of famous people. This was a very impressive sight. Hal was a tired man in his 50's, a musician who'd toured with different big bands in the 40's. This was typical for musicians who wanted to stay in the music business: they helped manage other groups. All the acts were escorted to the tour bus now waiting outside the office building. It was a half-step up from a school bus. With a wide chrome band wrapped around the outside, it looked like a 50's style diner with wheels. Johnny and the Hurricanes were already on the bus, as they had to load all their instruments, including a very large Hammond organ and matching Leslie speaker, directly from their truck. The drum set, guitar amps and the Hammond organ were stored on the bench in the back of the bus while the Leslie speaker was hanging half out the rear door. The Leslie speaker looked like a piece of wood furniture and was as heavy as a refrigerator. We found this out because we all took turns during the tour helping to load and unload the equipment.

The Leslie speaker is a combined amplifier and two-way loudspeaker that projects the signal from an electric or electronic instrument while modifying the sound by rotating the loudspeakers. A typical Leslie speaker contains an amplifier and a treble and bass speaker, though specific components depend upon the model. A musician controls the Leslie speaker by either an external switch or foot pedal that alternates between a slow and fast speed setting, known as "chorale" and "tremolo." What a great sound!

We all filed in with our suit bags and luggage and selected a double seat each. The Mystics sat across from each other midway, and everyone else found their seats, which would become their space for the remainder of the tour. We were the only act from Brooklyn and of course the initial conversations with the other acts centered on what it was like growing up in Brooklyn. Freddy Cannon was from Boston. Carl Dobkins was from Cincinnati, Ohio. Johnny and the Hurricanes were from Toledo, Ohio. Frankie Ford was from Gretna, Louisiana and Barbara Evans from Charlotte, South Carolina. Hal Charm, originally from Chicago, introduced everyone to our driver Dave Williams, a nice man who always wore his bus uniform, including a tie. We were getting settled in when Dave pulled the handle that controlled and closed the door. He put the bus into gear and off we went.

On this day, June 28, 1959 "Hushabye" had risen to number 27 on the Cash Box top 100 charts. The GAC "Vacation Dance Party" featuring many of the current bestselling recording artists was on its way. We started talking with the acts we'd just met, and I didn't even notice that we were already on a highway. Since this was the first tour for many of the artists, I guess we were all a little star struck, as everyone had hit recordings on the charts. The Mystics mostly talked among ourselves the first hour. We had built in friends – us. We slowly integrated with the other acts and became friendly with Frankie Ford, who as a veteran tour performer suggested that we steal a pillow and a blanket from the hotel that we were going to stay at that night so the next day's trip would be a little more comfortable. Frankie Ford was born Vincent Francis Guzzo. He learned to sing and dance at an early age, and when in high school he joined a group, the Syncopators, as singer and pianist. He was spotted by his manager, Joe Caronna, who took him to Johnny Vincent of Ace Records. Taking the stage name Frankie Ford, he made his first recordings for Ace in 1958. He toured locally in Louisiana, before recording a vocal overdub on the song "Sea Cruise," a song written and originally recorded by Huey "Piano" Smith with his group, The Clowns, and featuring overdubbed bells and ships' horns. Since Smith already had a record on the charts and was away touring, the record label decided to release Ford's version, and it rose to #14 on the US pop chart and #11 on the R&B chart, selling over one million copies and gaining gold disc status.

We all took a special liking to Freddy Cannon. I guess because he was from Boston and had personality and eastern humor we could identify with. Freddy had a heavy Boston accent, and we had never heard anyone pronounce words like that before. We were the ones with the heaviest accent of all. Our Brooklynese was fascinating to everyone. We immediately started joking around with Freddy asking him to say, "park the car," which sounded like "Pak da Kar." We all laughed, and it broke the ice. Freddy Picariello was born in Revere, Massachusetts. His father worked as a truck driver and played trumpet and sang in local bands. Freddy grew up listening to the rhythm and blues music of Big Joe Turner, Buddy Johnson and others on the radio and learned to play guitar. After attending Lynn Vocation High School, he made his recording debut as a singer in 1958, singing and playing rhythm guitar on a single, "Cha-Cha-Do" by the Spindrifts, which became a local hit. He also played lead guitar on a session for an R & B vocal group, The G-Clefs, whose record "Ka-Ding Dong" had made No. 24 on the Billboard Hot 100 in 1956.

Inspired musically by Chuck Berry, Bo Diddley and Little Richard, he formed his own group, Freddy Karmon & the Hurricanes, which became increasingly popular in the Boston area, and began to develop a trademark strained singing style. He also became a regular on a local TV dance show, Boston Ballroom, and, in 1958, signed up to a management contract with Boston disc jockey Jack McDermott. With lyrics co-written by his mother, he prepared a new song which he called "Rock & Roll Baby" and produced a demo, which McDermott took to the writing and production team of Bob Crewe and Frank Slay. They rearranged the song, rewrote the lyrics and offered to produce a recording in return for two-thirds of the composing credits. Many of the producers took advantage of the new teenage song writers by offering production for a piece of their composition. The first recording of the song, now titled "Tallahassee Lassie," with a guitar solo by session musician Kenny Paulson, was rejected by several record companies, but was then heard by TV presenter Dick Clark, who part-owned Swan Records in Philadelphia. Clark suggested that the song be re-edited and overdubbed to add excitement, by highlighting the pounding bass drum sound and adding hand claps and Freddy's cries of "whoo," which later became one of his trademarks. The single was finally released by Swan Records, with the company president, Bernie Binnick, suggesting Freddy's new stage name of "Freddy Cannon." After being promoted and becoming successful in Boston and Philadelphia, the single gradually received national airplay. In 1959, it peaked at No. 6 on the Billboard Hot 100, becoming the first of his 22 songs to appear on the Billboard chart, and also reached No. 13 on the R&B singles chart. In the UK, where his early records were issued on the Top Rank label, it reached No. 17. "Tallahassee Lassie" sold over one million copies and was awarded a gold disc by the RIAA. He stayed on the Swan label with producer Frank Slay for the next five years and became known as Freddy "Boom Boom" Cannon, for the thumping power of his recordings. Dick Clark brought him national exposure through numerous appearances on his television program, American Bandstand: a record of 110 appearances in total. Dick Clark made sure his artists did well.

Our first stop was the Devines Ballroom in Milwaukee, Wisconsin, which was approximately a three-hour drive from Chicago in this old modified school bus with seats that would not recline. It was warm, short sleeve weather in the Midwest. Although the bus was uncomfortable and did not have any of the modern conveniences that we have become accustomed to, like reclining seats and air conditioning, it was not nearly as bad as the GAC Winter tour that played the same venues. That tour was plagued with a bizarre cold spell in the Midwest.

On January 23, 1959, GAC's "Winter Dance Party" headed out to Devines Ballroom with Buddy Holly and the Crickets ("Peggy Sue"), The Big Bopper ("Chantilly Lace"), Ritchie Valens ("Donna"), and our Laurie Records associates, Dion and the Belmonts ("I Wonder Why)". After a few more dates on the cold road, this tour ended for three of the performers, on February 3, 1959. To avoid another night on a freezing bus, Holly, Valens and the Big Bopper chartered a plane to take them to the next gig in Minnesota. The plane crashed, and they all died, including the pilot. This event stunned the world and is known today as the "day the music died," as Don McLean sang on his recording of "American Pie."

We checked into the hotel and headed out to the ballroom to do a band rehearsal. Most of the acts had sheet music for most of their songs, and Johnny and the Hurricanes were good at following the music for those, like us, who didn't have charts. It didn't take long to go through our songs. Hal set up the lineup and told us we would be going on third, following Barbara Evans. Freddy Cannon, who had the biggest hit at the time, would be closing the show, which is the way most multi-act shows are structured.

Johnny and the Hurricanes opened with their 20-minute set, followed by Carl with a 15-minute set, and Barbara with a 15-minute set. We did a

20-minute set, with Frankie Ford following us with a 20-minute set, and Freddy closed the show with a 20-minute set and a finale with all the acts on stage singing "When the Saints go Marching In." Hal insisted we do a complete show, so he could time it. The show, with intros by Hal and Johnny Paris, was about two hours. Hal said "perfect." We got some more pointers and instructions from Hal and were on our way back to the hotel by 4:00 pm. We had some dinner at the hotel, showered and were on our way back with our show suits by 7:00 for our first show in the Midwest.

I don't remember if any of us actually called our parents to let them know what was going on. At that time, a long-distance telephone call was expensive and was only used in an emergency. I think we managed to make a call to our parents and girlfriends at least once a day, reversing the charges, of course.

The bus pulled up to the stage door of the ballroom and we all went silent as the noise from the huge crowd of teenagers startled us. It sounded like a riot. Dave maneuvered the bus, so the door would open directly in front of the stage door. There were a dozen security guards keeping the kids away from us as we exited the bus and entered the ballroom. We found the dressing rooms and settled in, amazed at what had just happened outside. We had never experienced anything like this. The crowds back east were loud, but this was different. We actually had to be protected from the crowd. Once inside, we saw the white walls outside the dressing rooms covered with the various signatures and sayings of performers who had appeared there in the past. Legendary names like Chuck Berry, Fats Domino, The Clovers, and The Platters were represented by hand-written autographs. Bobby called us over to where he was standing and pointed to three autographs on the wall, with the signatures of The Big Bopper, Ritchie Valens and Buddy Holly. The other acts came over and we were all awe-struck to see these names on the wall. The next time we all saw these autographs was on the white walls of the dressing rooms in the last show that these incredible performers played, at the Surf Ballroom in Clear Lake, Iowa. It was our 19th show on the tour, and at this point, we were well-seasoned performers.

Bobby had been in touch with Jim Gribble, who had set up our Dick Clark show performance to be taped in New York on Friday June 19 and shown the following day. Hal, who was also in contact with Jim, set up a car to take us to the airport early Friday morning, where we flew to NY and taxied to the studio to tape the show with Sam Cooke "Only Sixteen,"

James Darren ("Gidget" and "Angel Face") Stonewall Jackson ("Waterloo," # 5), and Tony Bellus ("Robbin' the Cradle"). We had to miss our show at the Dance Land Ballroom in Cedar rapids, Iowa, but it was worth it.

Jim greeted us at the studio with a big smile, and we were gushing with stories about the incredible tour, the crowds, and the fun we were having. Jim walked with us to our dressing rooms, and while we were settling in, Dick Clark walked in and introduced himself, which I found amazing because we all knew who he was. I mean really! Jim was becoming more than just a manager, he was our best friend. Dick Clark's Saturday night Beech-nut show was the ultimate gig in the rock and roll world: it was equivalent to doing the Ed Sullivan show. As Jim suggested, we wore our brown three button suits and were a lot more professional than we'd been on our first TV show for Allan Freed.

The cool part of all this was hanging out in the green room and meeting James Darren and Sam Cooke. We were in awe of these performers and were pleasantly surprised to see how nice they were. We were treated as equals, which coming from where we did, felt a little awkward. Jim congratulated us and gave us an update on how happy everyone at Laurie Records was with "Hushabye" and the good reports we were getting from the tour. Of course, Hal was the reporter. Jim said he had a bunch of shows and promotional radio and TV spots to do as soon as we got back, and we'd have to start working on a second record. Since the taping was in the afternoon, we got a chance to go home for the night and catch up with everyone about what we were doing so far. It was interesting, looking back, to see that even our own families treated us differently now. This was a phenomenon that I had a hard time getting used to. Although it felt good, it was sometimes unnerving. A few of my friends came by, and then I spent some time that night with my girlfriend.

The next morning, we were on our way back to Springfield. Flying was not a new thing anymore and we were settling into a show business life. In remembering this, what stands out the most is the fun we had. We really liked each other, and we laughed a lot. We were on an incredible ride. All we had to do is keep singing. We checked into the hotel in Springfield and everyone from the show was asking about how we did. Some of the acts had already done the Dick Clark show and were telling us how great it was to see themselves on TV a day later. At the time, it was unusual to see a pre-recorded show. Most of TV was live. So, we started to figure out that since it was Saturday and the show usually started at 8:00 pm, there might be a way to see the show. As it turns out, there was a bar about a half a block from the Orpheum Theatre. We ran out the stage door while the dance portion of the night was going on in the theatre and walked into the bar. We ordered some drinks and asked the bartender if he would put the Dick Clark show on his TV, which was a fourteen-inch black and white Philco TV on a shelf behind the bar, between the vodka and the whisky bottles. There were not many people in the bar and the bartender, a man in his sixties, asked us if we were with the show at the theatre. It was obvious that we were. We introduced ourselves and told him that we were going to be on the Dick Clark Saturday night show in a few minutes. He told us he had heard "Hushabye" and liked it very much. He fumbled with getting the TV reception to be a clear as possible and turned to the appropriate channel as the show started. When the announcer mentioned The Mystics, he turned to us with a puzzled look on his face. It didn't register with him until Dick Clark introduced us and he saw the same guys sitting at his bar on national TV. His head kept going back and forth from the TV to us. He had this goofy smile, like we were doing a magic trick. It was awesome. It wouldn't be a big deal now, because everybody understands that you can tape a show and play it later. However, in 1959, taping was not done too often, and this bartender in Springfield, Illinois, was astonished.

The rest of the tour was typical. The crowds were always loud but respectable and we just about sold out every show, which made Hal very happy. I think that part of Hal's compensation was based on attendance, as he had us visit local radio stations the day of the show to promote the event. Every act took turns going to the radio stations. Sometimes a few went and sometimes everyone was there. Bobby was our designated spokesperson, so he usually represented The Mystics. Sometimes the crowds were plain out of control crazy. I remember the show in Peoria at the Shrine Auditorium. The room was set up like there was going to be a boxing match, with the stage right in the middle of the room except there was no seating around the stage. The auditorium seating was on all four sides, like in Madison Square Garden. It was obvious that dressing rooms we designed for a team sporting event, with lockers and showers.

We heard the crowd noise building from our dressing rooms, and it was nonstop screaming. At this point, "Hushabye" was approaching the top 20 spot in Cashbox but was in the top three in Illinois, and number one on two of the Peoria radio and TV stations. "Hushabye" was being played on just about every radio station in the area. Posters promoting the show were in all the store windows on Main Street. Of course, five good-looking Italians from New York just fed the fire. Hal came to get us in the dressing room with two bodyguards. Freddy looked over at us, and we all bust out laughing at this bizarre scene. This was our first multi-bodyguard experience. Hal cautioned us that there was a large crowd here and that we should walk very fast to the stage. We walked with the two burly guards through the concrete corridor, and as we reached the entrance to the arena, we heard Barbara just ending her hit song. The crowd was roaring. We stepped onto the arena floor waiting for our turn. We could see that the stage, which now had a massive audience around it, was a few hundred yards away. It must have been about 85 degrees in the room. The spotlights highlighted a low hanging cloud of smoke over the stage. There was a double line of bodyguards forming a corridor by holding hands for us to walk through. It was now getting a little scary. Barbara was running towards us with a bodyguard on each arm, but her feet were not touching the floor, and she had a scared look on her face. Her hair was a little messed up and she was covered in sweat. It reminded me of when the gladiators were preparing to go into the arena not knowing what to expect and watching a wounded warrior come back. We asked her how it was, and she was about to answer when Hal yelled "Go!" and we started sprinting in between the line of guards with the guards yelling, "Don't stop."

The double line of guards had a hard time holding back the crowd. Arms were reaching through the guards, trying to grab us. It was a gauntlet. We reached the stairs as the local DJ was announcing us. It was hard to hear what he was saying with the screaming kids all around us. Bobby was near the top of the stairs, George behind him, and Phil on the next step down, all holding onto the handrail and looking in disbelief at the size and intensity of the crowd. I was still on the floor with, Albee in front of me with one foot on the first step, holding onto the handrail.

There were kids all around us yelling and screaming our names and trying to touch us. I thought to myself, "How the hell are we gonna get out of here?" The guards were pushing them back. They were just young kids, teenagers. We all talked about it later and wondered how the hell did they know our names? All of a sudden, I saw a hand shoot out towards Albee's head, grabbing his hair. His head went back, and he tried to turn and see what was going on. We both realized that we had seconds before we had to be up on the stage.

I looked at the closest guard, who was busy trying to contain some kids, and yelled, "Get that hand!" He saw the same thing I did and was trying to help me as I grabbed the arm while Albee reached back with both hands, trying to open the hand and release the grip. I saw the face that belonged to the hand and it was a young girl. Just then her other hand appeared, and it was holding a small scissors. Both the guard and I realized she was trying to cut his hair. With all that was going on, it was confusing as there were a lot of faces and arms reaching towards us. Albee was having a hard time breaking her hand free, which was surprising because he was so strong. The other guys started to move to the stage. They had no idea of the drama that just took place. In desperation, I tried to punch the girl, but I could not reach her. The guard grabbed her hair and pushed her head back and she released her grip while screaming out Albee's name. I followed Albee up onto the stage, glancing back with a nod of thanks to the guard. He gave me a thumbs up and mouthed the words, "Good Luck." We looked at each other as if to say, "What the fuck just happened?" Then Albee leaned over and yelled in my ear, "What the fuck just happened?" I shrugged and yelled back into his ear, "I'll tell you later." Phil and George sensed something happened and looked over questioningly. It was amazing how we had developed a way of talking without words, as if we could read each other's minds. My look back was enough to resolve the question, and we all knew we would discuss it later. I think this developed from the thousands of hours we spent singing while studying each other faces for a sign of where to go next or which part of the song should go higher or lower.

We walked to the middle of the stage, looking over and acknowledging Johnny and the Hurricanes, who were behind us vamping our opening song. They all had the biggest grins, mostly from the bottle of gin they consumed in the dressing room, as we approached the mikes and started our opening song; "Church Bells May Ring." I did not think it was possible, but the uproar when we started singing was louder than when we were announced. At the end of our set, "Hushabye" received a thunderous ovation and we left the stage aware there was a minefield to go through before we reached the dressing rooms. This time we ran as fast as we could. Hal looked delighted and congratulated us with backslaps as we got to the door. Frankie looked as calm as ever as he started for the stage. I explained to everyone what had happened with the "scissor girl" and we laughed about it. Freddy suggested we wear hats to do the finale and we all had a good laugh and stared at each other with a look of "Oh my God, we have to do that again."

We all got into a show business groove on this tour and became good friends with all the acts but especially Freddy, Gary Stites and Frankie Ford. Some of us became really close with Barbara. There were some trips between cities that required us to leave after the show and drive through the night to the next city. It was on these nights that the blankets and pillows we borrowed from the hotels came in handy. As suggested by Frankie Ford, a few of us would lay out our blankets on the overhead metal luggage rack and climb up so we could lie down. The bus seats were rigid and were incredibly uncomfortable. Many times, during the drive we would stay up most of the night and talk about the show, joke around and eat junk food. We once stopped at a pizzeria after a show; we were dying for a slice of pizza, and all piled out of the bus into the store. The Midwest does not have Brooklyn, or anything that even resembles East Coast pizza. We were desperate for pizza and kept bugging Hal until gave in. He warned us to behave and act like gentlemen and not get crazy like at some of the other roadside stops. It's not that we were not gentlemen, but I think we all were in a natural *high on life* state of mind. Here we were, young guys from different parts of the country, average age 20 years old, recording stars, and starting to understand what that meant. Or at least I thought I knew what that meant. We just felt like we were on top of the world: on the road, doing what we loved to do with our best friends and getting paid for it.

We found tables and when the waitress took our orders we all ordered Pizza. Freddy sat with Albee, Phil, Georgie and I. Bobby sat with Hal, Frankie Ford and the driver. And the rest sat at another table. The place was warm. There was a big propeller type fan in a corner right above our table and as we got a little crazy after finishing a few pizza pies, we started flipping pieces of pizza at each other and laughing. Suddenly Freddie takes a slice and flings it up into the fan and pieces of pizza flew everywhere. We were hysterical with laughter. That's when Hal got pissed and ushered us all out of the store while apologizing to the owner and stuffing some cash in his hand. Hal lectured all of us in the bus about the incident, saying that we were public figures, but we could not stop laughing. Eventually, Hal gave in and started laughing when Gary Stites announced, with a straight face, that he'd found a piece of tomato in his hair.

CHAPTER 14

MR. LONELY

The nights when we stayed over after the show were completely different. The show typically finished about 10:30. It took everyone a few minutes to change and load onto the bus for the ride to the hotel, which was usually 15 minutes away. There were usually a few dozen girls waiting for us by the bus, asking for autographs and just a chance to talk. They were mostly young teenage giddy-type girls, but there were also a few girls our age. In some instances, there were a bunch of girls waiting in the lobby of the hotel. This is where we had to be extra careful. Hal, like an uncle, pointed out many times, "Don't get caught with an underage girl. That would be very bad for the tour and really bad for you." The law in these towns does not like entertainers. Now I realize why Hal wanted to travel to the next destination right after a show. It would be hard to anyone reading this to believe that *none* of us went with any of the girls during the tour. Some of did and some of us did not.

By the time we reached the end of the tour "Hushabye" was in the top 20's nationally and in the top 5 as well as reaching number one in many of the cities we played. I loved this life, but it was time to go home and relax with family, friends and girlfriends. Paul Anka's "Lonely Boy" took the number one spot on the national charts. Carl Dobkins Jr's "My Heart is an Open Book" was number six and "There Goes my Baby" by the Drifters with the new addition of violins in the music was on its way to number one. I think that "Since I Don't Have You," by the Skyliners was the first rock and roll recording by a group to use violins. It was sensational. The interesting thing about the Skyliners (and a few other artists) was that their record company released their second recording "This I Swear" while their first record was still on the charts. Laurie did not do that with The Mystics. We kept asking Jim to follow up and get us a second record. It took too long.

We returned from the tour on July 6th and were on our way to Providence, RI the next day for the local TV station's 10th Anniversary block party hosted by Al Rucker (Clay Cole), which I have already described.

Clay interrupted with, "Wow I remember that crazy day like it was yesterday. We had a lot of people there".

We were exhausted, but it was a good exhaustion. The drive up to Providence took forever. We left very early in the morning because they told Jim that they expected a huge crowd and wanted us in place before the crowds blocked our entrance. He was certainly right about the crowds!

Soon after this show, we met Al Rucker in NYC. During this show, we became friends with The Videls, a local group from Providence, especially Vini Poncia and the lead singer Peter Andreoli. Pete and Vini told us that they had written a great song with us in mind called "Mr. Lonely" and sang it for us. I thought that not only was this a great song for us but a perfect follow up to "Hushabye." It had the unison beginning breaking into harmony like "Hushabye." We asked them to contact Jim Gribble and Laurie and present the song, which they did. Laurie declined, which really pissed us off. I stayed in touch with Vini and Pete and a few months later found out that they were coming into New York for an audition with George Sherman and JDS records, where they eventually recorded "Mr. Lonely" as The Videls. "Mr. Lonely" reached 73 on the national charts in early 1960. I was very happy for them, but I couldn't help but think we would have had a much bigger hit as a follow up to "Hushabye."

We were in Boston on August 4th, 5th and 6th for some shows and then on our way back to the Midwest for a show at the Lake Lawn Lodge in Delevan and The DeVines Ballroom in Wisconsin. We stayed overnight at the Lake Lawn Lodge, a beautiful country club resort on a lake. This was an older crowd than at our other shows, but after the show, we were still mobbed as we walked to our rooms across the lawn. Each of us was surrounded by very attractive girls asking for autographs. I kept trying to stay in eye contact with the other guys and they did the same so that if anyone was in trouble we could help. There wasn't much security here, and it was a little scary because these girls were getting real close and very aggressive. The girls were so close to me that I couldn't put my arms down to my side. That forced me to hold the pen and paper up close to my chest to sign. There had to be at least 12 to 15 girls pressing against me and each other. Suddenly I felt a hand between my legs and it definitely was not mine. I instinctively tried to move back but there was nowhere to move. Just as suddenly as the hand had appeared it disappeared. I caught Phil's eye and he burst out laughing at the sight of me in the middle of the chaos. When I explained later what he didn't see, he got hysterical and so did the other guys. We all kind of moved while signing to get closer to our cabins without upsetting anyone and finally ducked in. We talked a little about the event and went up to change our clothes and figured to meet up later to get something to eat, as suggested by the owner of the lodge. I found my room, got my key out, and found that the door was unlocked. I cautiously went into the room and heard muffled laughter and water splashing in the bathroom. It was my room, my clothes were hanging in the closet, my shirt was on the bed. I opened the bathroom door to find two naked girls in the bathtub. I recognized them from the group of girls that were outside earlier and since they looked old enough, and I had to take a shower before dinner, I joined them.

Everyone burst into laughter. Clay said, "I gotta say, that never happened to me! So, what happened next, Allie?" Emil said with a big grin.

"Well, needless to say, I missed dinner with the guys, but I had a late dinner that night with my two new friends in my room."

There were many parts of the tours that we didn't tell our parents about, and this was one of them. We went to Revere and Springfield, Massachusetts, on Aug 21st and 22nd of 1960, and were back in Brooklyn just in time to do a show in New Jersey on Sept 2nd. Sept 4th through Sept 13th was our best gig so far. We were part of the Alan Freed 5th Anniversary show at the Fox theatre in our hometown Brooklyn, NY. The same Freed show that we'd gone to see a few years earlier with Frankie Lyman and the Teenagers, The Cadillacs and many others. We never could have predicted that we would be on the show too. The lineup was awesome: Lloyd Price and his 16-piece orchestra, Jackie Wilson, Jimmy Clanton, Dion and the Belmonts, The Skyliners, The Crests (with Johnny Maestro), Bo Diddley, JoAnn Campbell, Johnny Restivo, Valerie Carr, Bobby Lewis, Johnny October, The Tempos, Ronnie Hawkins, Gerry Granahan, and the Isley Brothers as special guests

It was here that we met and became friends with The Skyliners, Johnny Maestro and the Crests, and Jimmy Clanton. There were four shows a day separated by the same movie. Most of the acts performed their hits. Jackie Wilson did about six songs and we did one. We were somewhere in the middle of the show, and inevitability while we were doing "Hushabye" someone would yell one or all of our names from the audience. Usually it was one of our neighborhood friends. We followed the Isley Brothers, who were currently on the charts with "Shout" parts I and II. They tore up the stage, jumping up and down, doing splits. Ronnie Isley got up on the piano and jumped off into a split then did a few spins into another split while the audience went wild dancing in the aisles. We watched this from the wings, huddled behind a curtain that had an old moldy smell, ready to go on next. Each time it was our turn to go on I would say, "Wow, how the hell are we going to follow that?" And Albee would say, "We'll be just fine." Alan, who really liked us, gave the audience a few seconds to calm down and get back in their seats before he gave us a terrific introduction, noting that he closes his TV show with this next group's hit record. We walked out to a great response and in two and a half minutes were doing our rehearsed bow and, on our way, back to the dressing rooms. We high-fived Jimmy Clanton on his way out to the stage and by the time he finished his song we were in the dressing room.

There was so much time to kill between shows that and much of it was spent trying to find a place to eat without being tracked by fans. Most of the time we went to the bar next door, which offered some protection from the younger kids with a body guard at the front door. The musicians passed the time gambling. Some played cards and some would shoot craps. That was Alan's thing. He was always gambling. He would get a crap game going in between shows behind the screen backstage, while the movie was playing. That's the first time I had watched a movie (a western) from behind the screen as it leaked thru. It was a bizarre scene: a group of young men shooting craps while just a few hundred feet away, on the other side of the screen, people were watching a movie.

The lines to get into the show were usually blocks long and every show was sold out. We made total, for all of us, of $1,142.00 for the ten days. That came to approximately $5.71 each per show. Not bad for recording stars. I'm kidding: that was ridiculous! But we were not concerned with money at that time, we were living our dream.

The second day at the Fox, while we were backstage waiting to go on, one of the security guards said that there was a guy claiming to be a TV host from Providence RI, saying that he was a friend of ours, by the stage door and wanted to know if he should let him in. The guard couldn't remember his name, but we knew it was Al Rucker. After the hugs and handshakes, he said he had great news. He had landed a job in New York for Channel 5 as a host for a new show called Rate the Record and wanted us to be on his first show. He also told us in his best announcer voice, "And by the way, Al Rucker has changed his name to Clay Cole". We congratulated him and invited him to hang out in our dressing room after we went on. He watched the Isley's rip up the stage and then our song. That was the beginning of a long and valued friendship between The Mystics and Clay Cole.

Clay Cole was born Albert Rucker, Jr. on January 1, 1938, in Youngstown, Ohio. He became a juvenile stage and radio actor; then in 1953, at age 15, he became the television host and producer of his own Saturday night teen music show, Rucker's Rumpus Room.

In 1958, he continued appearing on Saturday night television, launching Al Rucker and the Seven Teens program on WJAR-TV, Providence. In New York City in 1959, when asked to change his name, he chose that of a distant cousin, Clay Cole. He started with Rate the Record and then the Clay Cole Show from NY and live from Palisades Park in NJ, where we appeared an astounding thirty times over the next few years. Clay's 1960 all-star ten-day Christmas show at the Brooklyn Paramount Theater broke the all-time house box office record. Clay was among the few white performers invited to appear at Harlem's Apollo Theater; he headlined three week-long revues, starring Fats Dannyino, Gladys Knight & the Pips and Chubby Checker. In 1961, he appeared as himself in the film *Twist Around the Clock*. When WNTA-TV was sold in 1963, Cole's program was picked up by New York City television station WPIX-TV, where the program became known as Clay Cole's Discotek in 1965. During the 1960's "British Invasion," music acts arriving from the UK often appeared on Cole's television show before doing network shows such as The Ed Sullivan Show. The Rolling Stones and The Who were among those who first appeared in the U.S. on Cole's television show. Cole's show differed from American Bandstand: while both Cole and Dick Clark had an interest in young people and their music, Clay did not hesitate to join in on his show's dance floor. He was also more confident about booking lesser-known performers and comedians for his show. I stayed in touch with Clay, and he would always apologize for not being able to get us on the show, but I knew that the music had changed, and we were no longer relevant.

In the mid-1970s Clay and his longtime friend, Thomas John Butrim created the TV show, "People." Although it was short lived, it has been called the stepping stone for television stations such as MTV and television shows such as Entertainment Tonight. Some of the guests that Clay and Thomas had on the show included The Village People, Diana Ross, Donna Summer, Bette Midler, and Barbra Streisand. Clay called me a few times to appear on the show when he was short of guests. One night while having dinner with Clay and some friends, I commented on how many people recognized our (Mystics) Brooklyn accent when we were out of state. The conversation escalated, and he invited me to join him on a street corner in Brooklyn to talk about it "live" on camera the next morning. Clay called me often to run by some of his ideas about upcoming shows. We sometimes spent hours kicking around different scenarios while laughing so hard I would get pains.

Clay left the Clay Cole Show in 1967, which was a shock to everyone. He became a television writer-producer, involved in the production of over 3500 broadcast television shows. He produced "The Discovery of Marilyn Monroe," "Play Bridge with Omar Sharif" and 365 "This Day in Hollywood" segments. He returned briefly in 1974 as the star of the first HBO-produced music special, "Clay Cole's 20 Years of Rock and Roll," a two-hour event taped at Rockland Community College and as co-host of the WABC-TV weekday program, "AM New York." He won Emmy Awards as "producer of outstanding television programming" in 1981 and 1982. His final professional assignment was as writer/producer/director of the television special, "The 2002 San Remo Music Festival in Italy," featuring Britney Spears, Destiny's Child, Alicia Keys, Shakira, Kylie Minogue and other international pop divas.

Clay retired and has been living on Oak Island, North Carolina since 2007. His pop culture memoir, *Sh-Boom! The Explosion of Rock 'n' Roll (1953-1968)* was nominated for the 2010 Association for Recorded Sound Collections Awards for Excellence in Historical Recorded Sound Research. Cole made a personal appearance at the annual Long Island Radio & TV Day in New York City. I stayed in touch with him and Ray Ranieri, one of Clay's closest friends for years. Ray and I would often try to coax him to get back into the music scene. Finally, Ray got Clay to agree to host "Richard Nader's Original Summer Doo wop Reunion Show XX" in Rutherford, NJ, which since Richard Nader's death had been produced by his wife Debbie Nader. Until then, Clay had been self-conscious about his weight gain and didn't want to go out in front of an audience. But in 2009, he had lost a lot of weight and looked great.

"Aw, shucks," said Clay, with a display of false modesty.

"It's true, you do look great," I said.

"You don't look so bad yourself," said Clay. "For an old man, I mean."

Everyone laughed, and I replied, "funny, but true we are getting old, I wonder how long this music will last."

Kenny said, "As long as people come out to see it."

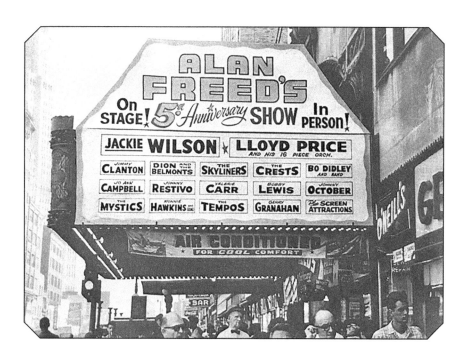

Brooklyn Fox Theatre (1959)

The Skyliners

Johnny Maestro and The Crests

Dion and The Belmonts

CHAPTER 15

SO TENDERLY

We were now desperate to get a second record out. We noticed that some of our friends who had hits at the same time as "Hushabye" were already on the charts with their follow-up records. We spent quite a bit of time at Laurie Records bugging Jim, Gene and Elliot, trying to get them to engage Pomus and Shuman to write a new song. Alas, Doc and Morty were not available to do their magic, so we were listening to various demos and songwriters selling their potential hits. We tried to get Elliot and Gene to listen to our original tunes, "A Prayer to an Angel," "Big Brown Eyes," "The Bells are Ringing" and "Why Do You Pretend?" to no avail. Laurie wanted a follow-up to "Hushabye" and it had to have the same flavor.

We loved "Hushabye" and it got us to the table, but we all agreed that our sweet spot was in the music that we loved to sing like the Rhythm and Blues group songs "Earth Angel" and "Oh What a Night." After hearing about 30 different songs that were like "Hushabye," they wore us out and we settled for "So Tenderly," written by Jeff Barry, who later became the super-famous writing partner of Ellie Greenwich. We also agreed on "Don't Take the Stars," written by a young Mark Harris, for the B side. Gene liked this song and for some unknown reason thought it was similar to "Little Darling" by the Diamonds. During the session, he had Bobby do a similar "ya-ya-ya-ya" tenor, which was nice, but neither song, no matter how we tried to think so, was another "Hushabye." They were good but not great, and great is what is needed to get another hit.

As it turned out, the DJ's turned the record over, and "Don't Take the Stars" started getting play, as "Hushabye" was now off the charts, something we feared. We lost our momentum and went from feeling so lucky to have been blessed with a hit to worrying about how our second release was going to stay on the charts. We went from a group of kids from Brooklyn who didn't know anything about the record business to a group of kids who didn't want to get out of the record business. We recorded "Don't Take the Stars" and "So Tenderly" at Bell Sound studios on August 20th, 1959. The October issue of Cashbox had "Don't Take the Stars" entering the national charts at #100 while "Mack the Knife" by Bobby Darrin was #1 and "Sleepwalk" by Santo and Johnny was #3. "Just to be with You" was peaking at #62, and The Passions were enjoying their first GAC tour in the Midwest. By November, "Don't Take the Stars" peaked at #75 and we were very disappointed. It was by no means a failure, and we had to remind ourselves that many records never even made the national charts. It did very well on the big city charts like New York, Chicago and Los Angeles, hitting the top twenty. What was strange is that it shot to number one in Hawaii, just like "Hushabye."

I didn't get the same feeling about our new songs as I did about "Hushabye." It wasn't just the song, it was a combination of the harmony, the lead vocal, the music and the "hook". Jim, Gene and Elliot were always referring to the "hook": that one special thing that catches your ear and makes you like it enough to want to buy it and hear it over and over. I believe that "Hushabye's" hook was the unison beginning followed by the full harmony and then Phil's falsetto. Most DJ's would only listen to the first few seconds of a record, and if it didn't do something right away, they tossed it and went to the next one. I'll bet a lot of great songs never went forward because the opening few seconds were not strong enough. In our case, they listened to a little of "So Tenderly" then turned the record over and liked "Don't Take the Stars." My guess is that based on the strength of "Hushabye" most DJs were curious about what the "B" side sounded like. And so "Don't Take the Stars" became our second hit.

The shows requests for The Mystics continued to come in, and Jim was scheduling us everywhere. We finished the Allan Freed Fox show on September 13, 1959 and appeared on the new Clay Cole show, as Clay promised, on September 17th. Most of the format for this show was inspired by Clay. The premise was simple: Clay would invite a panel of recording artists who would give opinions of new records that were recently released while also taking calls from the listening audience as well as the studio audience. Clay would switch between Bobby and me to be on the panel. I was on the first show, alongside Johnny Maestro and Jo-Ann Campbell. JoAnn was a very attractive woman who had been around the music business for a while. In 1956, she decided to quit dancing and become a singer. She received her first recording contract with RKO-Point Records in New York and released her debut single "Where Ever You Go" / "I'm Coming Home Late Tonight" with them in 1956. It was unsuccessful, and she signed a recording contract with Eldorado Records after performing at Harlem's Apollo Theater. She wrote and released her second single, "Come on Baby" in 1957. Later that year, she released "Wait a Minute" and appeared with us at the Brooklyn Paramount and on Dick Clark's American Bandstand show. Clay invited us all out after the show, and we had a great time at a local bar around the corner from the studio. We eventually wound up in Little Italy for the usual scungilli and hot sauce dinner.

This was followed by a show on Sept 19th in Providence, RI where we hooked up with the Videls again, who just happened to be on the show with their first charted record, "Mr. Lonely." We made arrangements for Vinny and Pete to visit us in the New York city in a few weeks. On Sept 20[th,] we did a record hop in Bellville, NJ, and first met a young girl group called the Starlets: sisters Phyllis ("Jiggs") and Barbara Albut, and Linda Jansen who later became the Angels and had a huge hit: "My Boyfriend's Back."

We were invited to do the Allan Freed TV show again on 9/22/59, and on 9/24/59 we did the Brad Davis show in Hartford. This show was mostly Jim Gribble's acts. The Passions, Johnny Saber, Johnny Aladdin, Phil Demarco, Phil Anastasia and The Demotrons all performed at this show. Jim would use the popularity of The Mystics and The Passions to get his other acts in the show. We had introduced Johnny Amplo, aka Johnny Aladdin, to Jim Gribble, along with Johnny Saber, real name Louie Adesso and Phil Anastasia, whose real name was Phil Anastasia. They were all sixteen years old. Johnny Amplo lived down the block from me on 84th Street and although a few years younger, would hang out with us at Frankie and Johnny's. One day I suggested that he meet our manager, Jim Gribble, and audition for a recording contract. Johnny was extremely handsome, and I thought he was just what Jim was looking for. Tony Armato (Punchy) thought the same of Louie Addesso, who was Punchy's girlfriend's younger brother. Phil Anastasia would also come to the bowling alley to sing with everyone. Punchy convinced Phil that he should sing solo instead of second tenor in a local group. All three landed recording contracts, and although none had a major hit record, they were all bitten by the show business bug.

Years later, Johnny Amplo changed his name to John Roper and went on to have a successful acting career in Hollywood with roles in several Alfred Hitchcock movies. He is still acting, producing and writing. Lou Addesso went on to a very successful career producing major commercials in both New York and Los Angeles. He has produced commercials for McDonalds, Intel, Ford, and PepsiCo. Phil Anastasi continued as a singer/songwriter/actor and in 1960 changed his name to Dean Parrish at the advice of Ronnie Spector (of the Ronettes), while doing a show at the Peppermint Lounge. As Dean Parrish, his vocal style changed to soul. He achieved success with his soul singles "I'm On My Way," "Tell Her," "Determination," "Skate" and "Bricks, Broken Bottles and Sticks." Phil/Dean is still performing in the US and Europe.

On September 25th, we were at Sunnyside Gardens in Queens, NY. As at the other shows, we met all the other performers in the early afternoon, so the acts could rehearse with the house band. The band for this show was the Bell Notes from Long Island. In those days, if you were a band and had a hit record, you got to back up the acts on shows and tours. The Bell Notes were regular performers in The Bronx in the 1950s, and performed at a bar owned by the father of Ray Tabano. He and Steven Tyler (of Aerosmith) occasionally played between Bell Notes sets and covered their song "I've Had It."

New York DJ (WADO) Fredericks saw the group play at a record hop on Long Island and saw its potential. He recorded "I've Had It" at a recording studio in Times Square, NY. The session cost a total of $50. He peddled the song around town, and Bob Shad eventually signed the group. He was starting up a new label and thought the band would be ideal because of the raw sound of the recording and the catchy tune they composed. "I've Had It," released on Time Records, was a nationwide hit, peaking at #6 on the Billboard Hot 100. They released four more singles in 1959 – "Old Spanish Town", "That's Right", and "You're a Big Girl Now," but only "Old Spanish Town" charted, peaking at #76.

We really hit it off with Ray Ceroni, the lead singer and leader of the band, and Lenny Giambalvo, the bass player, as well as Carl Bonura on sax, Pete Kane on piano and John Casey on drums. We had a lot in common, all being from New York. The Bell Notes had just finished a tour with

Bobby Darin and were telling us about his new album and new single called "Mack the Knife".

September 26th was another live show at St Thomas Aquinas in Brooklyn, where I met Linda Ardigo again, Carol Ardigo's sister. We'd rehearsed at her mom's house back in 1957. Linda was now about 17 years old and very attractive. She was so pretty, I just had to ask her out, and she accepted. We dated on and off for a few years and became very close friends and business associates 25 years later. Linda is still one of my dearest friends.

October was peppered with various shows and on 10/31 we did another Rate the Record TV show for Clay Cole, where we performed "Don't Take the Stars" and "So Tenderly." We did ten shows in November, including another Rate the Record with Clay on 10/21/59. Clay's show was breaking records as one of the fastest- growing shows on TV. Because of our friendship with Clay, we were racking up a lot of TV time. We spent our off days hanging with Clay, Johnny Maestro, and Johnny Farina in the city and in Brooklyn, where George, Johnny Maestro, Johnny Farina and I would regularly go fishing in Sheepshead bay.

The Mystics - August 1959 in Sunnyside Gardens

CHAPTER 16

SINCE I DON'T HAVE YOU

It was December 4, 1959, just eight days before we were scheduled to do a show at the Civic Opera House in Chicago to promote "Don't Take the Stars." I was supposed to go with Phil to hang out, but instead I went on a date with my new girlfriend, Linda. Thank heavens for Linda! If I hadn't been on that date, my life might have been very different.

That night, Phil was arrested with Vito Albanese, Frank (Tarzi) Barilla, Danny Vello, Michael Cassone and Joe Danota at a gas station in the Bath Beach neighborhood of Brooklyn. The cops also brought in Jerry Rosenberg, Albee Cracolici and a few other guys for questioning.

"Wait a second" Kenny interrupted, just as I was getting into the story. "Did you say Jerry *Rosenberg?*"

"Yeah, we called him Jerry the Jew; he was one of the guys we grew up with." Jerry's unbelievable story, which I will relate in due time, happened a few years later. Kenny's real last name is Rosenberg, but he's sure he's not related to Jerry the Jew.

Emil remarked, "Albee was there, too? I never knew that."

Clay pushed his chair even closer, and with a curious smile and eyebrows upraised like a kid waiting for a treat, he said, "I always wanted to hear this story – go on, Allie."

So, I told them about that fateful, and fatal, event.

It all began at the Hudson Diner, on 86th Street, where a bunch of young tough guys were hanging out. Tarzi Barilla, Danny Vello, Mike Cassone, Vito Albanese were having something to eat when Phil Cracolici walked in and sat at the next table. Phil had just gotten back from seeing his girlfriend, Andrea, on Avenue U. The jukebox was playing "Since I Don't Have You" by The Skyliners. Vito asked Phil where he was going later, and Phil said that he was going to meet his brother Albee at Smitty's gas station. Albee was working on his car, and from there they were going to Mitchells Drive In to meet some of the guys. Vito was planning on getting married and was discussing his wedding plans with his friends and how he really needed to get some money together to buy an engagement ring for his girlfriend, Marie. Tarzi moved over to Phil's table and Phil ordered a vanilla coke and fries. Phil was always hungry.

Phil was mild-mannered and on the quiet side, but he loved to laugh. When we started the Mystics, Phil was about 19 years old. He had brownish blond hair and was a thin 5'10. He was working as an electrician's helper before "Hushabye" hit the charts. All he wanted to do was further his career in show business with the group. He and his brother Albee came from a big Italian family of six brothers and four sisters, with Phil being the youngest.

Albee, the second youngest, was one of the toughest guys in the neighborhood. Blessed with abnormal strength, he was the only guy able to hold the mallet with one hand and drive the hard rubber device up the twenty-foot strong man challenge pole and hit the bell at Coney Island. I would never attempt it in front of anybody – I think the mallet was heavier than me. Nobody fucked with Albee. Albee was handsome, like Phil with darker hair. Albee had a scar on the side of his face that went from his ear to his jawbone in an elongated curve. The girls loved it, but strangers saw it as a symbol of a tough guy, and they were right.

But though Albee was tough, he hadn't done jail time, like Frank (Tarzi) Carelli, the leader of the Bath Beach Boys gang. Built like and as tough as Rocky Marciano.

Though Vito didn't have a criminal record yet, it was just a matter of time. Vito's father and uncles were "made men." Vito thought he would follow in their footsteps, and running numbers was a way to break into the mob. Vito's nickname was "Billy Botts." He just wanted to be called Billy, being fascinated with Billy the Kid as a kid. "Botts," which was tagged onto to Billy by his friends, was Italian street slang for crazy. Vito had thick black hair and was an athletic 170 lbs at 5'10. His best friend from grammar school, Mike Cassone, was 22 years old and six feet tall. He always wore a light tan sweater vest under his leather jacket. Mike had never finished high school and couldn't make a decision about setting his own course for life, so he decided to hang out with his best friend Vito, running numbers for the mob.

Vito asked Tarzi from the other table, "What if I pull a stick-up at Smitty's tonight? He must have some cash, and he could always tell his boss that he had to give up the money."

Tarzi explained that as far as he knew, Smitty, the night mechanic, who was a good guy for letting them fix their cars at night, really didn't have any money since his boss brought the receipts for the day to the bank in the afternoon.

Vito turned to his friends and said, "Then we will play a joke on Smitty, just scare him a little." Vito thought that Tarzi was protecting Smitty because Tarzi, Albee and Phil fixed their cars there. He was sure that there was money there, especially the gas money that Smitty kept in his pocket, and Vito was going to try a stick up anyway, under the guise of a prank.

Phil finished his French fries and got up to pay the check and leave for Smitty's. Tarzi asked Phil if he could go with him and Phil said sure. Phil didn't like Tarzi too much because Tarzi was always in trouble and he was a bad influence, but he couldn't refuse him a ride. The gas station had become a nightly hangout ever since Butchie Barone told Philly and Albee that it was his brother Matty Barone's gas station and they could go there to do repairs on their cars. Butchie was a frustrated street corner singer and was impressed that he could hang out with some of The Mystics, so he told his brother that he was going to practice a cappella with us at the garage and his brother agreed to let them stay there at night. Some of the girls in The Mystics fan club found out that Phil was there some nights and would walk over there at night to hang out, too. It was amazing and fortunate that none of those other guys or the girls were there on this particular night.

Vito and the guys waited for Phil and Tarzi to leave. They finished their coffee, talked a little more, and Vito decided to go to Smitty's, regardless of what Tarzi had said. They got into Danny's car and followed Tarzi and Phil to the gas station. On the way, Danny was sure this was going to be a great prank just like Vito's other pranks. Danny drove Vito and Mike to the garage from Al's luncheonette, and they got out. Then Danny parked around the corner.

The gas station was on the corner of Bath Avenue and Bay Parkway in Brooklyn, a regular nighttime hangout for a bunch of the neighborhood guys who would stay out into the morning hours talking and working on their cars. Smitty (Dennis Smith) didn't mind the company; with them there he felt a little safer. Smitty was thirty-six years old. He'd worked his way up from pumping gas to becoming a mechanic. Phil, Tarzi and Albee were searching the office for a part for Albee's car when Mike Cassone and Vito Albanese walked into the garage at about 10:00 pm.

Smitty was fixing a tire in one of the garage bays when Vito walked over to him, pulled out his .38 revolver and pointed it right in Smitty's face. He said with a big grin, "This is a stick-up."

Smitty, seeing a pair of shoes that had just moved into his line of sight, looked up, saw the gun, got scared, and instinctively tried to hit the gun with the tire iron in his hand. The iron hit Vito's hand instead, and as he instinctively squeezed to hold onto the gun, it fired a bullet into Smitty's head, right above his left eye. Mikey was frozen, staring at the blood coming out of the wound. He turned to Vito but could not speak. His mouth was open, but no words came out. The other guys came running into the garage bay when they heard the shot. Vito was stunned. His hand was shaking, with his arm in a frozen position still pointing at Smitty's lifeless body, which was now slumped and propped up by the tire he'd been repairing. Vito felt dizzy and nauseous.

Tarzi broke the silence, "What the fuck did you do, you idiot?"

"I told you this was a stupid idea; you know Smitty doesn't have any money," said Mike. Phil and Albee were in shock.

Tarzi's mind was racing. He couldn't be here with all this, not with his record.

"I didn't mean to shoot him, I only wanted to scare him a little" stammered Vito.

Danny walked in a few seconds later and froze, muttering, "Holy shit, you fucking killed him, you fucking killed him!" Tarzi told Danny to shut the fuck up. Danny was almost in tears; he didn't want any part of this nightmare. He just wanted to be part of the gang. He drove the guys around in his step-father's new car, so he could hang out with them. He always made an excuse when he thought something bad was going to happen and would never show up. He never figured on this. Danny was shaking like a leaf. All he could think about was his mother and stepfather and how pissed they were going to be. Phil was yelling at Vito and trying to revive Smitty. Danny just screamed and burst into tears.

Vito said to everyone at the scene, "Okay listen, me, Danny and Mikey are gonna take off, you guys better think of something if you're gonna stay here."

Albee wasn't going to leave, he felt sorry for Smitty, and instead ran into the office to call for help.

Tarzi, thinking fast, said, "All right, you guys leave. Me, Phil and Albee will stay, and we'll say we were in the office, (which was true), when we heard the shots and we didn't see the guys who did it."

Phil who was stunned by the events, didn't want to run away, he just wanted to help Smitty. He pressed his handkerchief onto the wound and prayed. The other three left and ran to Danny's car. In his haste, Danny dropped the keys and couldn't find them. He started to walk back to the garage and Vito pulled him back. "Are you nuts, you can't go back there!" They walked to 86th Street and got a cab. Danny was still in a state of shock.

Phil had Smitty's head in his lap trying to console him as Smitty's life slipped away. Phil could not hold back his tears as Smitty's head went limp. Albee had called the police and was helping Phil but before they arrived, an off-duty cop pulled into the gas station for gas, saw the commotion and took charge of the situation. The cop knew Smitty and knew that Phil and the guys were always hanging out at the station. The officer put the call in and an ambulance brought Smitty to Victory Memorial hospital, where he was pronounced dead a few hours later.

Detectives Kevin Riley and Angelo Carelli from the local station house took the case over from the off-duty cop and started asking questions of the three young guys remaining at the gas station. The off-duty cop relayed the information and mentioned to the detectives that he knew Phil and Albee and that they were friends of Smitty and Matty, the owner of the station. Phil called Butchie from the office and both brothers got to the scene in twenty minutes.

Kevin Riley had been on the job for 19 years. He couldn't wait to retire. He had a painting business on the side which was doing well. He imported relatives from Ireland and paid them less than minimum wage and they worked hard. They just wanted to be in America. Tall and lean with a weather-beaten face, he looked older than his forty years. John's partner, Angelo Carelli, had been on the job for ten years. He was determined to excel. Instead of running a side business like most cops, he took law classes at NYU. He hated his name Francis and told everyone he met to call him Frank. His Italian good looks and stylish suits gave him the nickname Romeo. His only vice was Lucky Strike cigarettes, a habit he picked up from his father. He never drank and worked out every day with an old set of hand me down dumbbells in the basement of his house. They both thought

Tarzi Barilla, who was always in trouble with the law, might know the guys who killed Smitty. "Not this time, guys," Tarzi said to the cops, "I never saw those guys before." A statement he would soon regret.

The three witnesses, Phil, Albee and Tarzi, were taken to the local stationhouse and questioned. At this point, the detectives were convinced that they didn't know the murderers, especially after the statement from the off-duty cop. They were brought to the basement of the police station to look at photos of known criminals. They not only saw Vello, Mike Cassone and Albanese in the photo gallery, but two dozen other guys from the neighborhood, including Tarzi. They stayed with their story. They didn't see anyone that looked like the guys who did it and besides they only saw them running away when they came out of the office after they heard the shot fired. Before the police arrived at the gas station, Tarzi told Albee and Phil that Vito's father and uncles were connected, and if they ratted on them, they and their families could be in danger. They decided to describe the clothes of the unknown robbers somewhat accurately, so their stories wouldn't get mixed up.

Inspector Steve Hanson was put in charge of the murder case and saw an opportunity to question every gang member in the neighborhood. Hanson was a fair-skinned man, 6'3, about forty years old and a little heavy but athletic from his college days. He always wore a dark suit with a white shirt and a dark bow tie. Hanson was feared by most of the known criminals in the neighborhood for his interrogations. There was no tolerance for failure in Steve Hanson. He would not accept an excuse from his staff. "Just get it fucking done!" he would yell whenever there was the slightest hint of some police officer not being able to complete an assigned task. Hanson was convinced that Tarzi Barilla was somehow involved. More than convinced, he *hoped* that Tarzi was involved. He didn't like Tarzi or any of the other Bath Beach Boys and always vowed to "get them all off the street and in jail where they belonged". Tarzi and some of his friends had been in jail before because of Hanson, and now Hanson was smelling blood. He ordered Carelli and Riley to round up the usual suspects: Jerry "the Jew" Rosenberg, Frankie Rice, Ralphie "Rest" Galione, Punchy, Johnny Black, and anyone that they were with at the moment and bring them to the station house. Jerry, who had the gift of gab, was found at his usual hangout, the 19th Hole bar on 86th Street with most of the usual suspects. The 19th Hole was across the street from the Dyker Heights Golf Club. Yes, a golf course in Brooklyn, a very unusual sight. I doubt if any of us growing up in the neighborhood ever swung a golf club. The only thing I knew about golf was that there were 18 holes and you were supposed to get the white ball into each one with a club.

Jerome Rosenberg was nicknamed "Jerry the Jew" by the wise guys he worked for because he was the only Jew with the mob, though he looked like a typical handsome Italian kid. A little like Tony Curtis. Slight build, 5'7, 150 pounds, a fair complexion and dirty blond wavy hair. Jerry was a known cop-hater. He had already done some time for burglary and possession of stolen property. On some of these jobs he teamed with Tarzi Barilla. Jerry had a normal upbringing but was hell-bent on a career of crime. He dropped out of high school in his second year and began his chosen profession by working as a numbers runner in south Brooklyn, where he became friends with some of the future gangsters of New York City. His parents, who worried that he had a mental disability, had him tested by a doctor who specialized in IQ testing. His tests came back with unusually high scores, so he was promptly re- tested and delivered even better results. He liked his new gangster friends. He felt like he belonged. He felt like it was his calling to carry a gun. The same way some teenagers' idolized singers, Jerry idolized John Dillinger and James Cagney in their movie gangster roles and made up his mind: crime was going to be his profession. Jerry always had a crazy look in his eyes, and Jerry the Jew was fearless.

Jerry and his regular group of friends had been at the 19th Hole, drinking and talking as usual, for most of the night. The two detectives walked into the bar around midnight with two officers and went straight over to Jerry. They all knew each other very well. "What the fuck now?" Jerry muttered as he saw them walking towards him. Punchy chimed in with, "Carelli doesn't look happy."

"Where were you guys around ten o'clock?" asked Detective Riley in his distinctive rough Irish voice.

"Oh, hi, detectives" answered Rosenberg with a fake British accent. "We were in London having a cocktail or two."

Carelli slapped Jerry as hard as he could, which caused Jerry's drink to splash on him and onto Riley's suit. "Very nice, Francis," Jerry said as he got off the bar stool, wiping the gin and tonic from his shirt with a bar napkin. He handed the napkin to Riley who just looked at him and picked up his own napkin from the bar. Jerry said in his own voice, "Very fucking nice, asshole, my mother hits harder than that." After a brief round of name calling, the cops put Jerry and the rest of his friends into the waiting van.

On the way to the station house they wondered what the hell was going on now. "Must be something big for those two assholes to have their balls in such an uproar," Jerry whispered to Frankie Rice. Frankie Rice looked and acted exactly like James Dean. His voice and expressions were so like James Dean that he could have doubled for him. Frankie Rice's good looks attracted the girls, and Jerry loved that. All Frankie had to do was stand there. Frankie looked so much like James Dean that teenage girls would ask if they could take a picture with him, so they could show their friends. He and Jerry were always together. Jerry liked the fact that the girls would go after Frankie because he would get to meet girls he would not otherwise meet. Frankie Rice was a 6'1 powerhouse who was not afraid of anyone or anything.

When Jerry and the guys walked into the station house, they were surprised to see Tarzi Barilla sitting with Albee and Phil. They exchanged glances and gave eye signals and shrugs to each other as if to say *what the fuck is going on*? Tarzi put his finger on his lip with a "be quiet" gesture, which everyone understood to mean don't say anything about anything.

Carelli, realizing that none of these people were at the gas station, explained to Jerry and the guys what had happened to Smitty. They were shocked. They all knew Smitty. Jerry explained that they'd all been at the 19th hole from 9:00 pm. "You could have asked the fucking bartender," Jerry yelled as Carelli started to walk away. Carelli stopped, stared at Jerry and said, "The rest of you can go, he stays. Inspector Hanson wants to talk to you." Jerry was always number one on Steve Hanson's hit parade, and Tarzi Barilla was number two.

The police, while looking around for clues, found a car parked next to the gas station with the driver side window open. Looking further, they found a set of keys between the curb and the front tire of the next car. In his rush to leave the scene, Danny couldn't find the car keys in the dark because after he dropped them, he'd kicked them past his car and under the car in front of his.

This looked a little suspicious, and upon further investigation, they tracked the car to Danny Vello's stepfather's house by looking into the glove compartment for the registration. Danny was just walking into his apartment building to get the spare keys for the car when the police grabbed him. Danny was brought into the Bath Beach station house through a back door, so no one saw him or knew that he was brought in for questioning. He denied knowing anything about the holdup and insisted that he never heard of Smitty. He didn't have a plausible explanation for his stepfather's car being parked alongside the gas station, especially after his stepfather told the cops that Danny had borrowed the car for the night. Danny was scared stiff. He sensed that the parked car was going to be a big problem and tried to explain that he lost the keys but that was just making it worse. Detective Riley hammered Danny on the car story for hours. It was now 2:30 am. They were not going to let him go. Thinking of how much trouble he was in, Danny couldn't hold back the tears. He wasn't a tough guy. A question and a slap, a question and a slap, over and over again. They kept him up all night. Based on Danny's answers that were changing, Hanson, Riley and Carelli were not only sure he knew who did it, but they were sure he was there. Danny had been arrested before, and they knew who his friends were and that they would pull something like this. They were also sure that he knew Tarzi, Phil and Albee. Everyone knew "Tarzi" Barilla; he was one of the toughest guys with the Bath Beach gang and had been under suspicion for some neighborhood holdups. Phil and Albee were well known too. How could Danny say he didn't know The Mystics?

After hours of intense interrogation, Danny fell off the chair and passed out for thirty minutes. When he came to, he looked at the clock and realized quite a few hours had passed by. Hanson had Riley move the clock ahead to 6:30 am in the small interrogation room while Danny was out. Inspector Hanson gave him a cup of coffee and a doughnut, which he devoured, and told him that while he was unconscious they had an eye witnesses come forward saying that he was seen running from the gas station. It worked. Danny thought that Tarzi told the cops to save his own ass and maybe there were other witnesses. Maybe even Albee and Phil said something. Sleep-deprived, hungry, in excruciating pain, he gave up everyone. It was a house of cards. Danny told them how he, Vito Albanese and Michael Cassone planned to play a joke on Smitty and discussed it while in the restaurant with Tarzi Barilla and Phil Cracolici, and when he got to the gas station it was all over, Smitty was shot. He said he didn't know exactly how it happened. Then he just stared, holding his head, as if he was trying to see it all over again while nursing his pain. Inspector Hanson was furious. While he was staring at Danny, Detective Riley whispered in his ear, "Smitty just passed away." Now Inspector Hanson tasted blood. His face flushed as his blood pressure started to climb. "Those lying bastards are gonna pay for this bullshit." His bloodhound instincts were out of control. "Get all those fuckers in here now and get this punk to a hospital." He yelled out in the hallway as he raced to the front desk to get the paper work started. "Make sure those three don't leave this building".

The word was already out to some of the newspaper people about the holdup and killing at the gas station. Joseph George, a reporter for the Daily News and a friend of Inspector Hanson, was already at the station house. Hanson had called Joseph because he had a story in mind and wanted to run it by Joseph. He was desperate to make this stick, especially for Tarzi Barilla, who already had two arrests to his record. This one would put him away for a long time. Hanson told Joseph that they all were part of a gang that was responsible for 20 stickups in Brooklyn over the last three months and Barilla was the leader. I thought that this was a completely fabricated story. He added that they had a shooting gallery in the basement of a bar on Bath Avenue and practiced shooting, another story, but Joseph George printed the fabricated story verbatim.

It was clear at this point that they had to reluctantly let Jerry go after his lawyer showed up with the owner of the 19th Hole and had an affidavit that Jerry was at the bar all night. Robert Hayman, Jerry's father's attorney, explained that there were other witnesses if needed. Hayman started yelling at the police for roughing up Jerry, who had bruises on his face. "If you picked him up to ask him a few questions, why did you beat him up?" asked the enraged attorney.

Hanson was so angry he couldn't even look at Jerry Rosenberg, but from the corner of his eye, he saw Jerry giving him the finger as he gingerly walked out, cursing Hanson and Carelli loud enough for them to hear. Hanson made a silent vow to get Jerry Rosenberg as his blood pressure skyrocketed again, giving him an instant headache. Inspector Hanson got his chance to arrest Jerry Rosenberg three years later, after two police detectives were killed in Brooklyn, but I'm getting ahead of myself.

When Jerry found out that Phil had been arrested for Smitty's murder, Jerry called the 19th Hole and told the guys to get word to Phil that Phil should immediately separate himself from the other guys, especially Tarzi Barilla, but this experienced, sensible advice was never passed on. He also commented on how that scumbag detective Hanson was going to go all out to put them all away. When Jerry found out how the arrests and subsequent trial played out, he was furious.

Phil spent the next two days in "The Tombs," alone in his cell for his alleged part in the gas station killing of Dennis Smith. The Tombs is the colloquial name for the Manhattan Detention Complex, a municipal jail in Lower Manhattan at 125 White Street. Constructed in a rectangular shape, 253 feet long by 200 feet deep, it appeared from the street to be only one story in height, the long windows showing just a few feet above the ground and extending nearly to the cornice. The main entrance, on Centre Street, was reached by a broad flight of dark stone steps that led to a big and forbidding portico, supported by four huge Egyptian-like columns. The other three sides featured projecting entrances and columns. The all-male prison contained a high-ceilinged but narrow hall with four tiers of cells. The bottom tier opened upon the main floor and each of the three above it opened upon its own iron gallery, one above the other. Two keepers were posted on duty in each gallery to guard the prisoners. The cells, intended for two inmates, often held three. Each tier had its purposes. Some ground-floor cells housed convicts under sentence. The second tier was devoted to those charged with murder, arson, and similar serious crimes. The third tier accommodated prisoners charged with burglary, grand larceny, and the like. The fourth tier was assigned to those charged with light offences. As if to reward the more violent men, the ground floor cells were the largest, while the fourth-tier cells were the smallest. Phil was on the second tier and was isolated from the other guys who were arrested for the gas station incident because Inspector Hanson didn't want any of them to talk to each other.

It was noisy, the inmates were constantly yelling, and it smelled like a sewer. Phil saw a few roaches sprint across the floor to get a crumb and he had to keep himself from heaving. His cell mate was covered with tattoos and looked like a serial killer. Hanson had them believing that they were all making their own deals by ratting on each other. When Barilla found out from his attorney that Albee could not be found, he assumed Albee had made a deal with Hanson and Carelli to get out of the whole thing and was free. He had no idea that Albee was hiding. Tarzi got pissed and decided to make a statement implicating Phil to get back at Albee. He told Carelli that he and Phil were aware of the plan to rob the gas station but that he tried to talk them out of it.

Phil was the only one without a criminal record. He'd served three years in the Navy to get away from this kind of crap and now here he was in jail for being at the wrong place at the wrong time, involved in a web that he wasn't sure he could escape. He regretted that he hadn't stopped them from doing the holdup when it had started at the diner as a joke. He felt like he should have seen through the bullshit joke story – but now it was a different kind of bullshit. The police understood Phil wasn't part of the Bath Beach bunch, but after Barilla's statement, there wasn't anything Phil's lawyer could do but wait for the trial. Santo and Johnny's "Sleepwalk" filtered through the chaos, reminding Phil of a recent show he'd done with Santo and Johnny Farina. Phil's own singing career, a dream come true, was now going down the drain. He wondered if his manager, Jim Gribble, knew about this development and what he thought. He felt so bad, as if he'd let everyone down. He got word back to Bobby through his lawyer that it didn't look good.

Phil sat on the filthy blanket covering his new bed in his new home, glanced over at his cellmate, who was sleeping, drew his legs up to his chest and closed his eyes. He actually managed to sleep.

A guard startled Phil by slamming the cell door next to his, and he sat up in his cell and opened his eyes. The guard delivered two baloney sandwiches on dry white bread on two separate metal dishes with two tin cups of water. Phil's cellmate got up and said in a thick Spanish accent loud enough for the guard to hear as he went to the next cell, "Hey, man, this is the same shit we got yesterday." He turned to Phil and said, "You better eat it slow cause there is nothing else until the morning." Just then a large water bug ambled onto Phil's cot.

Phil sat in his cell. It was the first time he'd been in jail. Just a week earlier, he had been happy and free, excited about being a Mystic. Rehearsing, singing, doing shows, meeting new people, hanging with his friends and girlfriend. Now he was locked up in a filthy cell. Tears came to his eyes.

Teresa said, "Oh my God! The poor kid."

Emil said, "Unbelievable. What a god damn shame."

Clay and Kenny shook their heads in disbelief.

CHAPTER 17

DON'T TAKE THE STARS

Since Albee Cracolici wasn't at the luncheonette when Danny and the guys met there earlier, Danny never mentioned him in his statement. Detective Carelli told Albee that he could either be arrested or be a witness as to what happened at the gas station, but Phil was going to be arrested. Albee picked witness. On Saturday morning, December 5, 1959, the five guys who were at the gas station were arraigned and held without bail for a hearing on Monday. They were all being charged with robbery, the Sullivan Law, and homicide for the slaying of Dennis Smith, 36, in a gas station at Bay Parkway and Bath Avenue. The Daily News reported it exactly as Inspector Hanson described it, even though it didn't exactly happen that way. A sixth man, Joe Danota, was also arrested and arraigned with the others. He was held on $7500 bail for a hearing on a Sullivan Law charge. Cassone and Albanese had turned their guns over to him the night of the incident. During the questioning, Danny had mentioned that Danota was supposed to be there with them, but he didn't show up and that the guns were his. The guns were found in Danota's apartment on Bath Avenue when the police busted in, searched and arrested Danota. This appeared to be an illegal move by the police.

Albee stayed at the police station and was interviewed by the detectives. He explained that he really didn't see anything and neither did Phil because they were both in the office of the gas station when they heard the gun go off. Albee called his parents and Bobby and broke the news. Bobby called me and George. I could not believe what I was hearing. Joe Cracolici, Albee' father, called Joe Fontana, a neighborhood attorney and family friend. Fontana was at the station house at eight the next morning. He spoke to Phil and told him not to say anything but realized it was too late for that.

Phil had already lied to the police when he told them he didn't know the guys who killed Smitty.

Joe Fontana, Phil's attorney, set up a meeting with Detective Carelli and Hanson so Phil could tell the real story and explain why he'd lied in the first place. Joe felt that this would separate Phil from the so called "gang." Phil was under tremendous pressure. He realized what was at stake at this point and was fighting for his life. He explained to the two detectives how it all went down and how he was so afraid of retribution from Cassone and Albanese and why he lied about knowing them. He told them that he knew them from the neighborhood but never really hung out with them. Carelli believed Phil but Steve Hanson was barely listening. He was focused on Barilla.

Hanson knew Phil was telling the truth but didn't care. Even Carelli put a few good words in for Phil, recognizing that he had a clean record and really didn't hang out with any of those other guys. But if they let Phil off easy, he would have to let Tarzi Barilla off and he was not going to let that happen. They knew that in order for Phil to go free, Danny would have to change his statement and that would include Barilla going free.

Joe Fontana made it clear to Albee that Hanson would be looking for him to implicate his brother and Tarzi Barilla in turn for immunity. Albee, after discussing his options with the lawyer, decided that he would never testify against his brother. Now it was clear that once Hanson found that out he would want to book him too, and he was right.

Both Hanson and Carelli sensed that since they were brothers, Albee would not testify against Phil. Therefore, Albee and Phil would have to be booked if they were going to book Barilla. Hanson's plan was to implicate whoever was at the gas station that night. Albee, under the counsel of Joe Fontana, played along with the witness idea to buy some time. He figured that after coming back from our show in Chicago he would simply disappear. Now he would not have to testify at the hearing or, more important, get arrested. Although Carelli had already decided to track Albee's whereabouts, he was not going to follow him to Chicago. He figured that he would wait for us at the airport and arrest Albee when we got back. He was shocked and pissed that Albee was not with us when we got back. We landed at Idelwild airport and Albee took a later flight to New Jersey. Bobby's answer to Carelli's question "Where the fuck is Albee?" was great. He simply said, "Oh, I thought he was right behind us." We just kept on walking while Carelli ran to a phone booth. The plan was to hide Albee at his girlfriend's family hunting lodge in the Catskills until everyone could figure out what to do next, and it worked.

It was now obvious how Hanson was going to make this look. Phil was devastated. I went to the station house on with Bobby and Georgie the morning after the arrest in the hope of talking to Phil. They refused to let us in, despite Bobby ranting and raving about how that was not legal. Bobby almost got into a fistfight with one of the cops. While we were talking to the desk sergeant, a door opened, next to the desk, and I caught a glimpse of Tarzi Barilla. He was hand cuffed in a wire cage. Our eyes met. I had never seen anything like that in person. His arms were over his head and the cuffs were attached to a hook inside the cage. He looked terrible. His eyes were red and he had bruises around his face, his clothes were filthy. It looked like he had been dragged across a dirty floor. He tried to say something to me and then his eyes looked to the side as someone from inside the room slowly closed the door. I turned to Bobby and said, "Let's get out of here".

At this point, we all knew that we had a big problem with Phil in jail, Albee going into hiding, performances coming up and a new album in progress up at Laurie records. Not to mention the show in Chicago with Paul Anka and Brooke Benton just eight days away. All of this made us nervous because we hadn't told our manager Jim Gribble or Laurie records yet what had happened to Phil.

Detectives Kevin Riley and Angelo Carelli were eventually credited with cracking the case, along with Inspector Hanson. They were congratulated by the Commissioner for fine police work and promoted. Inspector Hanson got a lot more: he was promoted to Chief of Detectives. The prize he was hoping for was still to come. He wanted all the Bath Beach Boys.

"Wow, what a story, said Clay, passing his hand over his graying hair.

Tom Schizzano came into the dressing room announcing that everything was ready for sound check for The Classics. Clay said to me, "You have to finish the story after sound check, OK?" I agreed, and The Classics followed Tom into the stage area.

Tom Schizzano was the fourth member of The Classics. He did second tenor vocals part and was also our musical director. Teresa, Emil and I all agreed that Tom was a musical genius. We'd never met anyone so talented. Besides leading the band through the arrangements, he wrote songs and played keyboard and guitar. Tom was responsible for the arrangements on all the CD's that the Classics recorded in Tom's studio, with Tom playing all the instruments on each of his arrangements. About 5'9, Tom was an even-tempered soul. Most things during the sound check were easily handled in his soft assured way. He looked a little disheveled at times but really had it all under control. "It's all good" was his answer to most problems, for he knew he would eventually solve them.

We walked through the area that led up to the elevated stage area that could have been set up for a prize fight. Tom was already in the band area on the floor area in front of the keyboards running down the song list with the band. Emil, Teresa and I walked up the stairs onto the stage and were handed our microphones from the sound crew. The sound technicians did a person by person sound check on each mike, and now they were ready to run through one of the songs with the band. We breezed through our opening song, an up-tempo version of "The Way You Look Tonight" and after we were confident that our sound was okay, we left the stage, going down the steps, and passing Speedo and the Cadillacs, who were going onstage for their sound check.

Every time I meet The Cadillacs I remember the time we all flew on the same plane to a gig for Richard Nader in the Midwest before Teresa joined The Classics. I was sitting across the aisle from Bobby Phillips, the Cadillacs' bass, who sat next to Earl Speedo Carroll, the original lead singer. Emil was sitting next to me; Mike and Scott were a few rows back along with the rest of the Cadillacs and Kenny Vance with his Planotones. The stewardess came down the aisle, asking if anyone wanted to purchase headphones for the movie that was about to start. I said "sure" and gave her $10.00 to cover Emil and me. She then asked Bobby, who overheard that it cost $5.00 per person. Speedo handed her a $5.00 bill and received his headphones. Bobby, a little hesitant, asked her, "What kind of movie is it?" The stewardess replied, "It's a comedy." Bobby paused for a second as if considering spending the $5.00, pointed with his thumb towards Speedo and answered, "No, thanks – I'll laugh when he laughs!" We all lost it and were laughing for a long time.

By now, dinner was ready in the "make believe" green room, so we all filled our plates and settled back into the dressing room, where Clay was waiting for the rest of the story. Kenny popped his head in the door and said, "Don't start without me; I just got to get some food." When Kenny got back, I started where I'd left off. I wanted to tell them about the Jerry Rosenberg story because it ties into Phil Cracolici's story with Inspector Steve Hanson. Clay was now right next to me, his legs straddling the chair while he leaned on its back.

I continued.

CHAPTER 18

ALL THROUGH THE NIGHT

Now that Phil was in jail, we virtually shut down and cancelled all upcoming shows except for the Civic Opera house show in Chicago with Paul Anka and Brooke Benton on Dec 12,1959.

It was cold that night in Chicago. The music was loud and brassy. The intro to "Church Bells May Ring" was hot. The lights were extremely bright and hot. The spots were blinding us as we came out from behind the curtain onto the vast stage. There had to be about 5000 people standing in front of their seats. The applause and cheering were so instantaneous and so powerful that we felt the air moving like a breeze against our faces. In all the shows, we had done we had never experienced anything like this. The continuous noise from the screaming and applause drowned out the entire first song. It was hard to see past the first few rows once we started singing as the spotlights were directly in our eyes. It looked like mostly kids standing, jumping up and down and screaming. We couldn't hear ourselves and were sure that the audience couldn't hear us either.

We relaxed, Bobby felt a little more confident and we started to move closer to each other to try to hear ourselves, but it was no use. It was like singing without any vocal chords. The only thing we felt was the vibrations from our own voices and hoped that it sounded good. Bobby tried to say a few words between songs, but no one heard him including us. Georgie was half laughing through the last two songs, partly from nerves and partly because the whole thing was so absurd.

Laughter was always infectious with us and it caused me and Albee to try to suppress our laughter too. I picked up my cue from the band and started singing, "Oh there'll be blue birds over," I barely heard myself in the monitors, so I sang the rest of the song with one finger in my ear. The noise level lasted all the way through to the closing song, "Hushabye," where it really got louder. "Hushabye" was number one in Chicago for a few weeks through the summer and it was obvious the kids loved it. All four songs, the entire 12 minutes of singing were engulfed in the crowd noise. We got a standing ovation after "Hushabye," along with the continued screaming, and walked off-puzzled and thrilled. The MC called us back for a bow and we were overwhelmed. He asked if we would do another song and Bobby explained, yelling in his ear, that we didn't have another one and off we went with the DJ screaming, "Ladies and Gentlemen-The Mystics, The Mystics." When we got backstage Paul, who was watching in the wings, told us that we did a great show. We explained that we couldn't hear a thing and asked him how it sounded. He told us that at this point it didn't matter.

The rest of December was spent realizing that Phil would not be returning to the group soon. Aside from eventually losing our chance at recording an album, we were now faced with possibly finding a replacement for Phil. We did a show with just the four of us in our old neighborhood on January 8, 1960 at the Cotillion Terrace, and a record hop in New Jersey with Clay Cole the next day, and another show for Clay at the Commack Arena in Long Island, but it did not feel right. A piece of us was missing.

We were torn between finding a replacement and hoping that Phil would get released by some miracle. Jim suggested we start looking for a replacement lead singer, and so the auditions began. Word was out: The Mystics were holding auditions for a new lead singer. Jim's entire stable of would be singers tried out.

In the meantime, we had selected three songs for our next session. The first was "Let Me Steal Your Heart Away" written by a new singer songwriter named Gene Pitney. We didn't get a hit with his song, but he sure had a lot of hits without us! The second, "All Through the Night," was selected by Elliot and written by Kal Mann, who also wrote "Teddy Bear' for Elvis and "Lets Twist Again" by Chubby Checker. It had the "lullaby" Mystic sound, but we weren't thrilled when we first heard it. Elliot reworked the original arrangement using alternating unison and harmony. The third song was," I Begin to Think Again of You."

The basic concept for these three selections was that we could sing them as a group without featuring a lead singer. We put this plan in place with the hopes that Phil would be released soon and in time for our next recording. To maintain the Mystics rich harmony, Elliot suggested we find a singer to fill in for Phil. We were confident, at this point, that Phil would be released soon, and recording this way would not show that he was missing. Jim suggested that we use a singer-songwriter who was always in and out of the office and pay him as a session singer. Elliot told us since he wasn't going to be our permanent lead singer; it wouldn't really matter as long as he blended. We knew he recorded under the name of Jerry Landis from Tom and Jerry, who'd had a minor hit with "Hey School Girl" in 1957. His real name was Paul Simon.

We would see Paul hanging out at the office and would say hi, but we never got very friendly. At Jim's suggestion, we rehearsed the three songs with Paul, keeping in mind that this would be a group type, all harmony recording. There was no question that he knew harmony and had quite a bit of experience in the studio. Once we got the major parts down we went up to Laurie and got Elliot and Gene to sign off on Paul. I don't think they saw him as a good fit for The Mystics, but we were in a bind, and it was not a permanent position.

I remember one afternoon rehearsing in Gribble's office; Paul and Bobby were having a hard time hitting a high note in the harmony. Jim, overhearing us struggling, suggested that Bobby and Paul stand on their heads to get the note. Jim said that this was an old trick used by the "Grand Old Opry" singers. I'm not sure if he was pulling our leg, but we were all in a good mood, and Paul agreed to try it. Albee and I held his feet and Bobby gave him the note and as he started to sing we all realized how absurd this was and burst out laughing. Then we all tried standing on our heads to do harmony. That was a Kodak moment (featuring the future writer of "Kodachrome"!). But unfortunately, no one had the sense to take pictures. We could not stop laughing. That broke the ice with Paul and we continued our rehearsal with great input from Paul on some harmony parts we were missing. We realized that not only could he sing but he was a fantastic guitar player. We went on to record the three songs with Paul on Jan 26th, 1960 at Bell Sound. After the session, we thanked Paul for his help and Jim gave him a check for his studio work. I always wondered why he never offered to write a song for us. We really should have stayed closer to Paul.

"I Begin to Think Again of You" is a ballad in the style of the Four Freshman, with intricate harmony parts combined with unison. Violins were showing up in rock and roll sessions since the success of "There goes my Baby" by the Drifters and The Skyliner's recording of "Since I Don't Have You," so Elliot included strings in this session, which was amazing. We didn't know that strings were part of the recording, so when we showed up at the session and saw all the extra musicians we were amazed. The room was full of violins and cellos. What the hell, we were eventually paying for it anyway. We felt that Laurie was really trying hard to get us a hit. It was both strange and flattering that we were worthy of the violins. Elliot arranged this in the vein of "Where or When" that he arranged for Dion and the Belmonts about six months later, on the album that was originally designed for us.

We were frustrated during the recording because Paul, being a solo singer, could not sync with us and would always be a split-second off. Every time I hear this song it seems to me that Gene should have never let this happen. Not that it was bad or that it would have made this song a hit, but it was not our sound. Albee was especially critical of the unison here. After years of singing together, we did not even have to think about it. It was natural and always sounded spot on . . . except for this one time with Paul Simon.

The next few weeks were spent doing record hops lip-syncing our records with the four of us. Our new recording of "All Through the Night" and "I Begin to Think Again of You" was released on Feb 1, 1960 and we were booked on the Clay Cole Show on Feb. 6. Both Cashbox and Billboard gave our latest release impressive reviews, but the record failed go anywhere on the charts. Recording songs that did not actually feature a lead singer but featured the whole group worked for us since we had great harmony, but I don't think we had the right material. On the weekend of 2/19/60 we did six record hops, including two TV shows in and around the Hartford area. Tom Vader and Brad Davis were the most popular DJs in the area. It was at the Hartford show that we met Joanne Gadomski and her friend Janice Gomers, who became lifetime Mystics fans. The following photographs were contributed by Joanne, who still shows up at our shows in Connecticut.

Joan with The Mystics - 1959

Courtesy of Joan Godomski

Janice with The Mystics - 1959

Courtesy of Joan Godomski

The Mystics with Joanne and Janice
Courtesy of Joan Godomski

CHAPTER 19

WHITE CLIFFS OF DOVER

We had the first week of March off, and if we were not hanging out in the office, we were with our friends and girlfriends in the neighborhood. We were somewhat famous and so everyone who ever knew us wanted to hang out with us, especially when we went to Mitchells drive in. It all looked great, but we were not making much money and that was becoming a problem. It's a good thing we were living with our families. We got an end of year Earnings statement from Laurie in January for 1959. It proved that although we were famous recording stars we were scarcely earning anything. Jim's 10 % commission was included in the statement from Laurie. Averaged out, we were earning about $50.00 per week from shows, which was minimum wage in 1959. This did not include our royalties from record sales, which after expenditures like our recording session and miscellaneous advances, netted us about $332.00 each for "Hushabye" (65,372 records) and "Don't Take the Stars" (40,000 records). A prior statement for "Hushabye," as I recall, was for about 400,000 records sold which at the rate of .03 per record was about $12,000, which netted us $2400 each. The statement shows how the math was wrong in calculating the royalties for "Hushabye." It shows 65,372 at .03 = $1001.16 when it should be $1961.16. Maybe it was a typo.

Bottom line: we had barely enough to survive.

Jim wanted us to start holding auditions for a permanent lead singer. We had a meeting and decided that if we were going to continue we just could not wait for Phil. It was awkward, but we had to hold auditions. Over the next week, we listened to a few different singers each day, but none compared, in our minds, to Phil. Gene and Elliot wanted to start preparing for our next single, and Jim told us that we were scheduled to do the American Bandstand show with dick Clark in Philadelphia on March 9, 1960. Albee kept updating us on Phil, but it looked hopeless. At this point he was scheduled to come out sometime in 1962.

Phil was transferred to Elmira Reformatory in Elmira in upstate New York where he served the remainder of his sentence as a farm worker for 8-10 hours a day. The fruits and vegetables were part of the meals served during the day for the rest of the prison population. Phil recalled the differences between Elmira and the Tombs: "In Elmira you got to shower everyday instead of once a week. And the food was better at Elmira." But there was not a day that went by that he would not think about The Mystics, his family and his friends. Phil always recalls, "The worst part was listening to the music on the radio and missing the group and the family during the holidays."

I think about that a lot. It makes me appreciate what I have and how lucky I am to have a great family and dear friends. And I also think about how one unlucky turn of events can alter the rest of your life.

We performed on American Bandstand with just the four of us, with Bobby standing in the lead position. The reception for "All Through the Night" was good but not as good as for our other songs. Despite terrific reviews in Billboard and Cashbox, the song failed to get on the national charts. It did make the big city charts but only in the forties. It debuted in Honolulu at number eight. Why did the Hawaiians like us so much? Was there anything Polynesian in our harmonies? Did we have relatives in Honolulu? Dick Clark came into our dressing room as usual to say hi, only this time the topic was Phil. By the time, the story about Phil got to him it was a total fabrication. Dick had heard that Phil shot two people in a gas station. We explained what had really happened and Dick was visually relieved and very sorry that it happened. He asked us to relay his regards to Phil and left to begin the show.

We were in desperate need of both another record and a new lead singer. We listened to about a dozen or so young men sing their hearts out for the chance to sing lead for The Mystics. A 15-year-old Stan Vincent (Stan Crochowski) sang okay but was not the right fit, size-wise or age-wise. Stan was a gofer in Jim's office, assisting with recordings, getting coffee, cigarettes and doing the many other things that Jim didn't want to do. Stan managed to get Jim to record him, but the singles went nowhere. Stan went on to write and produce "Teardrops Follow Me" by The Del-Satins for Laurie Records as well as "Remember Then" by The Earls in

1962. Stan also went on to have several of his songs recorded by Connie Francis, notably her hit singles "Drowning My Sorrows" (1963) and "Looking for Love" (1964). Stan also wrote "Tommy" for Connie and had gotten us a chance to do the background parts on that recording in 1959, a few months before we released "Hushabye." Stan went on to become a successful writer, producer and business manager.

One of the other hopefuls who sang well but just did not have the right voice for us was a 17-year-old named Artie Kornfield. Arty hung with Stan Vincent, Paul Simon and many other hopefuls in Jim's office. It was a breeding ground for wanna-be singer-song writers. If Artie Kornfield sounds familiar it's because after playing guitar with Dion and The Mamas and The Poppas in the sixties, at 22 he became the youngest VP of Capital Records and over the next few years was responsible for over 75 Billboard charted songs and over 150 albums.

In 1969 Artie left Capital to co-create The Woodstock Music & Arts Festival with his friend Mike Lang. Artie along with Steve Duboff wrote "The Pied Piper", "Dead Man's Curve" for Jan & Dean, as well as many others.

On March 10th, the last singer to audition in Jim Gribble's office was Jay Traynor, a very talented singer. We listened and then sang a few songs with him. We liked him. Jim asked Jay to step out for a minute and we discussed him with Jim. The pros were that he could sing "Hushabye" and sounded a little like Phil, especially on the falsetto. He was a likeable guy, he lived in Brooklyn and he was a 42 regular. We really didn't want to spend money on new clothes, so it was important that the new lead singer fit into Phil's clothes. So, we selected Jay, and he was thrilled and so were we. He not only fit into Phil's clothes, but he had a similar style, look and demeanor.

We had turned down Paul Simon, Artie Kornfield and Stan Vincent to be our lead singer, and they all went on to great success. Sometimes I wonder why these kids (all under 20 decided that this was going to be their career *and stuck with it.* I really don't think they were any more talented than any of us in the music business. The difference was they thought they could do it. They thought they could write a hit song or produce a record. They were not that good when they started out. There were hundreds of songs written by new talent that did not even get listened to. They learned the trade by trial and error like most trades for which there is no actual school. They came in every day, without getting paid, and suffered the failures of trying and getting turned down.

I don't think we were ready for that. It's weird but I think we felt we were just lucky to be in this business and it never occurred to us that we could write songs or produce records. We didn't even try. It wasn't until many years later that I realized that I'd missed the opportunity to be in the music business. Without another hit record, The Mystics would not recover from the slump. We could have hedged our bets by entering the music business as writers or producers, but we didn't.

With Jay now officially in the group, we started rehearsals to not only teach him our show but also to begin the process of learning the three new songs that we would be recording next. We finally accepted the fact that Phil was not coming back for at least two years and began acting like a five-man group. Although we started to sound like our old selves and Jay was more than we could ask for as a replacement, he was not Phil and we were heartbroken about that.

We did a record hop at Mariners Temple on the east side of New York City on March 12th for a new DJ on WINS radio named Bruce Morrow. This was Jay's first show with us and it was an easy one, as all we had to do was lip sync a few of our records and do an on-air interview with Bruce. This was a rather rough neighborhood and Bruce, who called everyone his "Cousin," was nervous. His innocent looking 6'4 frame, light suit, starched white shirt and polka dot bow tie made him stand out in the audience of mostly Italian and Puerto Rican kids from the Lower East Side. Realizing we were at home with this audience, he clung to us like glue throughout the time we were there and asked us to stick around so we could all leave together. We waited for him after the show to get a cab and then we drove back to Brooklyn. We developed a close relationship with "Cousin Brucie" in the following years. He was always a good friend and helped us whenever he could, especially by asking us to appear at his shows at Palisades Park, NJ, in the following months. Between Allan Freed, Bruce Morrow, Clay Cole and Murray Kaufman we always had a show or an on-air radio station interview. "Murray the K" gave us an open invitation to visit the station while he was on the air. He loved to hang out and talk about what we were doing, especially after midnight.

Jim was pushing Laurie to record us as soon as possible, but I don't think that they had the same enthusiasm as when we started with them. Finding a song to record was not easy. Gene and Elliot were still convinced that we could get a hit with another song like "Hushabye," and we weren't. We felt that we should be changing our style and lean a little more towards the rhythm and blues type songs we grew up with. They played a song called "Blue Star" written by L. Giordano and L. Cohen, which had a lullaby feel to it. We were pigeon holed to do lullabies. In researching the songwriters of this song, I kept coming up with Leonard Cohen who, although did not specifically show up as the official writer, certainly was writing poems and songs in the same genre at that time. Elliot had pushed the tempo up to "Hushabye"/ "Little Star" speed and it was a lot like "Hushabye." It even had the exact same time length, two minutes and thirty seconds. Gene suggested the characteristic high falsetto in the beginning, which Jay nailed flawlessly. We worked with Elliot for about an hour and got the song down. Elliot also had an idea for a version of the standard by Judy Garland, "Over the Rainbow" and we began working on it. Once again, it turned into a five-part harmony tune. Elliot confided in us and said that he and Gene were planning an album for The Mystics that would consist of standards done in our style. To be considered for an album with just two charted records was a tremendous feat. Gene told us later that week that he had great plans for us. He felt that Jay was a perfect replacement for Phil and he wanted to go ahead with the album. He gave us a list of songs to think about, including "Red, Red Robin, "Paper Moon" (which we'd already recorded with Phil", "Where or When," "Swinging on a Star" and the Cole Porter version of "In the Still of the Night."

Gene set May 11, 1960 as the recording date for "Blue Star" and "Somewhere Over the Rainbow" and wanted one more song to complete the trio. Since we had been rehearsing so much with Jay, teaching him our show in preparation for our next tour, Bobby suggested that we sing "The White Cliffs of Dover" for the team and that it would be a good song to record. We did the song in our show, and it featured me on bass lead and Jay on falsetto lead in the bridge of the song. Much to our surprise, both Gene and Elliot loved it. Jim once again just rolled his eyes as if to say, we have been doing this song all along, and lit up and sucked down another Chesterfield. We had been doing "White Cliffs" since we heard it on the Dell-Vikings album "They Sing They Swing" in 1957.

I should add here that if it were not for the Dell-Vikings and Tony Armato I wouldn't be writing this book. As a teenager with a bass voice, and with the help of Tony Armato, I would sing along with the bass singers of the time like Herb Reed of the Platters to learn the way they vocally enhanced their group's harmony sound. I was most impressed with Clarence Quick, the bass voice of the Dell-Vikings, and I learned to sing "White Cliffs of Dover" in the Overon days. One of the earliest songs we learned as the Overons was "Come Go with Me".

In the early seventies, a new DJ named Gus Gossert started playing the music of the fifties on his WCBS-FM Doo-Wop Shop show, and because of the feedback from the listening audience, he began producing and hosting live shows. Since most of the music in the seventies was called "rock and roll," Gus is credited with changing the fifties music designation from "rock and roll" to "doo wop." It was at one of these shows with The Mystics that I got the opportunity to not only meet Clarence but to sing along with him on "Come Go with Me" and "White Cliffs of Dover": we shared the lead. True, we were just hanging out in the dressing room, but it was very exciting for me.

Gene's plan was to test how "Over the Rainbow" would sound as the pilot song for the new album and release the other two as a single record as soon as possible. Jim hinted about an album photo shoot in June and we were really excited about it, except for the fact that Phil was still away. We started on an extremely heavy rehearsal schedule over the next few weeks, concentrating on the new arrangements for "White Cliffs," "Blue Star" and "Over the Rainbow." We also started learning, "The Red Red Robin," which was being scheduled for recording. Elliot also asked us to listen to and think about "Swinging on a Star," which I loved. On March 17, 18, 19 and 20[th,] we did shows in Pennsylvania, two of which were for Gene Kaye, a prominent DJ in Allentown. We got back home on the 21st and rehearsed for a solid week.

On Saturday April 16, 1960, we did the first of an expected nine live shows on the Alan Freed Eastern states tour, starting in Philadelphia. As in the other tours, we met all the other performers at the first show in the early afternoon so, as usual, the acts could rehearse with the band. Our old friend Freddy Cannon was the headliner, along with Teddy Randazzo. Freddy had a top current top ten hit called "Chattanooga Shoe Shine Boy" and Teddy was on the charts with "The Way of a Clown."

Teddy was born in our old neighborhood in Brooklyn. We knew him from when he sang with a group called The Three Chuckles. Their first hit, "Runaround," was a top 20 hit in 1954 and inspired a lot of teenagers to sing. The following year, he became the group's lead singer and sang on their hits "Times Two, I Love You" and "And the Angels Sing." The records' success brought him to the attention of disc jockey Freed, who featured him in the movie *Rock, Rock, Rock*. Later on, as a Irvingo artist, Teddy had three singles that made the Billboard Hot 100: "Little Serenade" (#66) in 1958, "The Way of a Clown" (#44) in 1960, and "Big Wide World" (#51) in 1963. He co-starred in rock revues staged by Freed, appearing with such artists as Chuck Berry and LaVern Baker. He also had roles in such rock films as *Hey, Let's Twist! The Girl Can't Help It,* and *Mister Rock and Roll* in the late 1950s and early 1960s.

Teddy began being recognized as a great songwriter and wrote a string of major hits for other artists with composing partner Bobby Weinstein, including "Pretty Blue Eyes," a top ten hit for Steve Lawrence in the US and Craig Douglas in the UK in 1959. He penned many songs for Little Anthony and the Imperials, producing and arranging several albums for the group in the mid-60's. The hit songs included "Going Out of My Head," which was covered by numerous artists including the Zombies and Frank Sinatra; "Hurt So Bad," which was covered by The Lettermen as well as Linda Ronstadt, who took it to # 8 in 1980. Many of Teddy's tunes became pop classics, recorded by a gamut of industry giants from Ella Fitzgerald to Frank Sinatra. "I've lost count on how many versions there are" Randazzo once said of "Going Out of My Head." It is now included in the Top 50 most recorded songs, with sales of over 100 million by over 400 artists, according to the Songwriters Hall of Fame. Later, he provided several songs for albums by New York soul group, the Manhattans, during their 1970's hey-day, including the "There's No Good in Goodbye," and "A Million To One."

The rehearsal went well, as Allan's seasoned musicians were on board with Sam "the man" Taylor as the band leader. We had met some other band members during the Fox show: The Fireflys ("I Can't Say Goodbye"), Eddie Quinteros ("Come Dance with Me"), The Singing Belles, and one of the legends of rock and roll, Sonny Til ("Crying in the Chapel"), along with Bobby Freeman ("Do You Want to Dance").

We all piled into the bus after the show with our luggage stashed below in the luggage area. We already knew some of the artists but this was the first time meeting Bobby Freeman from Los Angeles. "Do You Want to Dance" reached number No. 5 on the Billboard Top 100 and was covered later (as "Do You Wanna Dance") by Del Shannon, the Beach Boys, Johnny Rivers, Bette Midler, John Lennon, Cliff Richard, Marc Bolan & T.Rex, the Mamas & The Papas, Bobby Vee and the Ramones.

Bobby was a fun guy, and between him and Freddy Cannon hanging with us, we had a good time on the tour. The band liked to sit in the back of the bus and play cards.

Alan and his wife Inga, an attractive blond, sat in the front of the bus with their little dog and travelled with all of us everywhere. He loved to hang out with everyone while on the road telling stories while drinking, gambling and smoking. It was amazing how often these guys could shoot craps: in the bus, behind the curtain while the show was going on, in the dressing rooms and in the hotel rooms at night after the show. Alan was very fond of The Mystics and we genuinely liked him. He was a fun-loving guy who was completely in love with this music and the people who made it. I think he was broke because he gave his money to anyone who would ask. We never really found out why or if there was a reason why, but it was what it was. Alan was a legend and he liked us, and that's all that mattered to us.

Through all the things, we did and all the people we were with, we rarely took any pictures, and I think we all regret that. Alan Freed died in a Palm Springs, California, hospital on January 20, 1965, from uremia and cirrhosis brought on by alcoholism; he was 43 years old and was initially interred in the Ferncliff Cemetery in Hartsdale, New York. In March 2002, Judith Fisher Freed, carried his ashes to the Rock and Roll Hall of Fame in Cleveland, Ohio. On August 1, 2014, the Hall of Fame asked Freed's son, Lance Freed, to permanently remove the ashes, which he did. The Freed family later announced the ashes would be interred at Cleveland's Lake View Cemetery.

From Philadelphia, we went to Johnson City, New York., then to Scranton, Pennsylvania, and the following night to Sunnyside Gardens Arena in Queens. On the way to Scranton, Alan, who always walked up and down the bus while we were driving and loved to talk to everyone, did something so strange we were all shocked. He announced that we needed to all chip in $1.00 for gas as they (Alan) were short on cash. We gave a dollar each, so he must have collected about $40.00. I remember that I laid out a dollar for Bobby Freeman because he had no cash on him and also lent him ten dollars, since he said he was broke and was getting some money when we got to New York.

Our parents and all of our beautiful girlfriends were at the Sunnyside show. Jim, in his dark suit, white shirt and red tie, sat with our parents, who were full of questions about our future. That must have been tough. This was the first time they saw us on tour since Jay joined the group. Jay's mom and family were there also. The arena was packed, and the audience was great. We were featuring our new recording of "All Through the Night," which was not doing as well as expected on the charts but went over well with a live audience. We did our usual 6-song set and sat with the girls to watch the rest of the show. It was interesting to see the reaction of the girls and our families towards us. We did not feel special but the position we were in at that time elevated us to a special place as recording artists. The young people would come over for autographs and have that "star gaze look" as if they were talking to big stars. I honestly do not think that any of us felt as if we were big stars. I certainly can understand how people after seeing us on TV and on stage with Alan Freed and the other famous artists would think differently, but we were not affected. It was actually a little strange to see how people behaved in these situations. My girlfriend told me that she was approached by some of the audience with questions about The Mystics and me. "They even asked me for my autograph," she said with a nervous laugh, feeling a little embarrassed.

We had the next day off and spent most of it with Jim at the office. He was getting concerned because Alan had not given him the deposit check for the tour yet. We told him about the one-dollar collection and he got furious, which was unusual. We'd never seen Jim get mad. In between Chesterfields, he called Alan's office and left several messages for him to call right away. In those days, the only way anyone would get a message was if someone personally answered the phone and wrote it down. He gave Bobby instructions to ask Allan for the money when we got back on the bus the next day. After all the artists filed back on the bus, there was a lot of talk about money among us, as everyone had consulted their managers with the same results. Bobby approached Alan and came back to us and Freddy Cannon explaining that Alan was going to make an announcement to everyone about the tour. What was weird was that Alan was sitting in the front seat with Inga and the whole rest of the bus was wondering what the hell was going on. Alan got up and walked towards the middle of the bus, right where we were sitting. That caused an uneasy silence. He had a tired and worried look. He looked like he was sick and had not slept in days which, considering the stress we thought he was going through, was understandable. We did not expect what was coming.

He started with something about the fact that he knew we were all worried about the money and that that was being taken care of. He added that checks were being cut by his accountants and should be in everyone's hands as soon as we got back to the city. He then announced that due to poor ticket sales, the remainder of the tour was going to be cancelled and that Pittsburgh was our last show. Everyone started asking questions and it was obvious that Alan was on the verge of tears. Inga, who was standing in the front of the bus, walked over to Alan and put her hand on his shoulder and said to everyone, "Let's all calm down and be sensible about this." She wanted to say more but some of the performers were asking for their deposits right now, which told us that we were in the same boat and that everyone was out for themselves. Allan just kind of hushed Inga with a loving look and said, "They're right, Inga, they have a right to complain." Bobby jumped into the discussion and tried to get some kind of calm and succeeded to a certain point, explaining that there was nothing that any of us could right now so let's take Alan's word and see what happens. I think that no one wanted to believe the worst from a guy we all idolized. The rest of the trip to Pittsburgh was silent except for whispered conversations. We couldn't call anyone until we stopped and found a phone booth.

This was Jay Traynor's first tour, and although he knew all our material, he was visibly nervous on the first show. Most of the shows we had done with him prior to this were either lip-sync or with a small band. Just being thrown into this situation, and as lead singer, would unnerve anyone. We accepted Jay as one us but of course we all knew that if Phil were released that Jay would be out. We didn't talk about it. Jay was a good sport and went along with the teasing that a group of friends would normally do to the new young member. We all really liked Jay.

The Pittsburgh show went well and was well received by a sold-out audience, which kind of made everyone wonder about the ticket sales that Allan was talking about. All the performers, after numerous consults with their managers, agents and record companies, were semi-content with the fact that all of our money would be there when we got back to New York.

When we got back, it was not there. The money never came. Ever!

Alan Freed Show Poster

CHAPTER 20

SOMEWHERE OVER THE RAINBOW

Since the last two shows of the tour, Norwalk, Connecticut, and Ansonia, New York, were cancelled, we were back in Laurie's office rehearsing during the last week in August. We did a show in Trenton on May 5th and another on May 7th in Kingston, New York. May 8th & 9th more rehearsal and on May 11th,1960 we were in Bell Sound studio recording "The White Cliffs of Dover," "Blue Star" and "Somewhere Over the Rainbow." Who could have guessed that 46 years later, on March 26, 2006, "Somewhere Over the Rainbow" by The Mystics would be featured on the 68th episode of "The Sopranos" TV show? It's in the scene where Carmella is wetting Tony's lips. Who selected this song for the show, and why, is still perplexing.

I was home that night watching The Sopranos (which I loved) and the song that was playing sounded like a recording I knew. It started out very soft and gradually got louder about half way through. I jumped up off the chair and said, "That's us!" I called all The Mystics and asked if they heard that too. We were all shocked. The next morning, I called the agent who handles The Mystics account at Sony and asked if he knew that one of our songs had been played on The Sopranos. Up until this point, we were getting a small royalty for "performance" on any recording or completion of recordings that were sold. I had been pestering Gene Schwartz for years for our fair share of royalties that I knew were due us, and he would always say he would look into it. Every artist is supposed to get paid for their performance. It's a very small percentage, but I just wanted us to get what we deserved. Every once in a while, I would stop up at Laurie until they closed the NY office sometime in 1975 and moved to a small warehouse operation in NJ. I visited Gene and Elliot at their new place in NJ around 1985 with an idea for an item to sell, since at that time they were putting song collections and selling them on TV. In 1992, Gene informed me that Elliot and Bob had passed away and that he and Ernie Maresca, who was working with Gene, were selling the entire collection to Capital records (this was later taken over by Sony) and that if I would give him my information, he would be able to incorporate that into his deal to ensure that we got royalties for future sales. I called all the guys and put together a list of our social security numbers and addresses.

From that point on we received performance royalties for records sold. Unfortunately, we did not write anything we recorded for Laurie Records; songwriter royalties are much larger than performance royalties. We didn't get a lot of money, around $300 to $500 a year apiece. It wasn't really about the money, it was about us and what we deserved. I asked Gene about our money going back to 1960 when we last talked and he said there wasn't anything. I lost touch with Gene after that last conversation.

The agent called me back the next day and said we were due a one-time licensing performance check, which as I understood it, was paid by the producers of the TV show for the use of this particular recording. He explained that the fee is paid to the publisher who takes a percentage and then Sony distributes the remainder of the fee to the artist, after they take their cut as the licensee. I almost fell off my chair when he told me we were due about $30,000.

I told him that there is a slight problem because, although The Mystics recorded the song, there was a different lead singer, at the time, and I thought it only fair that we not only acknowledged him but also gave him a share. He said that was fine, but I would have to get a release from each of the Mystics who were on the record and the contract as the original artists before he could cut checks.

I called Jay, who was not even aware that "Somewhere Over the Rainbow" was played on The Sopranos, and he was also shocked. "Why would they pick that song?" he said laughing. I told him, "That's what I thought." We agreed. It was a terrific recording, but of all the songs in the world, especially one of the most recorded and famous songs of all time, it was puzzling that they picked The Mystics' version of "Somewhere Over the Rainbow." Perhaps they thought we would never learn that our song had been used and would never bother to collect the licensing fee.

Hushabye

"Wow, $30,000, that's amazing," Jay said.

"I'm still stunned!" I said as we both broke into laughter at the absurd twist of fate. I relayed the agent's request to Jay and he said, "No problem, let me know and thanks for letting me know." I called everyone individually, filled them in on the situation, and suggested we give Phil a share as he was going thru a rough period in his life and could use a few extra bucks even if he was not on the original recording, but I would have to clear that part with Jay. I called Jay the next day regarding Phil, and he agreed without hesitation. He also added, "Please give my regards to everyone."

I got the paperwork done and told Jay to call the agent, so his name would be registered in case someone else decided to use "Over the Rainbow" or one of the other songs he was on. We even went so far as to list the other two songs we recorded with Jay. I sometimes fantasized that some show randomly picked one of the songs that Paul Simon was on, so I could contact him and say, "Hey, Paul, you have a few thousand coming to you – where do I send the check?"

A few weeks later, we finally got our checks for $5000 each. It was the most we'd ever made for one event – and we hadn't even left the house.

The recording session at Bell Sound Studios in 1960 was routine and Jay, although a little nervous, did a great job. We had most of the same musicians as in our other sessions. The one thing that was a little crazy was when we recorded "The White Cliffs of Dover," I shared the lead mike with Jay. Well it was not exactly sharing. I did the lead part and when it came to the bridge for Jay's part, he had to run over to the lead mike and I had to run over to the group mike. The mikes were not that far apart but there was a screen to prevent the sound from leaking into the other mike, and because it had to be done in a split second, when I turned to run I forgot the screen was there and boom! Of course, this prompted a fit of laughter.

Gene stopped the recording and Jim got on the speaker with his typical remarks, "Boys you all settle down now." He knew us and knew that we could get off on a laughing jag and waste 30 minutes of session time that we were ultimately paying for. We were slowly becoming good friends with Jay and accepted him, at this point, as one of us. However, I knew, and Jay knew that we missed Phil.

Albee would update us on Phil when he would visit, and it was heartbreaking to hear how sad he was. We wrote letters to Phil and it was difficult because what could we say? "Hey Phil, we're having a great time"? I made my letters more like an update on my family, purposely leaving out girlfriend details.

It was around this time that Jerry Rosenberg's wife filed for a divorce and moved to Texas. Jerry went nuts. The whole neighborhood knew what had happened. Jerry had stayed in touch with Albee and was always asking about Phil. We would run into Jerry once in a while at a bar or nightclub and he would tell us how he was reaching out to people he knew in jail to keep Phil safe. We believed him. Even in jail, perhaps especially in jail, it was good to be connected.

BLUE STAR

On May 17th, we went to Laurie to hear the dubs, which were kind of a first pressing of the finished recordings. We showed up after first stopping at Jim's office and saying hi to all the other teenagers that were trying to get a hit record through Jim's efforts. Jim liked it when we were there and especially when the Passions were all there at the same time. He loved hanging with us, we made him laugh. The office was a beehive of musical activity. Inevitably, some of us would break off in a corner of the office and start singing with whoever was there at the time.

It was around this time that The Passions let Vinny Acierno, their baritone, go. I remember going to a meeting with Jim, Tony Armato, Bobby Ferrante, Albee Galione, Jimmy Gallagher and myself. Bobby and I were present simply because we happened to be there at the time. Jim considered us all family, especially since he knew we all grew up together, and encouraged us to talk about our problems. We had many talks with The Passions when Phil got in trouble and it was comforting. Tony wanted to bring Louie Rotundo into The Passions to replace Vinny. Louie was from South Brooklyn where Jimmy was from and was singing with the Del-rays. We had met Louie many times in the neighborhood and thought of him as a perfect replacement. It was Louie and Tony who eventually asked Emil Stucchio and his then group, The Perennials, to audition for Jim.

Except for a few local shows, the next couple of weeks were open, and we enjoyed our time off. We joined the Jack Lalanne gym that had just opened in Brooklyn and, since we were not working, would spend a few hours a day there. We invited Clay, as our guest, to hang with us and he would meet us for a work-out session and then dinner, either out somewhere in Brooklyn or with either my family or Georgie's family, which he loved.

Al Contrera

We went to Laurie's office to pick up our copies of "Blue Star" and "The White Cliffs of Dover" on June 2, 1960. They were released on June 3rd, when we did a high school prom in Freeport, New York. The next two weeks were somewhat open except for a show in Kingston and a Hartford TV appearance for Brad Davis, where we debuted our new recordings. This was Jay's first TV show and he handled it well, even with all the kidding when they put on our makeup.

The following night was another prom, this time in Long Beach, New York, and on Saturday, June 25th, we did another major TV show for Clay Cole at his Palisades Park studio. There were many acts on the show, including Fabian and Chubby Checker. We played our new releases for Clay before the show and he loved them. Clay had a good feel for picking hit records. "White Cliffs of Dover" / "Blue Star" got a Billboard Magazine, "Pick of the Week." The write-up said, "The Mystics, who have had hits in the past, have two more possible entries with these sides. 'Dover' is the standard and the boys sing it well, sparked by a bass lead. Flip side is a medium beat rockaballard, Laurie 3058, that shows off the group's vocal harmony." It was only after I read the write up did I understand why Gene and Elliot were so happy to record "The White Cliffs of Dover." It was a standard and that would fit into the upcoming album. We were on an upswing and feeling good about both songs when about two weeks later Jim Gribble fired Jay and banned him from the office.

Bobby found out while talking to Jim about some business and called us. "What the fuck else could happen to us?" asked Bobby. This cleared our July and August calendar. Of course, we were shocked and asked Jim why he'd fired Jay. He told us that he walked in while Jay was in his office looking through his desk. We explained to Jim that there was no way that Jay would do anything wrong and that there had to be a reason why he was in there, but Jim would not listen. His decision was final.

Soon after, we learned what had really happened. Jay had asked Stan Vincent, who was Jim's office assistant, if he could get a picture of The Mystics for a friend of his. Since Stan was busy and had to go pick up something down the hall, Stan told Jay to go to the bottom right desk draw drawer, where the pictures were, and help himself. So innocently, Jay did what Stan had told him to do. At that moment, Jim walked in. Stan backed up the story, but Jim didn't want to hear anything. Jay was out.

We were devastated again. Not only had we just recorded with Jay but also, we liked and accepted him. What were we supposed to do now? There was still no talk about Phil being released, and we were in the middle of promoting our latest record, which was not doing well.

At this point in time, it seemed that with the success of "Where or When" by Dion and the Belmonts (which reached #3), the Laurie team wanted to do more standards with Dion, but there was also some turmoil in Dion's group between Dion being hospitalized, the Belmonts wanting to do more group harmony, and Dion wanting to be on his own. My guess is that the Laurie team made another business decision and asked us to go back to work on the album that we thought was a dead issue when Phil left. We already had "It's Only a Paper Moon" and "The Red Red Robin" with Phil on lead recorded. Now we had "Over the Rainbow" with Jay on lead and no Jay and "The White Cliffs of Dover" with me on bass lead. Gene had asked us, before he knew about Jim's decision to fire Jay, to start work on "Swinging on a Star" and the standard version of "In the Still of the Night."

Jim told us that we would be taking pictures for the new album in Central Park on June 23, while Jay was still in the group, and to wear casual clothes. So, at 10:00 am on June 23 we showed up at the carousel in Central Park and met with a photographer, Gene, Jim and some woman hired to make sure we posed correctly for the album photos. It was a beautiful sunny day and we were so looking forward to this photo session. Imagine: we were taking pictures for an album! Doing an album had been one of our dreams. After a light makeup session, the mystery woman, who was smartly dressed and very classy, posed us on the carousel horses for our first shots. The other shots were on the grass, sitting and standing on the boulders, hanging off a tree, and one shot where we all lay down on our backs in the grass and the tops of our heads were just about touching. The photographer was on a ladder looking straight down at our faces and said we looked like a five-pointed star, whatever that meant! This was a wonderful day, and we were full of hope, knowing that Gene was all psyched up for the new album. He kept mentioning how this photo theme went hand in hand with the album theme of standards in our style.

I didn't see that at all, nor did the other guys. A few days after the shoot, we looked at the photos with Jim, Gene, Bob and Elliot and made preliminary selections for the album cover. They all came out great. I was thrilled. The mere thought of recording a Mystics album was mind-boggling. We joked around with Gene, asking what the title would be, and he said he wasn't sure. It would depend on how the songs came out, but he liked the sound of "Somewhere Over the Rainbow."

CHAPTER 22

SHE CRIED

After Jay was fired by Jim Gribble, he was approached by Kenny Rosenberg (soon to be Kenny Vance), Sandy Yaguda and Howie Kirschenbaum of the Harbor Lights to join their group. The Harbor Lights had a girl lead singer, which was not working out for them. They were also one of Jim Gribble's hopeful groups. We would see them at the office all the time. The timing for Jay was perfect. They knew Jay could sing – he was the lead singer for The Mystics – and they knew he was available. They got together, rehearsed and set up an audition with the independent producers and songwriters, Jerry Lieber and Mike Stoller. The audition went well, and they recorded the song "Tonight" from the *West Side Story* movie that had just been released. The other side, "She Cried," was a DJ favorite and became a huge hit for the new group, which was named "Jay and the Americans" by Lieber and Stoller. It was better than "Binky and the Americans," which was the first name suggested. They added another neighborhood friend, Marty Kupersmith, to the group as guitarist and vocalist and recorded a few more times but nothing happened.

It was becoming obvious, at that point, that the group members were not getting along, and Jay left after a conversation with Sandy about the group's problems. Jay later missed out on an opportunity to work on a project with Phil Spector and decided to join the Marine reserves to avoid the draft. He later landed a job with Warner Bros records and became a recording engineer working on many hit recordings including those of Bob Dylan. Through the 60's and 70's, Jay was the road manager for "Mountain." Then he worked as a Sinatra type vocalist with The Joey Thomas Big Band and played in casinos across the country. Jay lived near Albany and at some point, in the 70's, when The Mystics played near Albany, as part of the Brooklyn Reunion show, Jay showed up, and it was wonderful. We exchanged info and stayed in touch on a regular basis from that point on.

Unfortunately, we lost Jay on January 2, 2014 due to liver cancer. My last conversation with him was at the Christmas Holiday Dick Fox show in Westbury a few weeks earlier. This was the last time I heard Jay sing "She Cried." He was singing with The Tokens at the time and I was with Emil Stucchio and the Classics. The Classics and The Tokens were sharing the "star" dressing room with Dick Fox. This was as much fun as the show. There are two couches with a small cocktail table and a few chairs and lots of time to kill. After the sound check we sat and played catch up on everyone's life. Dick's dressing room was a hub of activity since he was the producer and all the other acts wanted to say hi to him and maintain their friendship.

We were sitting around laughing at each other's jokes and stories after dinner when Jay asked me if he could talk to me in private. I got a sinking feeling about this because he really did not look good. We went into the adjoining room and he closed the door. He started by saying, "My cancer is getting worse and my doctor tells me that there is nothing left to do." I was shocked. I knew Jay was sick but didn't realize it had progressed so quickly. Seeing my reaction, he continued with, "Look I've known you a very long time and wanted to tell you this in person before you heard it from someone else."

I felt the sincerity in his voice. Here was a man who thought enough of me and our friendship to let me know personally how he felt and that he was going to die soon. I was beyond stunned. Then he said, "If it weren't for The Mystics I would have never had this career." I felt tears start to well up. He continued, "I just want you to know that you are a good friend," and I just hugged him and said, "What can I do?" He said, "Just be my friend." We chatted for a few more minutes and he started to get ready for his show.

I went into the bathroom to get myself together, astounded at what I had just heard. I washed my face with cold water and tried to process the news. I went into the other room where everyone else was sitting, and both Emil and Dick asked me what's wrong. I said "nothing." Jay came out dressed for his show and we wished him the usual, "have a great show."

CHAPTER 23

GOOD BYE MR. BLUES

With Jay out of the group, we were back to four again and looking for another replacement for the lead spot. This time Jim Gribble left it up to us. I got the feeling that Jim was so busy with all the other acts that he was trying to promote that he slacked off on The Mystics. The Passions, although recording some great sides, failed to get another national hit. Jim cancelled the few gigs we had in July except for the record hops, which we could do with just the four of us. Louie and Tony (Passions) recommended Eddie "Shots" Falcone, who they both knew. I never knew how he got his nickname. Eddie had taken over the lead when Lou Rotondo left The Del-Rays from south Brooklyn. We met Eddie up at the office, and after hearing him sing a few songs, we hired him.

Eddie was a big guy with a big, operatic, yet somehow young voice. He did not sound anything like Phil, but now it didn't seem like anyone cared, as long as he could sing. In retrospect, we should have looked for a "Phil and Jay" type voice to continue our sound. But both Jim and the Laurie team approved, and we began preparing for our next recording. Gene and Elliot, much to our surprise, asked Stan Vincent to produce this session. Stan had suggested both songs, "Goodbye Mr. Blues" and "Star Crossed Lovers." At the time "tragedy" type songs were popping up on the charts and the Laurie team wanted us to do one. "Star Crossed Lovers" was about a young couple who got into a fatal car accident. I loved this song as well as "Goodbye Mr. Blues," which was an up-tempo rock n roll song that was in the genre that we always wanted to do. We did both at Bell sound but without our usual musicians. Stan brought his musicians, who were outstanding.

Our next big gig was for seven nights, from August 25 to August 31, 1960, as the featured act at the Aquarama amphitheater in Flushing Meadow on Long Island. This was a show that featured professional divers and synchronized swimmers in a dazzling setting. The comedian, Sammy Petrillo (a Jerry Lewis type), opened for us with a 20-minute set and we followed with a 30-minute show. We convinced the promoter to include Clay Cole as the MC. The audience was seated across from the pool which made it difficult for them to see us and just as difficult for us to see them. Add the spotlights on our faces, and we were playing to complete darkness.

We still appealed to record buyers and managed to attract a good size audience, as demonstrated by the sold-out shows, but between the lack of management from both Jim and Laurie records, we were slowly fading. Of course, it's easy to say now that we should have taken control and put more effort on our own behalf, but we were not making much money and there was pressure from our families, especially mine, to start thinking about a career. Plus, we were not teenagers anymore and I thought *this* was a career.

We had to get new suits, for there was no way that Eddie was going to fit into Phil's clothes. We worked with Eddie on our live show and although he sang well, somehow the live show didn't work out, and we eventually had to let him go. We did a few shows in September of 1960 with Clay, Bruce and Murray Kaufman, and morale was getting low. We had one more recording session left in our contract, and Gene finally agreed to let us pick our own songs.

With Eddie now out of the group, we were in search mode for another lead. Most of October was spent with family, friends and girlfriends. A bowling alley named "Frankie and Johnny's" opened on 86th Street and 16th Ave in the middle of our neighborhood and became the neighborhood hangout. It featured the new automatic pinsetters, a bar and a coffee shop. Not only was it convenient, it was an attraction for guys and girls of all ages. A great meeting place. We would usually stay for a while and then go to Mitchell Drive In for a bite to eat. Many of the neighborhood's would-be singers would hang out, knowing that both The Mystics and The Passions might show up.

CHAPTER 24

DARLING, I KNOW NOW

Most of the neighborhood knew us and still held us in high esteem in the overall scheme of things. One-night Bobby and I were standing outside the bowling alley talking with some friends about the Berlin crisis and that we could be eligible for the draft if things started to heat up, when we were approached by Ralph Lizano who, guitar in his hand, introduced himself and said he'd written a song for us and would like to play it for us. He had just moved into the area and found out that some "famous singers" (us!) hung out by the bowling alley.

He opened his guitar case, took out his guitar, and sang, "Darling, I Know Now." We loved the song and got George to come out from the coffee shop and listen. He agreed that this was a great tune. Ralph had a nice lead vocal and we started to harmonize and add some background parts, all in jest – except it started to sound good! This, of course, attracted a small crowd. Bobby asked Ralph if he was singing with a group, and he said no he just wanted to write songs and would love to get an intro to Jim Gribble and Laurie Records. The song had a nice shuffle and reminded us of The Shirelles' version of "Will You Still Love Me Tomorrow." Albee just happened to stop by, and now we were at full background strength, with the crowd listening to everything. We were at the birth of a song. Bobby called Jim that night and we were all in the car on our way to Manhattan the next morning.

Jim liked Eddie and was not happy we let him go but didn't pursue the reasons why. He loved Eddie's lead on "Star Crossed Lovers," the flip side of "Goodbye Mr. Blues." I think he was still kind of sorry that he let Jay go, especially since Jay was now doing so well, and he knew that Jay had meant no harm when he was in his office looking for a group photo.

Jim listened to us sing with Ralph and without a word picked up his phone, and called Gene Schwartz. He lit another Camel and said, "Gene, Jim here. If you all have a minute, I'm coming over with The Mystics and their new lead singer." When he said, "new lead singer" his eyebrows went up with an "Oh well, here we go again" look on his face, for this would be our fourth lead singer. Ralph, of course, was thrilled. I can imagine what was going thru his mind: I went to the bowling to hang out and sing and now I'll be the lead singer of The Mystics!

We knew that we were fading in the eyes of Laurie Records and it showed in the lack of enthusiasm from the team. Gene liked the song, he was always looking for new material, but was not as up as he usually was towards us, and Elliot was non-committal. Gene asked if we had any other songs that we could do in our next session. Ralph had a few more but nothing like "Darling I Know Now." Gene wasn't suggesting any and that was not like him. We always felt, as a group, that the music we grew up with was what we should be recording. Bobby had always liked "A Sunday Kind of Love" by The Harptones, and so we put a ballad arrangement together with our new lead singer. We could tell Gene wasn't thrilled about our version, but he went along with us. In our early days, even going back to The Overons, we all loved this song and would sing it often. There were certain songs that held special place for us, and singing them made us feel good.

We also liked "Love will Make Your Mind go Wild" by the Penguins, "Smoke from Your Cigarette" by Lillian Leach and the Mellows, and "Who's that Knocking" by The Genies. We must have sung "One Summer Night" by the Danleers hundreds of times over the years. We needed a third song, and Bobby came up with an idea for an up-tempo version of the standard song "Again." This arrangement was very different from anything we had done in the past.

Elliot loved old standards, but he didn't like this arrangement at all, as we sang in a very fast tempo, a real rock and roll group sound. Not that the harmonies were bad, they actually were as good as those on all our other songs, but our version of "Again" had lots of sounds and bass parts, and Elliot was into slow, easy-going melodic recordings.

We were now in November of 1960 and finally getting ready for our last Laurie recording session, which also satisfied our six-recording session contract, renewable only by Laurie. Unfortunately, Laurie did not exercise the renewal option in our contract, so we knew it was our last chance. Gene wanted to use Stan Vincent again for the production. I guess he felt that everything Laurie did, aside from "Hushabye," did not work well, or maybe with all that happened post "Hushabye," he gave up on us. We used Stan Vincent's band again and the session went well, with just a rhythm section for backup. It was simple and quick, and as usual we got the same thrill of hearing the studio re-play. Ralph was floating on a cloud. We set up some rehearsals and prepared for some promotional appearances. Of course, Clay Cole invited us to do his show with our new recording.

Bobby was now 25 years old, and being the most sensible person in the group, he was getting tired of the disappointments and the lackluster attention we were getting from the Laurie team and wanted to go on with his plans to become an engineer. We had some serious conversations about the future of The Mystics. We didn't have a real lead singer, we were not making any money and it didn't seem like this was going to pan out so well. During this time, George and I were still in contact with Pete Anders and Vini Poncia from The Videls, who were having similar problems with their group and their record company. Some of their original members were also thinking of moving on. Ralph was not very happy singing with The Mystics. We didn't have much work and since he was just interested in song-writing, our group, in his mind, was just a stepping-stone to further his song-writing career. He started talking with Gene about some of the other songs he had written and signed on with Laurie as a song writer. With Bobby deciding to move on and Phil still in prison, I got together with Vini and Pete one day in New York city and suggested that since we did not have a lead singer or a first tenor, and they basically did not have a group, Albee, George and I could hook up with them and we would have the best of everything. Pete Andreoli had a fantastic lead voice and Vini was not only a great tenor but a musician and knew how to put harmonies together. Both groups had great harmony, and if we could put this together, we would be unbeatable. They were all for it, and we started to plan. In the meantime, we were all basically broke. With practically no gigs on the books, we weren't earning any money. By the end of the year it looked bleak for The Mystics – except for this new alliance. I didn't want to give up!

John F Kennedy was debating Richard Nixon for the presidency, and Vietnam was heating up. Elvis Presley was in the Army and was scheduled to get out soon. We were beginning to worry about being drafted. Bobby had already joined the Army reserves and Albee had a deferral. Our music business friends were doing well with their follow up songs to their previous hits. Freddy Cannon was in the top ten with, "Way Down Yonder in New Orleans," Jimmy Clanton had "Go, Jimmy Go," Dion and the Belmonts were in the top ten with, "Where or When" and the Drifters were moving up the charts with "Save the Last Dance for Me," written by Doc Pomus and Mort Shuman. Johnny Maestro had two back to back hits with "Step by Step" and "Trouble in Paradise" with The Crests and Johnny Farina and his brother Santo had a hit with "Teardrop."

Pete and Vini lived in Providence, R.I., and, of course, we lived in Brooklyn. You might ask: why not get a couple of guys from Brooklyn and start from there? We were convinced that between us we had a killer group, with all the voices covered as well as the experience and the passion to back it up. The Videls had charted (#73) with "Mr. Lonely," but their next recording, "Now That Summer Is Here," which they also wrote, failed to chart. So, at this point, both groups were in the same boat.

It should be noted that The Mystics would record, "Now That Summer Is Here" on their "Crazy for You" album in 1982, on CBS's Ambient Sound label, produced by Marty Pekar.

In December 1960, The Videls were in the studio with Kapp Records and their producer Joe Sherman recording "A Letter from Ann," which due to the rest of the group dropping out was recorded with just Vini and Pete overdubbing the other voices. Joe had already built an outstanding reputation as a songwriter, having written such hits as "Rambling Rose" and "Sunday, That Summer" for Nat "King" Cole, "Eso Beso" for Paul Anka, and others, like "To the Ends of the Earth" and "Graduation Day."

The Videls were in the city recording for the week, which gave us the opportunity to get together and talk about how to put the two groups together. Towards the end of December, The Videls had a Friday night gig to do at the Villa Roma hotel in the Catskills and the Mystics had a Saturday night show in Long Island at a night club. This was the perfect opportunity to merge our groups. We did not have the money to buy new suits, so we borrowed Bobby's and Phil's brown suits. Vini was taller than Phil so he had the pants let out a little, Pete fit perfectly into Bobby's suit and with some new shirts and ties we had a new Videls/Mystics outfit. We contemplated buying new matching shoes, but again money was an issue. Vini and Pete were living at the Forest Hotel in Manhattan, costs picked up by Kapp records, so we spent a few days rehearsing at the Forest Hotel for the shows. We used some of the songs we did and some of the songs The Videls did in their show, since Pete was going to do lead on everything anyway.

It wasn't much money, but we needed the work and the experience of working together. Albee wasn't keen on the idea of the merge but agreed to work with us because George and I were into this and it was obvious that we had a great group, and all got along very well. Albee loved harmony, and this group had great harmony. Singing harmony with this group was effortless. We always talked about Phil getting out soon, but it looked like it was going to be the full two and a half years. We couldn't wait if we wanted to stay in this business and maintain status. You must be in it to keep the name alive in the public.

Since we were not under contract any longer with Laurie Records, the plan was to audition for Joe Sherman, who thought the world of Vini and Pete, and hopefully restart our careers as The Mystics, since we had the bigger record, or the Videls, or maybe a brand-new name, we weren't sure. We rehearsed at Pete and Vini's hotel room on Monday and Tuesday night and were supposed to meet Sherman on Wednesday.

The rehearsals were great. I always wonder how it happens. How does the brain remember and process the signals to the voice and coordinate it with the ear so that it is in perfect harmony with the voices it is hearing? Vini used to call our harmony "silk."

Joe wanted to meet us before he even considered an audition and so Vini set up a meeting. The most striking thing about Sherman's apartment was the lush white rug, which made the floor look like a white Alpaca sweater. Joe was very cordial and the five of us sat on the very large white leather couch and talked with him. He sat crossed legged in a white armchair. Vini always laughs when he recalls that time when Joe offered all of us one single coke, which is all he had in his white refrigerator. We had five glasses, and each took a little. I guessed that he wanted to see us in person. Of course, he already knew Pete and Vini, but he didn't know us.

He asked us to sing a song, which was surprising because this was just supposed to be a meeting, and he knew we were not prepared. "Just stay seated and relax" he said. "I would just like to get a feel for where your ranges are." After Vini hit a starting note on the white baby grand next to the couch, we did an a cappella version of "This I Swear" by The Skyliners. It was beautiful. Pete had the special talent of being able to mimic original

Hushabye

lead singers, which made the song sound so much better. Years later, when Pete and Vini became songwriters, they wrote some songs for Elvis for the movie *Harem Scarum* and did the demo records in Elvis's voice so that he could get a feel for what the song sounded like and to also highlight the way it should be sung.

Joe took a sip of hot tea from a white cup, and directing his gaze towards Vini, said, "I see a lot of potential here. I like your look and the vocals are great. I think with the right material we can do really well." He asked us about contractual obligations and we explained that our Laurie contract was over, but we did have a manager's agreement with Jim Gribble. We were not sure how solid that was, because it was for The Mystics and not for each of us. We left Sherman's apartment floating on a cloud, talking about how we should put all our efforts into this project. Joe was writing some new material with the Platters in mind, and Vini said that Joe thought we could fit that mold. This would move us out of the typical doo-wop group and into the more traditional type music that Joe was writing.

The next day we showed up at WNET studios in Manhattan to do a pre-scheduled show on Clay Cole's TV show to promote The Mystics' latest single. Our latest lead singer, Ralph Lizano, decided to pursue his songwriting career and Vini and Pete joined us. We found our dressing rooms with the help of Clay's production assistant. Clay popped into the room, and after the usual greeting and laughing congratulated us all on the merger. We were promoting "Darling I Know Now," as The Mystics, and were scheduled to be on the same show a week from that day promoting, "A Letter from Ann" as the Videls. Clay had a million questions as to how we were going to pull this off. "You guys are crazy, you can't do this, my producer is going to go nuts when he sees you back next week." I said, "Don't tell him, I don't think he will know. We all look alike to him anyway!"

We all broke up laughing and had a few drinks for the holidays (although we did not need the holidays to have drinks) before going to make-up. This was old school now. We didn't get nervous anymore. It was like a regular job. Although it was a big deal to go on television, it was getting kind of routine for us. We knew the lingo, we knew the camera angles and we knew our songs, we even knew some of the cameramen. We talked about everyday stuff up to the point that the music began, and the little red light came on the camera as it panned across our faces. We had our best smiles on, as we loved what we were doing. It was at the interview after the song that Clay began to worry about the interview with The Videls the following week. He told us before we went on that he was not going to go into the fact that we'd merged groups and just talked to me about the normal stuff, like where we were appearing as The Mystics, etc. He introduced each of us by our first names and thanked us. When we got back to the dressing room he said, "This is crazy, but I'll see you next week."

Clay interrupted. "Not only do I remember that story about you guys passing yourself off as two different groups, but I included it in my book."

That was just one reason why I liked his book!

We all took a short break and tended to our clothes for the show. There was still about an hour until show time.

The Videls – Peter (Anders) Andreoli, Vini Poncia, Herb Ricky, Bobby Cilitri, Norman Marzano

CHAPTER 25

A LETTER FROM ANN

We showed up the following week at Clay Cole's TV show as the Videls. Clay was laughing, and it was then I knew that he was as crazy as we were. He had officially turned into a New Yorker. What we were doing was not only unprecedented, it was nuts. Pete and Vini did most of the talking now that we were the Videls. No one at the production level, except Clay knew what was going on. Instead of worrying about what the circumstances would be, we went straight ahead as The Videls. We came out of the dressing room and walked the same route to the same spot during the commercial break. Clay was going over some things with his producer. When he turned around and saw us standing there in the same suits we'd worn the week before as The Mystics, his eyes went wide. "You guys are fucking crazy!" he said in a low tone, as he came over to us, so he would not bring attention to his surprise. Vini said "Well, we do have different ties," and with that, we all broke into uncontrollable laughter.

The performance was perfect. We didn't bother to change stage positions since Pete was still singing lead. The songs were very different but, of course, we looked the same. A few of the cameramen that we knew from our many appearances on Clay's show were aware of what we were doing and talked to us after our performance saying, with huge grins, that they never saw anything like that happen.

Clay did the interview with a straight face, directing most of the questions at Pete and Vini. We went back to the dressing room, changed and hung around waiting for Clay to finish up the show. Clay came in congratulated us on a great show, and after another round of laughter, we headed down to Little Italy to visit Vincent's restaurant for scungilli with hot sauce. We went there as often as we could. It was amazing how many people in Little Italy would recognize us and come over to talk. We got a lot of calls the next day from friends and relatives who'd watched the Videls on Clay's show. Everyone, of course, had lots of questions as to what was going on, but the most important call was from Jim Gribble. He wanted to meet us at his office. What he wanted to know was if we intended to continue and should he look for opportunities, since the Laurie contract was not going to be renewed. We were not sure which way we were going to go. A lot depended on Joe Sherman.

Since we all hung out together and Pete and Vini were without a group and still trying to record as The Videls, we helped with adding background parts with some of their recordings. We did the backup vocals, after a half-hour rehearsal in the studio for "The Party Starts at Nine." This song was written by Pete, Vini and Doc Pomus. It was released again when The Videls became The Tradewinds later in the sixties.

One night while rehearsing for our audition for Kapp Records with Joe Sherman, Albee decided that he didn't want to continue with us anymore. His girlfriend's father had offered him a position in his company, and like Bobby, he felt that our singing careers were not going well. He wanted to go back to work and make some money, especially since this was a good opportunity. I couldn't blame Albee for his decision.

It was around this time that The Mystics, were invited to Johnny's Maestro's 22nd birthday party at his girlfriend's house in Queens. At this party we met two girls, Vicki and Rose, who were trying to form a duet. They sang a little at the party and were very good and we asked Vickie if she wanted to join our group – basically because I was attracted to her. I called Vini the next day and asked him how he felt about putting a girl in the group to replace, Albee who'd decided to leave. After getting over the shock of Albee's departure, he said "Great idea, let's audition her." We all piled into my car and headed out to Queens, following the directions Vicki had given me earlier that day. She also told me that her parents would never allow her to sing with the group and suggested that Rose audition instead. We talked all the way out there about the possibilities with a female in the group. Aside from The Platters, The Skyliners were the only hit group with a girl in the background. We got to Vicky's house, narrowly escaping an accident on the way that would have probably ended all our careers.

We met Vicky's parents and wound up in the front porch, where the piano resided. Vicky played and sang a little with us as we waited for Rose to show up. We wanted Vicky but when Rose came in and sang, it was clear she had the better voice and did not have a parent problem.

We eventually met with Rose's parents, who were wonderful people, and although concerned, felt good enough about us to let Rose follow her dream. Rose's voice blended well with ours and we were all happy. I dated Vicki a few times after that first meeting, but it was soon apparent that we were not going anywhere. We did a few Skyliners songs, but it was on "My Prayer" that we realized that Rose fit. George and I were 22, Pete and Vini were 20 and Rose was probably 18 years old. We had a new direction! Vini told Joe Sherman that Albee had left the group and we now had a girl in the group and we needed a little more time. And so, the next step began. One of the hard things in forming a group that did not live in the same neighborhood was trying to find a place to rehearse and the time to do it. Here is where dedication, perseverance and will kick in.

Pete and Vini came down from Providence on Saturday February 11, 1961, and we rehearsed with Rose as much as we possibly could the whole weekend and perfected four songs for the audition with Kapp records, which was set for the following Wednesday.

The Mystics/Videls
L-R, Albee, George, Peter, Vini, Al

Johnny Maestro's Birthday, May 1961 (photo
courtesy of Grace Mastrangelo)
L-R, Paul Sherman, Santo Farina, Johnny Farina, Ralph Lizano,
Johnny Maestro, Al Contrera, Albee Cracolici, George Galfo (seated)

The Videls/Mystics
L-R, Pete, George, Rose, Al, Vini

CHAPTER 26

MY PRAYER

The audition was set up at the Kapp records office. Kapp Records was an independent record label started in 1954 by David Kapp with his brother Jack. David Kapp founded his own label after stints with Decca Records and RCA Victor Records. Kapp did not represent the typical rock and roll sound of the time but produced popular music artists like Jack Jones, Roger Williams, Jane Morgan, Buddy Greco and The Four Lads. Based on Joe Sherman's recommendation, David listened in on the audition. There were some A & R people, as well as some people we didn't know who looked very professional.

I got a strong sense that they were the promotional staff. We were all a little apprehensive while the introductions were going on, but I thought we did okay so far. Joe Sherman was surprised that we were not the same five people he'd met and was visibly disappointed that we showed up with a new member, Rose. We didn't think much of it at the time, but looking back it probably looked like we were not reliable.

Joe sat at the piano and guided us through "My Prayer," which went well. Pete was, as usual, fantastic. I thought we sounded great. We stood in a semi-circle with Pete on one end, and Rose in the middle. There were some nods and smiles but there was no applause at the end of the song, which was typical for auditions. There were some minor mistakes that only we heard, but I didn't think they were enough to sour the audition. The next song was a Skyliners song called, "This I Swear," which was flawless. Neither of these songs fell into the typical doo-wop rock and roll categories. Based on the type of artists Kapp was recording at the time, we thought, as Joe Sherman had advised us that these songs would fit into their genre.

We had coffee with Joe after the audition, and although he loved us, the Kapp team did not. Joe wished us well, and we could not figure out what had gone wrong. We were all disappointed after having such high hopes. Rose decided that this was the end for her. Her parents had let her try this, but there was no contract despite the countless hours of rehearsal, and reluctantly she told us she just could not continue. Georgie and I didn't know what to do but it was obvious that we were at the end of the road. Vini and Pete made plans to drive back to Providence in a few days to think about what they wanted to do. We were really feeling down. I had a job with my cousin Vic in his anodizing shop, but that was just giving me spending money. It was not a career. I talked to Bobby, who said he could probably get me a job as a draftsman where he was working. I was also getting concerned about the military draft. And so, by the end of February 1961, and for the first time in since 1957, I was not part of a vocal group. The Mystics' recording career was over.

Georgie called me a few weeks later and said that his father had a contact that could get us into the Air National Guard Reserve, which would help us avoid the draft. I was 21 years old without a career. My visit with the draft board had left me with a 1A status, which meant I could be drafted by the Army at any moment. Quite a few of my friends were getting notices. There was not much of a test to get into the Army, but there was a minimum two-year hitch plus reserve duty. I certainly was not contemplating going through the rigorous training necessary to be a Marine. The last time I went fishing I got sea sick, so I ruled out the Navy. I talked it over with Bobby, whom I trusted, my girlfriend Marcia and my cousin Conig, as well as my parents, and we felt that the Air National Guard was my best option.

Georgie felt the same way, so we went to Floyd Bennett Field in Brooklyn and met with the officer his dad knew. He explained that this was the Air National Guard Reserve which meant that we had a four-year obligation as reservists to go to meetings one weekend a month, plus two weeks every summer. We would not be drafted into the Army and would not be likely to go overseas. He also said that we would have to take a test to get in and, almost apologizing, said we would have to go to basic training, which might last three to six months. Perhaps he felt that we were important recording artists and that this was interrupting our careers. He didn't know that our careers were just about over. We found out later that the officer's 14-year-old twin girls loved The Mystics and of course we were more than happy to give them autographed records and photos. This was a lesson in using status to get things that would not normally come my way.

Georgie got a four-month trainee school gig, and I had a choice of either a Chaplain's Assistant, which had a four-month course or a Ground Support Service Equipment Repairman, which had a six-month course after six weeks of basic training. Of course, I selected the Chaplain's Assistant, and of course after my interview I was put into the Ground Support Service Equipment Repairman's course. George went off a few weeks ahead of me to San Antonio, Texas, for basic training and then on to school for a few months. He called and gave me a heads up on what to expect. It did not sound like fun. Bobby was already in the Army reserves, and Albee was not eligible to be drafted. Correspondence with Phil suggested that he would be getting out some time in the beginning of 1962. Georgie was scheduled to get home in August and me, if I left in June, in January of 1962.

I said my goodbyes to my family and friends with a small home gathering and spent some time with my girlfriend, Marcia, the night before. Conig drove me to Floyd Bennet field in Brooklyn the next morning where four other recruits were waiting to start Basic Training. At first, I felt like I was going to do a tour with some other artists until I saw the C-130 military transport sitting on the runway. I met Angelo Paladino, one of the recruits, whom I'd never met before and who happened to live two blocks from me in Brooklyn. We quickly became friends and have been ever since.

This was no luxury plane. It reminded me of the no frills bus we had on our Mid-west tour. It was a military transport plane that had benches positioned at both sides of the fuselage just like the in the war movies. There were parachutes which made us feel uneasy until one of the pilots said to use them as cushions, and now we were really nervous. Angelo and I found out that we would be in the same area in San Antonio and that made us feel a little better. Upon arriving, which took two days because the pilot made stops along the way to visit friends. We were greeted by screaming sergeants, instead of screaming fans, trying to scare the shit out of everybody, again just like in the movies. I couldn't help but think that this was kind of like what Phil was going thru except he had no choice, and it made me feel bad. We were reminded that we could not leave and that this was our new home and if we did not complete this training correctly we would have to start all over again. Angelo and I were split up and assigned to different barracks.

Most of the recruits were between 17 and 18 years old and from all over the country. Angelo and I were 21 years old and having grown up in Brooklyn were not easily intimidated. It didn't take me long to figure out what the game was, and my goal was to get out of San Antonio ASAP. The Drill Instructor, (DI) was a massive six foot four inch 25 year old southerner, with a crew cut and a red neck. He would be referred to as SIR from now on. He lined us up outside our barracks and yelled out, "You sissy Mary's probably packed too much stuff, so we're gonna pass by with a sack so you can lighten your load once we get inside." There were individual rooms that had bunk beds with four to a room and one room which only had two beds. The DI's room was opposite this room.

I took his statement to mean that if you want to have an easy time here, put something valuable into the sack. I don't think anyone else looked at it that way. We lined up inside and the Sarge walked down the line interviewing each recruit and taking note of what they dropped into the sack, held by his six-foot three inch assistant. He had a sheet of paper on a clipboard with our names and wrote notes as he went down the line. He would ask some questions, especially the kids from the south, like if they had hot and cold running water and if they had an inside toilet inside back home. To my surprise, many of them did not. I thought to myself that a lot of these people would become career military people. The first question he asked me was, "Are you Eye-talian?" I answered, "YES SIR" in a loud clear voice, the way he instructed us to answer questions. I wanted to just burst out laughing but realized this was not a good time to do this. His next question was, in a deeper southern drawl, "So are you from a Mafia family in Brooklyn?" I turned my head and looked at him directly into his eyes, although we were told *not* to look directly into his eyes, and answered, "NO SIR" and dropped my contribution into the sack. My eyes went back to the straight-ahead position, and I wondered when he would begin yelling at me to not look directly into his "fucking eyes." It never came, he did not answer. My contribution consisted of a shirt, some underwear and a black, leather-bound case. He raised his eyebrows and reached down into the sack and pulled out the case and opened it to find a brand-new Remington electric shaver. He put it in front of my face asked me if I was sure that I wanted to, "throw this away," and I answered, "YES SIR." No one could see what this was, as everyone had orders to look straight ahead. He glanced at his assistant, who had a slight smile, and made a notation on his list. He asked me how old I was and moved on to the next recruit.

He went into his office, left us "at ease," and returned in 20 minutes holding his clipboard and barking, "Okay listen up for your room assignments." The first assignment was for the room with the two beds, and he named me and a tall young man from Atlanta named James Cosgrove. He added that, "These two Airmen," as we were all called from then on, "will be your barracks chiefs."

I didn't know how good an assignment that was until a few days later, when we found out that we were excluded from all cleaning activities including latrine duty and KP (kitchen police). Of course, we were now in charge of 40 scared kids. We were all instructed as to cleaning the barracks and ourselves, and especially our closets and drawers. Everything had to be "white glove" clean. Jimmy and I quickly became friends, realizing how lucky we were to have landed the best jobs in the barracks. Jimmy's contribution to the sack had been a brand new extra-large sport jacket. We began putting our stuff away.

I found myself completely cut off from the world. I thought of my family, my girlfriend, my friends, and The Mystics, all of whom I missed very much. I could not help but think of Phil and how he must have felt. I decided to get through this the best I could and contemplated what I would be doing when this was over. I knew I didn't want to be in the anodizing business with my Cousin Vic. He was a great guy and made a good living, but I learned that being in business was tough. I knew how to be a shoemaker, having learned that from my father, but didn't see myself doing that for the rest of my life especially since I saw how hard it was for my father. I wanted to stay in music but staying in the music business was fading fast from my wish list mainly since The Mystics were not singing and The Videls simply could not afford to stay in New York.

The Four Seasons had just released "Sherry," which I heard from a jukebox while in the mess hall. "What a great record," I thought. "Damn, I miss music." Little did I know that in the months that followed, the music business would drastically change with groups like The Beatles and The Rolling Stones. I thought I probably would take Bobby up on his offer to get me into his place as a draftsman when I got out. After all, I did take some Mechanical Engineering courses in my first year in community college and I did have a great hand as a draftsman. The life of a recording artist was fading away. Except for a few brief telephone calls and letters, I had very little contact with anyone for seven months. Albee was working with his girlfriend's father, Bobby was working as a draftsman, Georgie would be working in his father's dry-cleaning business when he got out, and Phil was still away. I tried to stay in touch with Vini and Pete, who were not only pursuing their song-writing careers but making progress. I often wondered: if I'd had no choice but to stay in the music business, would I have been successful?

Airman First Class Al Contrera

CHAPTER 27

SAVE A DREAM

My cousin Conig would give me the neighborhood news through my weekly phone call. He said that Jerry the Jew was supposed to get released from his four-year rehabilitation stint in Comstock State prison. Jerry and Frankie Marino had been arrested and consequently convicted for holding up a Queens check cashing place in October 1957. Out of boredom and mostly for the extra "good time credit," Jerry enrolled in a high school equivalency course in Comstock and completed it in record time with surprising high marks. The warden was convinced he'd cheated.

Jerry looked at the time spent in jail as a way, to bolster his reputation as a wise guy. It was like building a resume, substantiating, in his mind and the minds of his fellow career criminals that he indeed was a pro because he'd done time without giving up anyone else. Getting arrested was part of Jerry's training, an annoying necessity. And to not be a rat was the most important thing in life. He lived by his own code of criminal ethics. It was like going to college for a degree: he got a course on how to deal with the realities of prison life in preparation for the future. One would think that this type of course, in prison, would demonstrate the way to avoid that dreadful life. I guess to guys like Jerry it did not seem dreadful. It was exciting. Jerry had gotten the word out from Comstock in 1959, when "Hushabye" was released, that he was proud of his neighborhood friends and if it wasn't for him our success would have never happened. He boasted to the other inmates that not only were The Mystics his friends, but he played a major part in their career. He told them about how he would hang out with us and, of course, how he'd gotten us furniture for the rehearsal room.

When my eight and one-half weeks of BMT (Basic Military Training) was completed, I was given two days' leave, which I spent with my new Brooklyn friend Angelo and a few of the other recruits in San Antonio before leaving for my school assignment at Chanute Air Force base, located in Champaign County, Illinois, south of and adjacent to Rantoul, Illinois, about 130 miles south of Chicago. Its primary mission was Air Force technical training. Chanute Field was established on 21 May 1917, being one of thirty-two Air Service training camps established after the United States entry into World War I. I took a long train ride to Chicago, where I, along with some other Airmen, was picked up by a military vehicle for the two-hour ride, to Chanute Air Force Base. Once again, I thought of Phil: I felt like I was doing time because I had no control over my life. Phil was preparing for his parole board interview, which he desperately wanted to pass.

I settled into a barracks that was surprisingly comfortable, compared to basic training. It was like the basic training housing in Texas, except it didn't come with the strict rules and "chicken shit" stuff. We were basically treated like students, going to college and living on campus. At our course introduction, our instructor, "Pappy," as he wanted to be called, informed us that many of the graduates of the Ground Support Equipment Repairmen's course would be offered jobs in the airline industry. I didn't think that this course, even if I was offered a job, would alter my life and cause me to venture into the world of United Airlines to repair the equipment that was sitting on the runway. Pappy was a career Air Force Sargent and an excellent instructor. He explained to our class of ten students that the reason we were selected for this course was that we scored high grades in mechanical aptitude. I did remember taking an entry exam but never thought it would be taken seriously.

School was from 8:00 am to 4:00 pm, with a 30-minute lunch break. We learned how to repair and service all the equipment that pulled up to the C-130 transport planes to support them while repairs and service were done on the planes, including the portable air conditioning, heating units and portable generators. We had weekends off, which were not that interesting because we were given various tasks related to our course. I had six months to go. It seemed like a lifetime. At least I was able to correspond with anyone I wanted to. I didn't have a phone in my room, but there was a pay phone in the barracks. I used it often, but I felt my identity slowly fading away. The course was intense, with homework to do after dinner.

There was a rotating KP duty list, which gave me some insight into what it was like to operate a restaurant feeding hundreds of men without worrying if anyone liked the food. I was committed to getting, at the very least, a passing grade to graduate, because if I failed, I would have to take the course over. I missed my Mom, Dad and brother Richie very much, and I missed my girlfriend Marcia.

At the midway point of our course, our instructor informed us that we would be getting a three-day pass. There wasn't enough time to get to New York, so I asked Marcia if she would like to visit me in Chicago. My last visit to Chicago had been the show at the Civic Opera House with The Mystics. This visit would be completely different.

Much to my surprise, she agreed, and we had a wonderful weekend at a decent hotel. I hated to see her go, but the fun was over, and I put her in a cab to the airport and took a train back to the base.

At this point, it could have gone two ways. I could either just quit, which was not a prudent option, or I suck it up and go on for three months, which was what I chose. The final three months were brutal, and I always thought that if I thought this was bad, what was it like for Phil? This is what got me through the last three months. During that time, the music was changing. Dion left The Belmonts and released "Runaround Sue," there were fewer groups and more single artists on the radio like Bobby Lewis, Del Shannon, Bobby Vee and Chubby Checker. Vini and Pete were writing and performing in Providence and were making progress as songwriters. The Passions were still performing, but only locally, and The Classics had landed a contract with Jim Gribble based on their original tune "Cinderella."

Phil was finally released from prison in the beginning of 1962. Two and a half years ripped from his life. "A horrible nightmare" was his description when I met him in Brooklyn a month later after I got home from my "not as horrible nightmare." My mom and dad invited Albee, Bobby, Phil and Albee with their girlfriends as well as Marcia to dinner the Sunday after I got home. Phil was with Eileen, Albee was with Barbara, Bobby brought his girlfriend (today his wife) Georgian and Georgie came with his girl, Gerri. I was thrilled to see my brother Richie, who seemed to have grown so much. We had a great lasagna dinner, which I'd missed so much, and caught up on many things. We had not seen each other for quite a while, and eventually the conversation drifted to music. Bobby, Albee and Georgie were still in the jobs they had before I left. At my suggestion,

Phil had reached out to Johnny Amplo's dad, Chris, who was influential in the electrical union, and he'd gotten Phil a job with a local electrical contracting company. After dinner, we decided to sing a few songs for old times' sake and they sounded as sweet as ever. I could see the happiness on everyone's face as we sang. I suggested we try to record again.

I spent the next few weeks getting myself together and realizing that our music career as The Mystics was probably over. There was no way to earn any money singing like we used to. Bobby suggested that I interview at the consulting engineering company he was currently working at in Valley Stream. About a week later, I interviewed with Frank Ruggiero at Caferielli Associates, owned and managed by Saverio Caferielli. Mr. Caferielli was an old-fashioned no-nonsense professional engineer. The interview was brief. Based on my community college courses in mechanical engineering and my drafting ability, and that Frank Ruggiero was a Mystics fan, I got the job. I started at minimum wage or $1.15 an hour, just about the same as we were getting as recording artists, but, of course, there was a lot less glory and no adoring fans.

The job was mostly drafting and tracing building architectural drawings to add the HVAC, plumbing, and electrical components necessary for the building to operate. Bobby had taken some design courses in the school he attended and was already doing design work. At this point, all I was did was draw whatever he and some of the other designers come up with onto the architectural drawings. Life settled into a normal zone. It was during this time we met and became lifelong friends with Pat Shurott, a senior designer at Caferielli. With the help of Pat, Albee and Phil got jobs as draftsman with us.

The Mystics were no longer stars but normal, everyday working people. The four Mystics took turns driving to work every day, while George worked at his new job at American Express as well as helping with his families dry cleaning business. And although there were no spotlights and screaming teenagers, it was proving to be another interesting chapter in the lives of five friends. We were still bound together by this incredible friendship. We all assimilated into a normal life in the neighborhood and would still hang out as friends during week nights and weekends.

We continued to work together in various engineering firms for the next forty years.

I stayed in touch with Vini and Pete, who were now working as song writers for Hill and Range and beginning to produce records, and

I suggested that we try to do something together with The Mystics. Vini told me he had a song that would be perfect for us and would let me know. I met Vini and Pete in the city a few weeks later, and they played a song they wrote for Elvis, "Save a Dream." It was supposed to be for one of his movies but was not selected by his team. It certainly had all the marking of a "Hushabye" follow up. I thought that since the original Mystics, including Phil, were back, we might have a chance at a hit record based on the strength of the song. We decided to try it. Vini proposed using Jimmy Crane's song "My Faithful Heart" as the B-side, since Jimmy was going to help produce this session. We had met Jimmy a few years earlier when we had been singing as The Videls in Providence. Jimmy, a big fan of The Mystics and The Videls, loved the idea of our singing his song.

I discussed it with the guys on our way to work one morning, and we thought it would be a great idea, especially for Phil, who had missed so much. I started to get that feeling again that we could have another hit record. In the back of my mind, I knew how much of a long shot it was but thought "if we don't try we'll never know." We met George that night and talked about it. Everyone was excited about recording, especially Phil. I set up a rehearsal for us, and the following week and we all got together at my house. It felt good, like old times. It was the first time in a long while that all of us were in the same room to sing. I played the demos, and everyone loved the songs.

It was strange to be learning a new song with Phil – especially without Jim, Gene and Elliot. The next rehearsal was in the city with Vini and Pete to go over the music arrangements. We had worked with the demos, so we knew basically how the songs should go. Phil had the lead down perfectly for both songs. We sang "Save a Dream," and although took a while to get the harmonies right, I could see how much more professional Vini and Pete were now than before. I was so proud of them. They really belonged in the music business. We worked out some key issues, changed a few things and scheduled a recording date for the following week. And so, in March of 1962, the original Mystics went back into a recording studio with Vini Poncia and Peter Anders as producers and recorded a new record.

A get together at Al's house (1963)

CHAPTER 28

ONE SUMMER NIGHT

In 1962, Jerry Rosenberg was released from his four years at Comstock prison and quickly hooked up with his old gang and started to go back to business as usual. Jerry heard that Phil was out and wanted to get together. He got in touch with Bobby through a mutual friend and we all went to meet Jerry at the 19th Hole. He was genuinely happy to see all of us and was full of questions, especially for Phil. Jerry invited a few of the other wise guys that were there that night to sit with us at a table in the back and ordered food and drinks for everyone. It was the party that both Phil and Jerry didn't have after getting out. A coming home from "college" party. We, of course, sang some a cappella with Jerry chiming in on one of his all-time favorites: "One Summer Night."

Jerry couldn't get enough of our stories about our last few years as The Mystics and we were fascinated by Phil and Jerry's stories of prison life. He loved the fact that we had met Dick Clark and Alan Freed and were really good friends with Clay Cole. He wanted to meet Clay and kept asking us about the girls we'd met on tour and the parties we'd gone to. He gave us regards from a few mutual neighborhood friends that he'd met while in prison and wanted a bunch of autographed pictures to send them.

It was strange because in his eyes we were still the popular group that he'd heard on the radio over the last couple of years. It seemed like time had stood still while he was away. It was impossible to explain that we were no longer in the spotlight and did not have any bookings. He didn't want to hear it. We talked about our new opportunity with our new recording. Of course, he wanted to help us in any way he could, but we knew what the outcome of that would be and just smiled and were friendly. "I could manage you guys!" he exclaimed. "You would be working every day."

The scotch was kicking in. "I have a dear friend in Vegas, I will call him tomorrow!" He then explained that he had to go to Texas to see his wife and kid and would get back to us when he got back in a few weeks. It was a great night and we all wished each other luck. Later, Bobby explained that not only was Jerry not allowed to be in a bar but would be jumping parole to go to Texas and if caught was sure to go back to prison. I was not surprised. Jerry had no fear of the law – or of anything else. He thrived living on the edge.

CHAPTER 29

THE WANDERER

On May 18, 1962, two Detectives, Luke Allan and John Wilson were assigned to cruise the Borough Park section along New Utrecht Avenue because of a recent rash of store holdups. They were in plain clothes and were driving an old taxi cab as cover. They decided to stop at the tobacco store on their way back to the precinct to pick up some cigars and candy. Luke Allan had 20 years on the job and was getting ready for retirement. He thought he had seen it all. He was tired of being a cop. He accepted the undercover assignment because he felt it would be something different, plus he wanted to be with his partner, John Wilson, who volunteered for the assignment.

Luke was a strapping six foot three inches. His undercover disguise was his own knock-around jeans, sneakers and short sleeve shirt. He saw many cabbies dressed like this. He and his wife thought he really looked the part. John had been on the force for five years and was looking to make sergeant soon. He wore a light gray sport jacket with blue slacks. His clean-cut blondish hair gave him the "passenger" look he wanted, like a college professor. He rode in the back seat and Luke drove. They switched roles every other day, the only difference being that Luke, no matter what he wore, looked like a cop in disguise.

The store owners knew the detectives and always welcomed them. Even though they were in plain clothes, it was still a form of temporary protection. In the background the radio played Dion's latest hit, "The Wanderer," while the detectives chatted with the Hayman brothers, who had owned this business for over 20 years, and left with some Cuban cigars and a box of chocolates which were "on the house," as usual, even though, as usual, they wanted to pay.

Irving and Louis Hayman were brothers who'd inherited the business from their father, Lester, who started supplying wholesale tobacco and candy to local candy stores during the Depression. Lester was a bookkeeper, and he contacted his book-keeping accounts that were in the candy and tobacco business and offered to do their books for free if they bought their supplies from him. This was a stroke of genius; Lester never lost money on the deal. It was a very successful business and eventually spun off into an accounting firm that his brother Arnold ran. Lester retired and lived in Miami with his wife, Dottie. Irving and Louis were thin and frail-looking and relied on Saverio Barelli, their only full-time employee, to do all the heavy moving and delivery of supplies. Sebbie, as he was called by his friends, was a tough-looking, hard-working Italian. At 25, with a wife and a kid, he needed this job and was very loyal. Orders were usually paid in cash, which Saverio would give to Irving, who would put it in the safe in the clothes closet at the back of the store. Sebbie did not know the combination, nor did he want to know it.

On this day, two men in their early twenties, one heavy, one slight, looked down at the Park Tobacco store on 48th Street from the elevated train station that ran along New Utrecht Avenue. It was late afternoon, a cool day for May but sunny and clear, with just a few clouds dotting the blue sky. The heavy-set guy was wearing a light jacket with jeans; his aviator style sunglasses covered a good part of his face. His partner was slight in stature, about 5'8, and wore similar aviator style sunglasses and a dark NY Yankees baseball jacket and hat with jeans and sneakers. They saw two customers walk into the store. The thin guy said, "Let's wait until they leave. It's almost closing time."

So, they waited. Then the two guys in aviator glasses came down from the train station and entered the store with handkerchiefs covering their faces and guns in their hands. "Okay, this is a stickup. Do as we tell you and nobody has to get hurt," announced the thin guy in as rough a voice he could muster. The two bandits had gotten a tip that the Hayman's were holding a lot of cash in the store because it was the end of the week. The thin guy herded the owners and Saverio into the back of the store while the other guy turned the small office behind the front counter upside down looking for the money. He thought for sure it would be in a cigar box. The heavy guy shouted in frustration that there wasn't anything there and started going to the back of the store. The thin guy, hearing this, slammed

Irving Hayman up against the wall, and in the struggle, he tightened his hand and the gun went off with a deafening noise.

The bullet lodged itself into one of the wood beams that supported the second floor after passing through the tin ceiling like a hot knife through butter. Everyone's attention was now diverted to the hole in the ceiling. Irving went limp and fell to his knees. He just could not bear violence. Saverio, feeling bad for his boss, instinctively yelled at the gunmen, who pressed the gun into Saverio's chest and told him to shut up. Saverio's legs weakened and he became nauseous. He helped Irving into a chair and motioned to Louis to sit in the chair next to Irving. He wanted to get them water but was afraid to ask for permission.

Both robbers were getting nervous. Their eyes met, and the expressions suggested a quick exit. This was taking way longer than anticipated. The thin guy started screaming and pushing at the trembling owners. He yelled, "Where is the fucking money, I'm gonna blow your fucking heart out." Saverio helped Irving stand up and handed his handkerchief to Louis, who was now in tears.

Meanwhile, Allan and Wilson, who were about four blocks away, decided to go back to the store to get some cigars for the other guys at the station house. They were always being teased that they had the best gig because of all the freebees, and they wanted to spread the wealth around. They had just double-parked in front of the store when they heard the gunshot that went through the ceiling. They glanced at each other. Allan drew his gun and hooked his badge on his jacket as he got out of the car. He tried to open the door, but it was locked, so he kicked it open and yelled, "This is the police."

The bright sunlight left Luke Allan at a disadvantage, and his eyes strained to adjust to the dim light of the store. The heavy thief, hearing the door slam open, ran to the front with his gun ready, and seeing a man with a gun pointed at him, opened fire with three rounds. finding Allan's chest and dropping him, dead, to the concrete sidewalk. The heavy-set thief was calm, as if in a trained military maneuver. His legs were apart, he was breathing calm and steady, his mind was focused on the task at hand. Looking at the lifeless body, his eyes darted back and forth waiting for something else to happen. He heard a voice calling "Luke, Luke" and saw the shadow of another person approaching the body. Within a second, he knew he had just shot a cop, and he figured there would soon be another. He also knew that this was a huge problem.

Wilson, on the heels of Allan, didn't have time to identify himself as a police officer, and he just fired all six rounds at the man who had just shot his partner, missing every shot. The heavy-set bandit fired his remaining rounds from a calm, kneeling position, hitting Wilson in the neck and the chest. Wilson toppled backward onto the sidewalk over his partner's body. Now Wilson, too, was dead. The sunlight that had obscured the vision of the two dead detectives now lit the remaining smoke from the discharged weapons still in the hands of the police officer.

The gunshot sounds were unmistakable. Some people ran away from the noise, but many ran toward the shots. The heavy-set bandit pocketed his gun and walked out the door, carefully avoiding stepping on the two bodies and the pooling blood and walked calmly around the corner while looking down with his hand over his face as if in shock, in case anybody was watching him. Then he disappeared into the neighborhood. None of the approaching people noticed him. They were focused on the two bodies, the bright red blood and the two smoking guns still in the hands of the victims.

The thin crook was in a state of panic after running to the front door to see where the shots came from. He saw his partner walking over the two bodies that were lying on the sidewalk. He spun around in a slow-motion circle, looking for another exit. Remembering that there was no back exit, he put his gun in his jacket and made for the front door. The handkerchief dropped from his face and he picked up a towel from the counter as he ran past Saverio, who had also run to the front door area with his bosses, who were now wailing in Hebrew. The thin man wondered if anyone had got a look at his face as he slipped through the front door. He wondered which way his partner had gone and noticed that people were gathering to look at the bodies. He thought that with all this confusion he would just walk out and act like he was just another bystander. Once outside, he dropped the towel to his side and walked past the people who were watching a good Samaritan tend to the detectives. A man who was bending down next to the fallen policemen glanced up as the thin gangster walked past but paid no attention. He made a quick right turn and tried to hug the building. With all the confusion, no one even noticed him as he quickly and calmly walked around the corner. He glanced back to take one more look as he got to the end of the building, where he made another right. More people gathered by the two bodies, Saverio was outside but was looking the other way. He made a mental note that no one was looking his way. He removed the baseball hat, jacket and sunglasses while he was walking slower now but very close to the building and held them under his arm until he put them into different garbage pails three blocks away. By the time, he disposed of the last article he heard the neighborhood explode with sirens.

It did not take long for everyone to find out that two detectives had been murdered in cold blood. There had never been a single cop killing in this neighborhood, much less a double killing. Within the hour, there were hundreds of angry cops at the crime scene. This would become the largest single police action in the city's history. Chief of Detectives Steve Hanson was put in charge. Within the next few hours, there were dozens of reporters on the scene with more on the way.

Chief Hanson's assistant, Captain Albert Seedman, told a reporter for the Daily News at the Borough Park crime scene that he had a good idea who had committed this terrible crime. Seedman continued to explain to the reporters that he and Chief Detective Hanson had been investigating reports that certain individuals were thought to be involved in a similar tobacco store hold-up a few weeks earlier. He could not explain to the reporter why they had not been arrested before.

Seedman called in a few favors with his friends at the Daily News and a story implicating Delvecchio and Rosenberg was released. The story indicated that the two robbers first surrendered to the detectives in the tobacco store, and as Allan went for his cuffs Rosenberg and Delvecchio opened fire with hidden guns. This story in the Daily News would go on to enrage every cop and citizen in the city. Seedman called in all his newspaper favors to feed the media fire. He thought that, like in the past, the more the press pushed the story, the more the public would believe it. Numerous press conferences were held. And some newspapers went so far as posting a reward for information leading to the arrest of the killers, Rosenberg and Delvecchio. Numerous press conferences were held.

Albert Seedman had all he could do to control the hundreds of cops who wanted to get involved with the case. Many offered to work on their own time. The initial crime scene investigation revealed no actual physical evidence. At this point in time, aside from what the Inspector said, there were no actual suspects. All they had was a description from Saverio and the Haymans, and a bullet hole in the beige tin ceiling, which Saverio proudly pointed out to the police at least six times. Some of the witnesses described the clothing, the hats, the sunglasses and the fact that they really did not get a good look at the gunmen's faces. The first break for the police came the next day, when one of the detectives working with Hanson found an old black baseball hat and a pair of black plastic sunglasses in two different garbage pails a few blocks from the crime scene. The Haymans, with the prodding of the Police, identified the sunglasses as the exact pair that were worn by the thin killer: black thick frames with thick side-pieces. This was not true. The killers wore aviator style sunglasses. The thick black glasses were traced to a neighborhood kid named Joey Shoes. because he was well known and that "Joey shoes" was scratched onto the inside of the wide black frame, so he was picked up and brought in. Joey worked in his Fathers shoe repair shop, so his nickname was "Joey shoes".

By now, everyone in the neighborhood was on alert. The police were questioning anyone that had a record.

Joey was scared, he had just turned twenty. His Uncle Tony was supposedly a wise guy, and Joey idolized him." He was a thin kid, slight built with brownish hair.

Joey shoes was put in a room by himself at the police station for a while, and his head was spinning with the thought of doing time. His Uncle Tony tried to pull some strings with the cops he knew, but it didn't work out. Seedman, who knew Joey and his Uncle Tony, walked in and said, "Look, we found your sunglasses in a garbage pail two blocks from the murder scene and we have a witness who thinks the person who put them in the pail looks like you."

Joey replied, "I don't know what you're talking about, I was at work at with my father when all this happened, just ask my father." After saying that, he had the scary realization that he'd taken off a little early to meet his girlfriend on 48th Street and 15th Avenue, two blocks from the murder scene. They'd had an argument, and she threw the sunglasses he gave her into a garbage pail. In the heat of the argument he never recovered them. He felt sick and broke out in a cold sweat. He was sure they would check out his story, but he didn't want to get his girlfriend, involved. Her father would be so pissed at him.

Seedman, knowing that Joey was nervous, suggested that he may have given his glasses to Jerry the Jew a few days earlier. Seedman knew Joey did not do it but if he could get him to testify that he'd given his glasses to Jerry, he might have something more than what they had now. Seedman said it again, "Are you sure you didn't lend your glasses to Jerry Rosenberg?" Seedman knew that Joey was always hanging out by the 19th Hole, which, of course, was Jerry's hangout, too. All he had to do was agree and he was out of there. Joey did not like Jerry because Jerry always ignored him. He wanted to hang out with Jerry and the other guys at the 19th Hole, but Jerry just treated him like he was invisible. He convinced himself that he hated Jerry, and so he agreed with Seedman that he gave Jerry his sunglasses.

The next day, several people claimed to have seen the killers as they ran from the store along New Utrecht Avenue after the shots were fired. The police added their spin, and now Anthony Portelli, a neighborhood teenager, was identified by a bystander and added to the list. Both Saverio and Irving, in describing the killers, said that the heavy-set guy looked like Anthony Portelli, who hung out on the next corner next to the Bar. Anthony always wore a baseball jacket and jeans, like the suspect, and also had a heavy-set build. They meant that they thought that Anthony looked like the suspect – not that he *was* the actual suspect.

Seedman sent a statement to the press that he had one of the killers in custody. He said he had the fingerprints of Rosenberg and Delvecchio on the guns, and that Delvecchio was the getaway driver. The guns were never found and there was no car: the killers fled on foot. Delvecchio, at the advice of his attorney, explained that he not only did not drive the killers, but had witnesses as to where he was at the time of the murders. An article was already being printed as the Daily News headline read, "Two Down, One to Go, in Cop Killer Hunt."

Emil said, "Hey wait a minute, I remember that. Didn't the newspapers print that Jerry dressed up like a woman to hide out?"

I had to smile at the image. "You're right, he did."

I heard from some of his friends, at that time, that Jerry was hiding out in his elderly aunt's apartment in the Bronx. She was practically blind, and in order to go outside, he slipped on one of her black housedresses, and with a black kerchief hiding his face was able to get to the corner to make phone calls without being spotted. He had a tough time squeezing into her black shoes, but it was only a block away, and although his feet were killing him, the disguise was perfect. He used a cane he'd found in her closet and went out after she went to sleep at 9:00 PM. He devised a limp based on his memory of Aunt Rosie after she had surgery on her feet, and the tight shoes helped. No one would question a hunched-over crippled old lady making a phone call.

He was hoping that this would all blow over and they would catch the killers until he read the newspaper that he'd gotten from the newsstand and knew he had to do something. This was not going away. It was getting worse by the hour. He knew Hanson had it in for him, and he had to head him off. Jerry thought, "That fat fuck Hanson has had it out for me for years and now he's going to try to pin these murders on me." Jerry spoke to his father and a friendly attorney and they decided to have a friend of his father, who worked for the Daily News, bring Jerry in to the Daily News office so he could tell his story without being in a police station. Jerry Rosenberg was a very bright guy.

A group of Daily News reporters questioned Jerry, who said that although he knew Delvecchio and Portelli from the neighborhood, he never did a job with them. He said, "I am being framed. His explanation for walking into the News and giving up to the police was simple. "I gave myself up because I am innocent. If I did it, I would be very far away by now." Seedman walked in with a team of police, and after some name-calling by Jerry, arrested Jerry and took him away in chains. The news photographers had a field day with the photos as the police moved very slowly with Jerry, his hands cuffed to leg irons, which made it hard to walk. He was eventually tried and convicted but I'll get into that later if we have time.

Clay said, we've got time, we're still OK."

Kenny said, "Yeah we got little more time, I've got to hear this."

I continued.

On April 15, 1968, six years after his arrest and while in prison, Jerry Rosenberg sued Steve Hanson, retired Chief Inspector of Police. This was the first time Jerry used the law instead of violence to get even.

Jerome ROSENBERG, Plaintiff-Apelles V. Raymond V. HANSON, Defendant-Appellant, No.649 Docket 72-2262 United States Court of Appeals, Second Circuit claiming that Hanson had "Caused him to be convicted by illegal means in lying and inflaming the public about him through various news media, and had deliberately fed the news false information, to slander and influence the courts, people and public against him". The jury agreed that Hanson "exceeded the limits of proper Police procedure" and returned a general verdict in Jerry's favor awarding him $7500 in damages. Jerry Rosenberg represented himself at that trail.

CHAPTER 30

MY FAITHFUL HEART

The recording session went extremely well. It was so gratifying to see Phil's happiness. If nothing else happened, if we did not get a hit record, if we were never on TV again, this day was outstanding. We all were thrilled to be together and recording again. Jimmy Crane sat in the control booth. Vini hired a few of the studio musicians they were currently working with and directed everyone. We changed a few background elements from the demo of "Save a Dream" and added some guitar and vocals to get a more "Hushabye" flavor.

We did "My Faithful Heart" as a group singing the lead lyrics in harmony, and it was fantastic. It was like many of the prior Mystics' recordings only this one had Pete doing a high falsetto. Both songs came out wonderful. Phil's lead was perfect, but Vini suggested that Phil do an overdub to fatten up Phil's voice and it sounded even better. We were all so pleased. After the session, we went to Vincent's for scungilli and talked about the possibilities.

It was always exciting to see our original autographed 8 x 10 photo on the wood wall in Vincent's. Maria, Vincent's wife, loved our group and would always put a bottle of red wine on the table "onna the house." The Passions' picture was in between photos of The Mystics and The Classics. Although we knew it was a million to one shot that we'd have a hit record, we were as upbeat as could be.

Sometimes we talked about Jerry's situation. Based on his attitude at our last meeting and his feelings about getting back with his wife and daughter, we found it hard to believe that he would be involved in another robbery. His manner was not that of a person who wanted to go back to prison so soon. Jerry was too smart for that. Besides, according to Jerry, at our "out of college" party he was rolling in dough. His take on the ongoing income producing activities of his associates for the last couple of years came to quite a bit of money. The neighborhood word was that Jerry was not involved in this tragedy. People were saying it was two guys from South Brooklyn but that the police were after Jerry. We thought the same.

Vini, Pete and Jimmy Crane loved the finished recording and assured us that it would sound even better after editing. A few weeks later, we heard the final edit and it was outstanding. They shopped it around town including Laurie records, who took a pass. We were disappointed and slipped further into acknowledging that it was not going to happen for us again. We would not be singing for a living again.

Over the years, we continued to have on-going, in-depth discussions with the Laurie team about royalties due us from our recordings. All talks ended with their saying "we will consider it" and "we'll get back to you." In similar on-going conversations with other artists, it became increasingly apparent that the record companies were cheating the artists.

We contacted Jim Gribble, who was now knee deep in new would-be rock and roll stars. Stan Vincent was running a lot of Jim's business and it was apparent that we were not going to get much help from them. Many of the groups who were now practically out of the music business were talking about attorneys who were representing them and considering starting a lawsuit against the record companies on their behalf.   W h i l e at work one day, Bobby and I calculated that "Hushabye," based on how long it stayed on the charts and how high it was in many areas around the country, probably sold at least twice as many records as we were told and got paid for. We thought that between "Don't take the Stars", "Hushabye" and "White Cliffs of Dover" we should have sold at least 750,000 records at .03 per record x 750,000 = $28,500 - $9000 already paid left $19,500 still due us. That would be approximately $160,000 in today's money. Of course, that was based on our calculation. Our new attorney agreed and thought we might even be a little light and offered us half of whatever he recovered once initiating the lawsuit. We all agreed that it was better than nothing, which is what we had at this point. It seemed that the music business, although having its bright spots, had a very dark side when it came to business. Most of the groups and single artists that we knew complained of how they were cheated, especially regarding royalties. Sure, they were also underpaid on personal appearances and ripped off by agents and managers but getting cheated on royalties hurt the most.

CHAPTER 31

PLEASE PLEASE ME

The Rosenberg double cop murder trial was to finally begin on October 17, 1962. The Classics were preparing to record "Till Then," The Passions were winding down, and the Mystics were holding on to a dream. The cop killings transcended all the other things that were going on in the neighborhood. We had heard through the grapevine, that there was no real evidence and that the prosecution was counting on an obscure law that the defendants were part of a conspiracy to commit armed robbery. This was a very similar situation to the one that had entrapped Phil in 1959. Everyone in the neighborhood followed the trial as if it were the World Series. Phil, having had first-hand experience, kept saying that they were so screwed and felt so bad for them. "Once those bastards have you in their sights, your dead" he would say.

Before the trial, Jerry's lawyer, asked Jerry if he would consider offers to plead for a reduced sentence. Of course, there where strings attached, like giving up his friends. Jerry continued to say that first, he was innocent and second, he was not a rat. Jerry lived by the rule of the street: no matter what, even if you hated the guy, you do not become a rat, especially when the police are involved. His lawyer pleaded with him to give them Delvecchio, "then you can plead guilty to armed robbery which you will get a max of eight years." "No fucking way" Jerry yelled, thinking he was getting framed. Jerry felt his lawyer was an idiot and that he himself could do a better job. He didn't see a way out of this. None of the three defendants had made any sort of statement or confession. They all stood by their initial statements that they were innocent. None of them would give up anyone even if his life hung in the balance.

It took over six weeks to appoint attorneys for Rosenberg and Portelli, and the alleged suspects spent those six weeks in four different jails without bail. During that time, Jerry continued to suffer. The Delvecchio family hired a lawyer who started immediately working on the case. The District Attorney was having a difficult time making a case because there just wasn't any hard evidence linking the suspects to the murders. The only thing the DA had was a so-called, eye-witnesses. Not one of the suspects admitted to anything nor was there any physical evidence despite the hundreds of police who searched the crime scene. No guns were ever found.

With the constant prodding of Seedman and Hanson, the three suspects were finally charged under an obscure provision of the NY State Penal Code whereby all suspects in an armed robbery (felony) resulting in murder could be charged with first degree murder. All the state had to prove was that they conspired to commit armed robbery. They were indicted by the same court officials who had presided over the gas station murder trial of Dennis Smith (Smitty) in 1959.

There were numerous delays and setbacks during the weeks that followed, pushing the trial start seven months into the future, mostly because of the lack of evidence. The defense attorneys insisted that the trial begin but they kept getting denied. During that time, all the suspects were asked many times to plead guilty to lesser charges and give up the other guys. They all refused. The presiding Judge took a leave of absence due to illness and Judge Leibowitz was assigned to the case. His reputation as one of the toughest and smartest judges on the circuit was widely known and widely feared. Jerry now had not only the entire NYC police department against him but also the toughest judge in town. Delvecchio's attorney, was equally terrified. During a time when he was a prosecutor in Leibowitz's courtroom, he witnessed Judge Leibowitz preside over various juries that returned a guilty verdict in most cases. It was known in law circles at that time that Leibowitz had an uncanny ability to predict how jurors would vote just by questioning them. During trials, he used body language, which would not show up in court records, to convey his opinion. He also worked closely with young prosecutors, guiding them in his chambers towards a direction that would eventually, somehow, end with a decision that he favored.

Portelli's attorney, attempted various defense motions to change the venue and appeal to the court, showing that these defendants were treated unfairly during the initial arrests, negative newspaper portrayals of their characters. Every attempt was flatly answered by the judge with, "Motion denied." The suspect's lawyers tried in vain to convince Judge Leibowitz that after their arrests, their civil rights were violated because they were portrayed as murderers by the newspapers. He flatly denied their motions and set the trial to begin on January 14, 1963, 11 days before the Classics were to record "Till Then", and 11 days after the Beatles launched an unprecedented attack on the American music business by releasing "Please Please Me."

Delvecchio's lawyers found that Delvecchio and Barilla had been before Judge Leibowitz before. At that time, it was reported that Leibowitz told the young defendant that he was a "potential holdup killer." Delvecchio's lawyer asked that Leibowitz disqualify himself because of the prejudicial nature of that statement. Leibowitz denied the motion.

The witnesses were getting nervous, especially after Seedman's latest newspaper interview, where he named the suspects as a major part of the mafia element in Brooklyn. The Haymans, who by now really believed they'd seen Jerry and Portelli, wanted the police to do something. Typical of their business nature, they negotiated a deal for their testimony. They said they were concerned that someone from the mob would visit them, so Seedman promised the Hayman's full time protection in return for their testimony. He had a detective go to work at the Boro Park tobacco store every day. The only difference between him and the other workers was that he carried a gun. The Detective was assigned to work in the store until the trial was over. When it came time for the Haymans to identify the killers at the trial, they positively identified Portelli and Rosenberg. He admitted that they were wearing handkerchiefs and sunglasses but was sure he caught a glimpse of them when they were running out of the store. When asked what kind of sunglasses, he responded with, "Aviator type."

Jury selection was taken over by Judge Leibowitz. Jerry, who was now working as hard as his attorney, felt that this judge was steering the selection his way by his remarks and gestures towards potential jurors. There was a great deal of tension in the court room as the trail finally began. Leibowitz had the jury sequestered, with 24-hour protection, claiming there were threats to their families, although there was never any proof or even a hint that that was true. Of course, this did not sit well with the jurors. Jerry and his attorney viewed this as a maneuver to get the jury to quicken its pace towards a guilty verdict.

Typically, defense attorneys can cross-examine potential jurors. In this case, Leibowitz, to save the taxpayers' money, decided to shortcut the process by eliminating certain people despite the hundreds of objections. Jerry and the other defendants had to stand at attention while the jurors were asked if they personally knew them. There was not one question as to whether any of the jurors knew *about* them being in the newspaper.

During the first days, both Haymans identified Jerry and Portelli as the killers who held them up even though they never saw, only heard the gunshots and admitted in the press articles that due to the shocking nature of the event, they "couldn't remember much of anything." Under cross examination, they admitted that the perpetrators wore masks and glasses, but they claimed to catch a glimpse of them as they ran out. If the shooting was done at the door and the Haymans were not near the door how could they see them running out?

Next on the stand was Johnny "Bat" Batilli, who initially said to Detective Hanson that Portelli and Jerry did it. He said that because he was forced to go to the police station where he was convinced and finally agreed to sign anything they wanted. He would have confessed to the murders if they wanted him to. The court was in shock.

Leibowitz looked around the courtroom and condemned the police tactics. He then calmly asked Johnny if his testimony was based on what the Police did and Johnny said "Yes." He then asked Johnny if he thought that his testimony was truthful, and Johnny replied "yes." And with that, he declared a 15-minute break.

Batilli would not return to the courtroom because he said as he was leaving, he was threatened by a gesture of someone in the court. Leibowitz ordered the doors locked and Batilli brought back in, with armed police protection. Leibowitz asked Batilli to point out the person who made the threat. Batilli responded, "I'm not sure, I couldn't see very well."

Leibowitz slammed his gavel, silenced the court and adjourned for the rest of the day. His parting statement was that Batilli "is clearly terrified by someone in this courtroom," pausing between words as his eyes narrowed and he searched for the guilty party. It was as if he possessed some special superhero vision that could discover the bad guy.

Nine years later, while serving time in Attica with Jerry, Johnny Bat told a different story. He signed an affidavit swearing that everything he'd said at the Portelli/Rosenberg trail was fabricated by the police and that the police threatened to arrest his wife for prostitution and even threatened to hurt them both if he didn't testify against Portelli and Rosenberg.

The defense attorneys decided not to put their clients on the stand for fear that their prior records, which could be exploited by the DA, would make it worse. The defendant's alibi witnesses were not brought in because each one was a known criminal with a record that would also be exploited. The attorneys thought that this would undermine any testimony any of them would give because a jury would not believe a known criminal, especially with Leibowitz at the helm.

The last prosecution witness was "Joey shoes". He testified that he remembered not only lending his glasses to Jerry but also hearing Jerry and Delvecchio planning the robbery in a candy store. This was, of course, another lie told by a potential suspect. After asking Joey to put on the sunglasses and hat recovered from the scene, the defense attorney pointed out that he looked very similar to Jerry Rosenberg. They had the same slight build, same facial features, and same wavy hair. He pointed out that "If Seedman had Joey's picture in his pocket instead of Jerrys, it would have been Joey shoes not Rosenberg that would be on trial today." No one brought up the fact that Seedman gave Joey an out when he'd asked him when he lent his glasses to Jerry. And no one remembered that Joey's sunglasses were not aviator glasses as originally described by the Haymans. That statement was no longer in the records. Jerry was fuming. He leaned over to his attorney and said, "This is such bullshit. Can't you do anything?"

"Look Jerry, this is not going to go well. Leibowitz has a real vendetta against you guys. I'm running out of options, I'm sorry." Jerry wanted to stand up and explain everything, but knew he was powerless.

The only piece of physical evidence even remotely connected to the robbery was a single thumb print found on a ripped piece of wax paper on the floor. The prosecution provided an expert who testified that the finger print was, without a doubt, Portelli's. This expert assured him in private that the print was too small to read, but changed his mind on the stand, saying that it was in fact large enough match Portelli's print on file with the FBI. Portelli's attorney argued that anyone could have handed him that paper at any time after the so-called crime. "They could have offered him a ham sandwich wrapped in wax paper!" yelled, Delvecchio's lawyer. Delvecchio's boss, testified that he and Del, as he called him, were picking up brick in N.J., for a job that they were doing. This was on the day the police said Delvecchio bought the guns in Brooklyn.

After that, Jerry sat through agonizing hours of listening to testimony from friends who, he knew, were lying because the police threatened them. He felt helpless. All the defendants' attorneys agreed not to put them on the stand because that would have given the prosecution an opportunity to cross examine them, and because of their prior records, this would surely have prejudiced the jury against them.

The trial continued, with Leibowitz knocking down every request by the defense to instruct the jury to disregard a questionable statement. During the last days of the trial, Judge Leibowitz, upon hearing compelling evidence from witnesses that Delvecchio was at a birthday party in Connecticut during the time of the hold-up, declared a mistrial for Delvecchio, which released a frenzy of mistrial claims from the other defense attorneys. These were all squashed by Leibowitz.

The summation was long and covered all the points required to convict. Of course, he never mentioned that the sunglasses were not Aviator type, that anyone could have given Portelli something to touch during the months that he was in jail, that the murder weapons were still missing, and that the witnesses' stories were inconsistent. The defense attorney's final remarks were just under an hour, as were the others, who brought out the various facts to support the plaintiff's innocence, as well as the confusion about the alleged robbers running past the fallen detectives.

The jury came back with a verdict within three hours. Jerry and Anthony Portelli, who were shackled to a bench, were brought into the courtroom in leg irons and chains. "How do you find as to the defendants Anthony Portelli and Jerome Rosenberg?" asked Leibowitz. And on February 18, 1963 the jury spokesperson said, "Guilty under the felony murder statute, your honor, with no recommendation for mercy."

In anticipation of what was to follow, the judge grabbed his gavel and pounded away as the law enforcement community cheered and the families and friends jeered.

Ironically, a movie called "The Trial," directed by Orson Welles and starring Anthony Perkins, was currently playing in theatres about the corrupt court system. Jerry's and Phil's arrest and subsequent trials were also, oddly similar to another movie based on the true story of prize fighter Rubin "Hurricane" Carter, who'd been convicted of murder in 1967. In

1985, A Judge with the United States District Court for the District of New Jersey set aside the convictions, and Carter, 48 years old, was freed

The neighborhood went wild after hearing that Jerry had been convicted. Every corner hangout discussion focused on the outcome of this trial and the obvious ridiculous decision. The newspapers applauded the judge and jury, but we all deplored them. Based on what we knew had happened to Phil, we all felt that this was another gross mistake.

Leibowitz waited three weeks before pronouncing sentence. In a statement to the defense attorneys, later carried by the press, he said, "They got a fair trial, the evidence was overwhelming." He asked Jerry if he had anything to say before the sentence. Jerry slowly got up, adjusting the chains so he could stand straight. His jaw was tight and clenched, and the strain of this massive weight was written all over his face. He cleared his throat and looking straight into Leibowitz's eyes said, "You keep saying that this was a fair trial. This was not a fair trial, this was a lynching. And the fact that you keep harping on the fair trial only means that you know deep in your heart that it wasn't." Before Jerry finished the last word, Leibowitz cut him off with his gavel while shouting at the top of his hoarse, tired voice, "Jerome Samuel Rosenberg, I hereby sentence you to be executed in accordance with the law during the week of March 31, 1963."

Jerry, now completely enraged, tried to leap the thirty feet to the bench but was held back by his chains and two enormous security officers. While pointing at the judge, Jerry yelled, "You're the murderers! You, the DA, Hanson, Seedman and the whole fucking police department are the murderers!"

Leibowitz screamed back, "Get this killer out of my court and transferred to the Sing Sing death house now! I will sign the order this afternoon." He then got up and left the courtroom, his black robe swirling behind him like a sorcerer's.

Delvecchio, who was tried as an accessory and found guilty, was retried a few months later. This time when a young girl, who said she was with him, got on the stand; and broke down under questioning and told the truth. She said that both Seedman and the DA threatened her. The presiding judge, was outraged at the actions and asked the District Attorney to look into this post haste. Because of Jerry's criminal record and a side conference with Seedman, they never considered Jerry's case, but on June 5, 1964, a jury in a re-trial found Delvecchio not guilty and he was set free.

CHAPTER 32

WALK LIKE A MAN

On February 19, 1963 while "Walk like a Man" by the Four Seasons was approaching number one in the country, Jerry Rosenberg and Anthony Portelli, astounded at where they'd wound up, began to wrap their heads around the fact that they were probably never going to see, their 28th birthdays. They were sure they would not leave Sing Sing alive. They established residency in their new homes, eight-foot-wide by twelve-foot-long steel cages, like something you would see at a zoo. Each cell was equipped with a metal cot, one sheet, one blanket, one pillow, a toilet bowl, a metal stool, one towel and a sink with only cold water. Their new keeper, a guard named Roger, oversaw them from this time forward. Shaving happened every morning when Roger passed a razor with a bowl of warm water and soap through the cell bars and watched until the final splash of water rinsed the soap off. He collected everything. Next up was a half hour of supervised exercise in a tiny outside yard. You could bounce a ball if you were lucky enough to get one.

The worst part for Jerry in his new home was his title, "cop-killer." He could think away most of the lies that had been thrown at him, but he despised this description. His execution was on his mind ever since reading in a newspaper article: Two thousand volts of electricity will instantly boil blood and within two seconds destroy the heart, causing death.

Jerry could not get over the fact that Delvecchio was acquitted and he and Portelli were in the death house. He spoke to his family, who hired a high-priced attorney, to formulate an appeal. At the time $10,000 for an attorney was a lot of money, about $200,000 in today's money. Jerry convinced himself by fantasizing that this appeal, based on Delvecchio's situation, might just work.

There are no secrets in the death house, and Jerry's new neighbor, wasted no time in educating Jerry about his new nightmare. He boasted, through the bars in his cell, about how he was doing his own law research. Jerry, half-listening, thought, "This guy is nuts." He explained that based on the law books he read, he was going to get his conviction thrown out on the grounds of prejudicial pre-trial publicity.

"What did you just say?" Jerry's brain lit up like a Christmas tree. Jerry got hold of some of his law books and started reading. He didn't understand a lot of the words, but the following passage made perfect sense. *"Every person accused of a crime is entitled to have a fair and impartial trial before an unbiased court and unprejudiced jury, regardless of any preconceived opinions that may exist as to the conclusiveness of the evidence against him."* The more he read, the more he realized how little he knew and how much there was to know. Another passage about changing venue when jurors might be influenced by adverse sentiments was especially interesting. It was like someone reading a structural steel engineering manual and thinking he could build a bridge the next day. It seemed overwhelming, but he had nothing to lose.

Accepting the fact that he would probably die in the electric chair, he made up his mind that he would fight with the tools of the establishment: the law. It was better than thinking about what he was missing. This is exactly what drove Phil crazy: thinking about what was going on at home while he was in his cell.

Jerry threw himself into this new, unfamiliar world of law and became obsessed with finding a way out of this nightmare. The more he read about the law, the more pissed off he became at the absurdity of it all. Especially when he read the line, *"No one can be convicted of a crime he did not intend to commit."* This lit a fire in his brain that never went out. In fact, it grew with every thought of how he'd been framed and how the authorities engineered the story using their influence with the newspapers.

It makes me wonder, and in a way, feel guilty that we did not think about doing this for Phil. And why didn't his attorney do more? But who were we? Just ordinary teenagers with no idea how the law worked. As with many people, we just accepted the outcome as it is, trusting the lawyers to do the job they do, just like you trust your doctor to give you the right medicine.

Jerry concluded, after the first two weeks of study, that his constitutional rights *had been* violated because of his right to due process and equal protection under the fifth and fourteenth amendments of the Bill of Rights.

We had lost all contact with Jerry at this point as he slowly faded from the number one topic in conversations on the corner. Some of us followed his life through the various articles in the newspapers and were astounded when we read that in the following years, Jerry got himself out of the death house in 1965 with a brilliant appeal directed at Governor Rockefeller based on what he had learned of the law on his own. Jerry was transferred to Attica, where he arranged for a steady supply of law books, mostly from his parents and a few from the prison library and immersed himself in this new world.

Four years later, Jerry earned a law degree from the Blackstone Career Institute. Prior to Jerry, no inmate in the state of New York had ever earned a law degree while in prison. During the 1971 Attica Prison riot, Jerry provided legal advice to those leading the uprising and assisted in negotiating the riot's resolution. Jerry was then transferred to the Sing-Sing Correctional Facility. As a jailhouse lawyer, he frequently assisted other prisoners with legal issues and it's estimated that he was involved in over 200 lawsuits. They transferred him to Wende Correctional Facility in 1991, serving, among other positions within the prison, as paralegal assistant for three years in the law library. In 2009, Jerry was transferred to the prison hospital, where he died of natural causes at the age of 72.

Jerry served 46 years in state prisons, the longest of any inmate in New York State penal history. He even argued a case in front of Judge Leibowitz and won the case. Leibowitz remarked, "When I send them away, they never come back – except for Jerry Rosenberg, who not only came back, he came back as a lawyer." He also told Jerry's parents that had their son decided to take up the law instead of crime he could have been one of the greatest lawyers of his generation.

CHAPTER 33

CRAZY FOR YOU

The years following our last recording of "Save a Dream"/ "My Faithful Heart" with the original Mystics were full of advances in the family and engineering worlds – instead of in the music business. In the years that followed, Phil married Eileen, Albee married Roberta, Bobby married Georgian, George married Elaine and I married Florence "Lucky" Pagnotta. We were in each other's bridal parties, performed at each other's weddings, and continued to be close friends through the years. We did some local work with The Mystics when the opportunity came up, but the music as we knew it had completely changed with The Beatles, The Rolling Stones and the onslaught of the British groups. American groups like The Four Seasons, Jay and the Americans and the Motown sound survived, but our music, had died. The Beach Boys also continued having success with their music and in 1964 released an outstanding version of "Hushabye" on their "All Summer Long" album that blew our minds.

In the late sixties, several early rock and rollers like Little Richard, Chuck Berry, Jerry Lee Lewis, Carl Perkins, Bill Haley & His Comets and Bo Diddley, who had been out of fashion since the British Invasion, experienced a resurgence in popularity, performing their old hits to old and new music fans. Rock and roll revival festivals became popular, mostly because of Richard Nader's revivals shows at Madison Square Garden. The DJ's at New York's WCBS FM, like Don K Reed, Joe McCoy, Norm N. Nite and many others across the country, never stopped playing rock and roll music but now started calling it "oldies" and "golden oldies" music, after an album series of the same name, which was sold through bulk TV commercials and did extremely well. The Laurie record team produced many of these new "oldie" albums. The DJ's also started to define the music further and called the music recorded by groups "doo-wop" music.

Many people in the music industry agree that the first record to use the syllables "doo-wop" was the 1955 hit "When You Dance" by The Turbans. The term "doo-wop" first appeared in print in 1961 in the *Chicago Defender*; fans of the music coined the term during the height of a vocal harmony resurgence. The phrase was attributed to radio disc jockey Gus Gossert who noted that "doo-wop" was already in use in California. Doo-wop peaked in 1962 and slowly faded as the British music came on the scene. Doo-wop's influence continued in soul, pop, and rock groups of the late1960s. There is no doubt that the recording artists of the fifties influenced The Beatles and The Rolling Stones.

Singer Bill Kenny became known as the "Godfather of Doo-wop" for introducing the "top and bottom" format in the early 1950's, which featured a high tenor singing the lead and a bass singer reciting the lyrics in the middle of the song. Bill Kenny (1914 –1978) was a pioneering African American tenor vocalist with a vocal range spanning four octaves. Often regarded as one of the most influential high-tenor singers of all time, Kenny was noted for his "bell-like" vocal clarity and impeccable diction. Although he is most famous for his role as lead tenor with the Ink Spots, Kenny also led a successful career after disbanding the Ink Spots in 1954. Throughout the 1950's and 60's, Kenny recorded, toured the world and appeared on many popular television shows. In 1966, Kenny became the star and host of his own musical variety show The Bill Kenny Show. Eleven years after his death, Bill Kenny was inducted into the Rock & Roll Hall of Fame.

In 1968, my sister-in-law, Judy Pagnotta and her friend Billy Mandile, knowing I was always looking for talented bands, recommended I see a local four-man group playing at the Flatbush Terrace in Brooklyn. I walked into the bar not expecting to hear much and was pleasantly surprised. They were very good, and I approached them after their set, introduced myself, and said I was looking for a back-up band for my group, The Mystics. They knew the group, and after a short conversation where I assured them that they would have time to continue their gig at the bar, they agreed to be our back-up band. We set up rehearsals, so they could learn our show. Our first show was at a popular Brooklyn night club called The Penthouse.

Joe Esposito was the lead singer and played guitar, Eddie Hokenson was baritone and played drums, Bruce Sudano was the tenor and played keyboards, and Eddie's brother Louie was also a tenor and played bass. We got together whenever The Mystics had a show, which was not too often. There were not many gigs and they did not pay very well. At around this time, Vini and Pete opened their own record company in New York City with Frankie Mell, a music producer, and called it MAP City Records. I would usually stop there after my job at the engineering company and hang for a few hours to watch the recordings and talk with Vini and Pete. I was so proud of what they had accomplished up to this point, and they would always show me their latest projects and songs. Vini said that they were always looking for new material.

I told Joe Esposito about my friends at MAP City, and we decided to start writing songs. We wrote a few songs and I set up an appointment. After Vini and Pete heard Joe sing our songs, they signed us up as their new songwriting team. They were especially impressed with Joe's vocal talent. There was no doubt in any of our minds that Joe was gifted with a fantastic voice. Vini and Pete helped us out with the writing, and I was now into a renewed music career, while working at my day job and taking care of my family, which now consisted of my wife Lucky and my daughter Christine, with my daughter Dina on the way. Joe also had a day job and a family, and we often talked about how great it would be to just concentrate on music.

We wrote some tunes together which were not recorded by anyone except for the demos that Joe and I did at the MAP city studios. Months later, when Vini teamed up with Richard Perry to produce an album for Ringo Starr in Los Angeles, he called me from LA and asked if I would be interested in going out west to be part of the vocal back-up group, and although it was so tempting, I just could not go. I had a family and a career in engineering. It was a decision that I often ponder. I told him that Joe Esposito was available and obviously much more talented than I was, and off Joe went with Eddie on the adventure of their lives. They not only did the back-ground vocals with Vini and Paul McCartney but through many related contacts, including another Brooklyn-born Casablanca record executive, Susan Munao, eventually met Neil Bogart of Casablanca records.

Bogart (Neil Scott Bogatz) was born in the same neighborhood as Joe, Bruce and Eddie, and there was this connection that occurs whenever you meet a fellow Brooklynite. He grew up in the Glenwood housing projects in the Flatlands section of Brooklyn, the same area as Joe, Eddie and Bruce. He was a singer in the 1960's, using the name Neil Scott. He had little success as a singer but went on to become a producer at Buddah records at around the same time as Vini and Pete. Casablanca became known as the studio of dance icons Donna Summer and Giorgio Moroder, KISS, and the Village People. Giorgio Moroder, also known as the father of disco, produced many of Donna Summer's recordings for Neil and worked with Joe Esposito on some of his own projects.

In 1969, Vini and Pete released "The Anders & Poncia Album," produced by Richard Perry. In my opinion, it's one of the greatest albums ever produced. Anders and Poncia also formed The Tradewinds and The Innocence while working for the Kama Sutra label formed by Arty Ripp. Arty Ripp was an original member of The Temptations, a white New York vocal group who recorded "Barbara." In 1965, the Tradewinds' debut single "New York is a Lonely Town" reached #32 on the Billboard Hot 100.

During the 1970's, Vini and Pete went their separate ways for a while, and with the help of Richard Perry, Vini became Ringo Starr's co-writer and produced several of his albums: Ringo (1973), Goodnight Vienna (1974), Ringo's Rotogravure (1976), Ringo the 4th (1977), and Bad Boy (1978). Vini also produced albums for Melissa Manchester and Lynda Carter. He wrote songs for Jackie DeShannon, Martha Reeves, and Tommy James. Vini is also listed as co-writer on "You Make Me Feel like Dancing" with Leo Sayer, which won a Grammy. He then produced Peter Criss's 1978 Irvingo album and at Criss's request produced Kiss's 1979 album Dynasty. He sang backup vocals and helped with songwriting on both albums. In 1981, he produced the album, "Turn out the Lights" for the band Tycoon. In 1985, Vini also produced the Detroit rock band Adrenalin with "Road of the Gypsy," from the film *Iron Eagle*. Poncia produced Criss's second post-Kiss album, 1982's Let Me Rock You.

Vini and Pete stayed on their musical course. They also worked with Phil Spector and became members of Spector's house band, the infamous "Wrecking Crew." This crew included Nino Tempo, Leon Russell, Glen Campbell, Hal Blaine, Joe Osborn, and Sonny Bono. Pete and Vini composed songs for most of Spector's artists, including Darlene Love, The Crystals and The Ronettes, for whom they wrote two of their biggest hits, "Do I Love You" and "The Best Part of Breaking Up." They also produced several other records including Cher's first recording, "Ringo, I Love You" (released under the name "Bonnie Jo Mason").

I often wonder what would have happened to me if I had accepted Vini's invitation to go to Providence and write with them when The Mystics and The Videls' association disbanded. Instead, George and I went into the Air National Guard.

In 1970, Larry Marchak, who was an editor at *Rock Magazine,* decided to partner with CBS to put on live shows with original groups from the fifties. Larry had the task of finding and reuniting many of the groups for a "Revival Concert" at the New York Academy of Music. This proved to be a huge success and pumped life into an otherwise dying style of music. We were approached by Larry and agreed to do the show which also starred, The Dubs, The Harptones, The Cleftones, The Bobbettes, The Dell Vikings, Don & Juan, Sonny Til and The Orioles, Danny and The Juniors, The Cadillacs, the Skyliners and The Passions with the original Freed Band.

We were excited and happy. We got together and rehearsed. The producers wanted it to be as authentic as possible and even published a program, like Freed did. We met many of our old music business friends at the show, which was as much fun as dong the show. A live album was released, but it did not do well.

Still, some of our music friends were thriving. After a very successful career with Jay and the Americans, Kenny Vance began producing and scoring for the movie industry. Kenny and I always stayed in touch, and he called me one day and said that he was working on a movie called *American Hot Wax* (1978), which was a story about Alan Freed, and it reminded him of The Mystics' story. He wanted to use the original Mystics as one of the groups in the film, but between our family ties, our engineering careers, the travel to LA, and the money involved, it was not going to work out. I said that Joe, Eddie and Bruce were now working with Vini in LA, and Kenny contacted Vini, who vouched for the Brooklyn back-up singers, who had just signed up with Casablanca Records as The Brooklyn Dreams. Vini set up the meeting and they were cast in the movie as "Professor La Plano and The Planotones," with Kenny as the professor. Years later, they became known as Kenny Vance and the Planotones.

The Brooklyn Dreams are best known for their collaboration with Donna Summer on "Heaven Knows," which featured Joe sharing the lead with Donna, and "Bad Girls, which they co-wrote. Giorgio Moroder asked Joe Esposito to collaborate on his 1982 "Solitary Man" project, which became Joe's first solo album. Joe is best known for his performances of the hit songs "Lady, Lady, Lady" from the Solitary Man album and the 1983 film *Flash dance,* and "You're the Best" from the 1984 film *The Karate Kid*. One of my favorite songs which he wrote.

In the late seventies, we met stockbrokers turned producers Frankie (Lanz) Lanziano and Joe Contorno, who teamed up with veteran music producer Tony Delauro. They picked up where Marchak left off, putting together their own Doo Wop revival shows, starting at the Beacon Theatre in New York City. It just so happens that as kids, both Joe and Frankie had watched us sing on Brooklyn street corners. We did shows for them at the Beacon theatre and formed lifelong friendships with Joe, Frankie and Tony. Phil, Albee and I hired bands to back us up and continued to play at local nightclubs as The Mystics throughout the seventies.

We did not do many shows as The Mystics, but we kept our name alive in the doo-wop world and fulfilled our desire to perform. In 1981, I got a call from Marty Pekar who said that he would like to record The Mystics. I was about to hang up because we were always getting calls from would-be producers which usually amounted to nothing, when he said that he'd gotten my number from Nick Santo of The Capris and that they were going to record with him. He went on to explain that he was not only a fan of doo-wop music but also a collector as well as a producer. He said that he'd convinced an executive at RCA to let him record some of the original groups in the setting that they recorded in the fifties. After our conversation, I called Nick, who confirmed that Marty was legitimate and said, "At this point, what do we have to lose?" He was right. I saw it as a way to get some more work for the group. Marty was a pure record collector and wanted to record the original groups without using the tracks or overdub techniques currently being used in production. He already had asked Randy and the Rainbows, The Harptones, The Jive Five, and The Capris and they had all agreed. I met with Phil and Albee, and we thought that this was a good idea, but it would be better with the original group, which was Marty's preference. I set up a meeting with Marty, and he explained that this album, between rehearsals and actual studio time, would probably take a few months to record. The studio was in Brooklyn and it was an all-live recording, which made it difficult for George, since he had just moved to Florida and started a new job. Bobby, who was still in New York, and getting ready to move to Arizona, did not want to work nightclubs or live shows but was interested in the recording session.

At the time, we were working at local clubs like Hadaar and Crocittos in Staten Island, with a new backup band that I had found in Staten Island led by lead singer Lenny Indelacati, who we thought of using in the recording session. Marty had hired studio musicians for all the groups and Lenny's band was a little annoyed that they would not be involved and quit. Just around this time, I met John Tarangelo through my good friend Tony Sciametta. Tony asked me, as a favor to him, to audition John for our group. We did and found our new first tenor. Bobby did second tenor, and we had our recording personnel. We now had an almost all original group ready to record. Marty was very particular about our song selection and we started the process of submitting songs. He was interested in obscure but recognizable songs from the early fifties and had to hear us do them before he would consider using them. We agreed on the following songs:

"Crazy for You," originally done by The Heartbeats. Marty loved our version and Phil's voice on this song so much he named the album "Crazy for You."

"Hush My Darling," a new song of ours. Marty did not want to re-record "Hushabye" because he said, "You can't re-create the Mona Lisa." So, he asked us to write a song like it. I came up with the concept, and we all had a hand in putting this one together.

"You Baby You," originally sung by The Cleftones and covered in an upbeat version by The Excellents.

"Prayer to An Angel," one of our original songs, which we finally got to record in its purest form.

"Chills and Fever" was originally sung by Johnny Love and written by Billy Ness and Bobby Rackup. Marty selected the song but wanted us to change it around, so we decided that I would do a bass lead.

"Doreen Is Never Boring" was written by Joey Ramone, who happened to be one of Marty's friends. Much to our surprise, Joey Ramone loved The Mystics and came to one of our recording sessions, where he and Marty asked us to sing this song. We learned and recorded the song that same night with Joey filling in a few harmony parts. We also recorded an a cappella version of "Duke of Earl," with Joey singing lead, but it was never released.

"Wish I Had My Baby," originally done by The Five Satins. We used to do this song in our early days on the street corners in Brooklyn.

"Why Do You Pretend," another original Mystics song that Laurie would not record.

"Will Love Ever Come My Way," originally recorded by Dion. Marty selected this, and we changed the background to give it a different flair.

"The Bells Are Ringing," another original Mystics song, written in 1958.

"Now That Summer Is Here," recorded by The Videls and written by Vini Poncia and Pete Anders, which was why we chose it. It was one of our all-time favorite songs.

The sessions were long but incredibly enjoyable, especially the time we spent with Joey Ramone. Marty did a fair amount of promotion, including a video for "Soundstage" which was done with a live audience in Chicago. The producer of this show was Ken Ehrlich, who went on to produce many Grammy and Golden Globe shows. All five groups, The Harptones, Randy and the Rainbows, The Jive Five, The Capris and The Mystics, performed a few of their album songs as well as their hit songs. Marty also set up a series of live performances for the five groups including two shows at Allan Pepper's Bottom Line nightclub in New York City. The only hit to come out of all this was "Morse Code of Love" by The Capris, which was later covered by the Manhattan Transfer.

Joe Contorno, Frankie Lanziano (Lanz) and Tony Delauro started producing their Royal New York Doo-Wop Show at Radio City Music Hall in the early eighties. Having already done many shows with them, we became and remain friends, still getting together for a reminiscing dinner every so often. Having done so many shows, they were looking for something different for their next show. I suggested that since it was the 20th Anniversary of "Hushabye," we could get The Mystics, Classics and Passions together on stage. They loved the idea.

We were always trying to get more money per show from the booking agents and they would always say, "Well, you only had one big hit." So, I came up with the idea of asking Emil to join The Mystics and with that, we would have two big hits. Emil loved the idea, since he'd just taken a break after touring for a few years, as The Classics with Albee Galione and Louie Rotundo, both from The Passions. Albee and Louie re-started The Passions and along with Jimmy Gallagher and Tony Armato, started to book work again as The Passions. Jimmy was living in Florida for a few years and was still working with The Passions and other groups, including backing up Dion, who also moved to Florida, on some recordings and shows. The booking agents could not believe that we pulled it off, but The Mystics now featured Emil Stucchio the original lead singer of The Classics, and now we had two major hits, "Hushabye" and "Till Then." The original members of The Classics, Johnny Gambale, Tony Victor, and Jamie Troy were no longer interested in working with the group and had gone on to successful careers in the business world. We were all still working on our "day job" careers but we could not give up the music.

We called for a meeting, with the Passions and the Mystics, at a diner in Staten Island to go over the idea of getting together with the three groups, and it was like old times. The first hour was spent reminiscing about the old days and laughing so loud that the diner's owner put us in a separate room. We all agreed it was a great idea and wanted to start working on it right away. We set up rehearsals in Albee's house on Staten Island and began putting the medleys together. Since we were limited for time on our set, we decided after much discussion, to do a portion of two songs that each group recorded and then close our set with our main hits. We opened the set with "Made for Lovers," originally recorded by The Passions, because the opening lyrics were, "This night was made for lovers," and it was an up-tempo song. Each of the lead singers of each group did a verse. Rehearsals were fun. We reminisced about old times, caught up on our families and realized how much we loved to sing and missed hanging out with each other. Kenny Filmer, from Staten Island, was our guitar/arranger/vocalist and became an invaluable asset in putting this show together. Kenny stayed on as a Mystic for quite a few years.

We didn't want to call it The Mystics' 20th Anniversary Show, and since we were from Brooklyn and were doing a 20-year reunion, we called it The Brooklyn Reunion with The Classics, The Mystics and The Passions (alphabetical order-of course). The other acts at Radio City Music Hall were Johnny Maestro and The Brooklyn Bridge, Freddie Paris and The Five Satins, The Penguins, The Skyliners with Jimmy Beaumont and The Dubs.

It was the first time any of us had played at Radio City Music Hall, and we were so impressed. We rehearsed with the band, and when we were done with sound check, a lot of the acts came over to say how great we sounded and that it was a great idea to get all three groups together.

The producers were ecstatic about how good this sounded and especially how unique it was. Joe Contorno commented, "This type of reunion has never been done before, we are the first." How could it not sound good? We had twelve singers on stage singing all our hits with the original lead singers. Backstage at Radio City was amazing. Looking out at this huge stage and the soon-to-be-filled 6,000 seats was overwhelming. The producers had a 1958 Chevy convertible on one part of the stage and a street corner lamppost on the other side.

Frankie Lanz was the MC and with his signature enthusiasm introduced us by saying how he remembered as a kid listening to these three groups sing on the street corners of Brooklyn. "To celebrate twenty years of friendship they will be performing their hits for you tonight!" Then he continued with, "Ladies and gentlemen the Brooklyn Reunion". The sold-out house roared. Watching from backstage, hearing the audience, and looking at my lifelong friends by my side caused a surge of nostalgia to surge through me, and I just savored it for a few seconds. How lucky we were to be able to do this! Frankie named each of us individually as we walked across the enormous stage and then he announced, "Phil Cracolici and The Mystics." The Mystics got to the microphones and started with "This night was made for lovers," a gigantic screen lowered itself above us with our original group picture, and the audience applauded. Frankie announced, "Jimmy Gallagher and The Passions" as they walked out from the darkened portion of the stage, which was suddenly lit from the lamppost. When their picture appeared, the audience, applauded even louder. A spotlight shone on the 1958 Chevy as Frankie announced Emil Stucchio and The Classics. As Emil got out of the car and started walking to the center stage, The Classics' picture appeared on the huge screen, and the audience went wild. We closed our show with our version of Kenny Vance's, "Looking for an Echo," which was very appropriate for this show.

Just before starting the first line of our closing song, I said a few words about how we all grew up together, had been in each other's bridal parties, had watched our kids grow up – and we still like each other. I closed by remarking, "There is an old saying that a man's wealth is measured by the friends he has, and so you are looking at a bunch of millionaires." We got a standing ovation.

It went over so well that "The Brooklyn Reunion" continues to the present day as a live show.

I took a walk out to the lobby during intermission to say hello to some friends when a thin young man approached me and introduced himself as Dick Fox. He said that he loved the music and thought that our group did a great job. We chatted for a few minutes and I thanked him and turned to talk to my friends. Many months later, I was invited to a recording session by Vini Poncia, who was producing Melissa Manchester's latest album in New York City. Vini introduced me to Melissa and to Melissa's manager, Dick Fox. I did not recognize him at the time. Vini and Dick knew each other, and being avid doo-wop fans, played sort of a doo-wop trivia game with each other. Vini said to Dick, "I got one for you, Dick, you will never get it."

Dick smiled and answered, "Go ahead."

Vini asked, "Who sang lead on The Mystics' version of 'White Cliffs of Dover'?" Dick paused, as if thinking deeply. Then he pointed at me and said, "He did!"

Vini and I were shocked, and we all burst out laughing. Dick reminded me that we had met at Radio City. We all went to dinner (scungilli in Little Italy, of course), and I remain good friends with both Vini and Dick.

In the eighties, doo-wop was revived several times. The Mystics, The Passions and The Classics rode the revival wave for years, interchanging personnel now and then as we did in the past.

In the nineties, there was another resurgence in doo-wop, which resulted in many of the original groups joining this new old music scene. The Mystics, The Passions and The Classics all got back together. Producers like Richard Nader re-invented the Alan Freed rock and roll shows and showcased this fifties music to the later generations who had missed it.

Doo Wop 50 aired on December 5, 1999. This was a PBS pledge drive special created and produced for PBS member station WQED-TV by TJ Lubinsky, grandson of Herman Lubinsky (founder of Savoy Records) and owner of Times Square records in NYC. The special was inspired by a best-selling 1994 CD boxed set of doo-wop music produced by Rhino Records, which was also a development and production partner in the special.

Doo Wop 50 was videotaped live at the Benedum Center for the Performing Arts, Pittsburgh, Pennsylvania on May 11 and 12, 1999. It showcased many doo-wop groups that had existed since the 1950s and was hosted by former Impressions lead and soul singer Jerry Butler. Doo Wop 50 became the highest-producing pledge drive special in the history of PBS, garnering more than $20 million for its member stations. Doo Wop 51 and the American Soundtrack series followed it. We did Doo Wop 51 at the same theater. It was especially interesting (although sometimes weird to see how our old music friends looked). We would all gather and talk in the Green Room about our aches and pains and laugh at each other's stories. Some of the singers could barely walk – but they moved like teenagers when they hit the stage!

L-R, Joey Ramone, Albee Cracolici, Phil Cracolici, Al Contrera (1981)

The Mystics backstage at Westbury Music Fair/Dick Fox Show (1995)
L-R, Bob, Albee, Phil, George, Al

L-R, Kenny Vance, Vini Poncia (photo courtesy of David Gahr-1974)

CHAPTER 34

GOOD NIGHT, SWEETHEART

Now, at the Meadowlands in 2009, it was time to stop talking about the past. Although interesting it was time to go to work. After hours of chatting and reminiscing, it was almost show time, and we all needed to make final preparations. As Kenny headed for the door to check with his group, he said to me, "You know you should write down that story, it could be a book." Clay said, "He's right, that is unbelievable" and went back to his dressing room. The band started to change into their show outfits. Emil, Teresa and I talked about last-minute show details. We were wearing our new black suits with black shirts and silver ties. Teresa had a matching black top with silver pants and looked great.

As I was getting dressed I thought about what I had just talked about. All the years that went by and all the things we did. Not only with the Mystics, Passions and Classics but in our own lives. We had music careers, raised families and had business careers. I thought how lucky I was to have had the opportunity to be a part of all this. How fortunate we were that music altered our life course from a potential path of crime. How lucky we were to have wonderful loving families and good friends. It's amazing but I'm still enjoying the gift I was given by Tony "Punchy" Armato and Tony Conigliaro, when they opened a door for me so many years ago. I will be forever grateful. I cannot imagine going through life any other way.

Emil seeing that I was in deep thought and a little teary eyed said, "You're thinking about all those years-right?"

I said, "Yeah it's a little nostalgic".

Emil response was classic, "It's incredibly nostalgic-we are just so blessed to be able to do this." I thought for a second that he was reading my mind.

Hushabye

We could hear the audience buzzing as Teresa, Emil and I walked through the corridor on our way to the doors leading to the stage area. Most of the acts were standing by the wings to see the kick-off of the show with Clay. I was surprised to see Dick Fox backstage, but I guess he was as curious as everyone else. The band was already in place, and Clay was standing in his very cool black tuxedo, waiting to be introduced by Debra Nader. We thought that Richard Nader might show up but unfortunately, he was still in the hospital. Richard was a good friend and we miss him so much. Clay was as cool as can be even though it was the first time in many years that he was hosting a live show. The arena was dark except for the spotlights highlighting the stage. Clay was calm and confident.

At exactly 7:30 PM, the spotlights brightened, and the band started playing an up-tempo rock and roll tune. Debra walked out onto the stage, greeted everyone and introduced Clay. The sold-out audience of 19,000 erupted in cheers and applause. Clay began talking and was as smooth as ever. After a brief greeting he said, "And now, ladies and gentlemen, my good friends, Emil Stucchio and the Classics," and we walked up to the stage.

We opened our set with our up-tempo version of "The Way You Look Tonight" and continued with "My Heart Sings." The adrenaline kicked in immediately, along with euphoria. We talked about how great it was to be back at the Meadowlands, and we joked a little about how long we had been around and how long we'd known Clay. We each took a part of the stage and faced the audience individually instead of lining up together. We glanced at each other while changing positions and knew everything was right. We then sang "Cara Mia" and closed with "Till Then." The audience gave us a standing ovation, as they did for every act that followed us. They were all great.

Being able to perform for a sold-out audience is incredible but performing with your best friends is the icing on the cake.

The Classics, L-R, Emil, Teresa, Al
Photo courtesy of Sonny Maxon

The Mystics 2018
L-R Albee, Phil, George, Al and Bob
Photo courtesy of Joni Sperling

BIBLIOGRAPHY

"Doing Life, The Extraordinary Saga of America's Greatest Jailhouse Lawyer" by Stephen Bello.
"Rock On" by Norm N Nite.
"The Complete Book Of Doo-Wop" by Dr. Anthony Gribin.